SAVE

750 EVERYDAY WAYS YOU CAN HELP

OUR

CLEAN UP THE EARTH

PLANET

QUANTITY SALES

Most Dell books are available at special quantity discounts when purchased in bulk by corporations, organizations, and special-interest groups. Custom imprinting or excerpting can also be done to fit special needs. For details write: Dell Publishing, 666 Fifth Avenue, New York, NY 10103. Attn.: Special Sales Department.

INDIVIDUAL SALES

Are there any Dell books you want but cannot find in your local stores? If so, you can order them directly from us. You can get any Dell book in print. Simply include the book's title, author, and ISBN number if you have it, along with a check or money order (no cash can be accepted) for the full retail price plus $2.00 to cover shipping and handling. Mail to: Dell Readers Service, P.O. Box 5057, Des Plaines, IL 60017.

SAVE

750 EVERYDAY WAYS YOU CAN HELP

OUR

CLEAN UP THE EARTH

PLANET

DIANE MacEACHERN

A DELL TRADE PAPERBACK

A DELL TRADE PAPERBACK
Published by Dell Publishing, a division of The Bantam Doubleday Dell Publishing
Group, Inc.
666 Fifth Avenue
New York, New York 10103

ISBN: 0-440-50267-5

Packaged by Rapid Transcript, a division of March Tenth, Inc.
Designed by Stanley S. Drate/Folio Graphics Company, Inc.

Printed in the United States of America
Published simultaneously in Canada

March 1990

BG   10   9   8   7   6   5   4   3   2   1

To Dick
For Daniel

CONTENTS

PREFACE / *ix*

ACKNOWLEDGMENTS / *xi*

INTRODUCTION: THE PLANET IN PERIL / *1*

1 In Your Home / *21*

2 In Your Garden / *73*

3 In the Garage / *99*

4 At the Supermarket / *111*

5 At School / *128*

6 At the Office / *142*

7 In Your Community / *152*

8 In Your Apartment / *173*

9 Vacations / *178*

APPENDIX: RESOURCES / *189*

INDEX / *203*

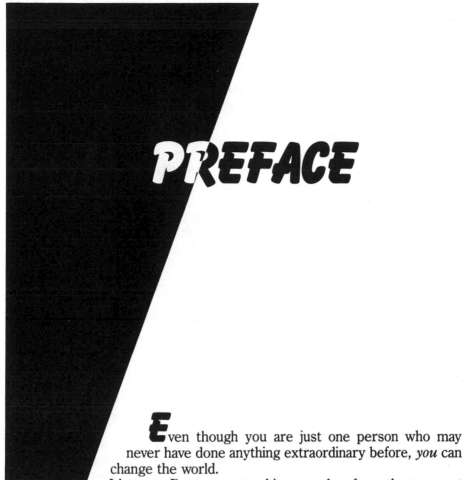

PREFACE

Even though you are just one person who may never have done anything extraordinary before, *you* can change the world.

It's true. Because everything you do—from the way you wash your clothes to how you heat your house to the kind of car you drive—either makes the world a better or worse place in which to live.

It's not that corporations, the government, or legislators should be let off the hook: We must demand a cleaner, safer environment and a healthier world, and we must hold industry and government accountable for the many actions they take that affect the health of the earth and the future of the planet.

But we're responsible, too. This is our world, and it's the only one we've got. By making small but substantial decisions about the things we do, the goods we buy, and the laws we support, we can make a better life for ourselves while helping to ensure a world that's fit for the future. If we expect others to be accountable, then we must be held accountable, too, starting with our own lives.

This book offers that point of departure. First, it provides a brief glimpse into some of the greatest environmental dilemmas the world has ever faced.

Unfortunately, the picture it paints of the earth is not an optimistic one. Clearly, the planet is in peril, and the blame for its destruction rests squarely on the shoulders of each and every one of us who contributes to— or even tolerates—environmental abuse.

But as grim as this planetary predicament may seem, it's not irreversible. On the contrary, each environmental problem has many solutions, and the bulk of the book focuses on the simple ways you can integrate these solutions into your own life.

Save Our Planet is divided into chapters corresponding to where we lead our lives; there is one chapter each for home, garden, garage, supermarket, school, office, and community. A special section for renters and apartment dwellers has been included, as well as one on vacations that will give you— and the planet—a break. And the appendix lists additional books, catalogs, agencies, and organizations that you can join or from which you can get more information. Though this book has not attempted to provide a comprehensive list of "ecologically correct" consumer products, where particular items or companies stand out as being significantly "better" or "worse" than their counterparts, they are mentioned.

Look for this symbol 🔆 any time you need a "bright idea" to help you solve a particular problem or want to see how others are responding to an environmental challenge. It's a fluorescent light bulb, one of the most promising energy-saving inventions on the market today. Substituting just one fluorescent light for a traditional bulb can keep half a ton of carbon dioxide (the chief cause of global warming) out of the atmosphere over the useful life of the bulb.

Specific sources of information that will help you find a product or track down a source more easily are highlighted with a shooting star. Each chapter ends with a chart linking the most important actions you can take in that chapter to the environmental problem they will help solve.

There are hundreds of tips here, but don't let the numbers throw you. Even if you follow just one or two of the suggestions provided, tangible progress will be made towards restoring vitality to the earth.

In almost every case, each action you take will make no appreciable difference in the way you lead your life. But it will have a substantial positive impact on the world around you. In every case you'll be doing the planet a favor. And in many cases, you'll be improving your own quality of life, not only in your immediate environment, but in terms of the health benefits you'll enjoy and the money you'll save on medical bills, fuel costs, throwaway items, and chemical poisons you don't really need.

We can make these next ten years the "decade of the environment" or the "decade of demise." Which will it be? *You* can make the difference.

ACKNOWLEDGMENTS

From the beginning, *Save Our Planet* was bolstered by the enthusiastic support of my friends, family, and many, many others who believed that a book like this needed to be written. Lani Sinclair helped me translate staggering numbers into the easy framework that has made the book readable. Glenn Starnes guided me through the pitfalls of a new computer system without which this book simply would not have gotten done. My colleagues at other organizations generously provided guidance, information, and access to their materials and critical review—in particular Howard Robinson, Robert San George, Brian Day, Allan Margolin, Norman Dean, Marc Ledbetter, and Scott Sklar. I would also like to thank Denis Hayes, Michael McCloskey, Rob Ringer, Carol Parker, Peter Harnik, Jeanne and Travis Price, Alice Trembour, and Rob Schwerr.

I find it hard to believe that anyone in this business could find a better team to work with than the people at Dell. My agent, Gail Ross, put us all together. My editor, Jody Rein, believed in this book as much as I did, and the credit for its appeal rests with her and Jeanne Cavelos. Thanks, too, to publicity director Roger Bilheimer and his associate director, Larry Hughes.

My mother, Ann MacEachern, deserves special recognition because she came up with the title for this book. But all of my family has been behind me 100 percent, and though that's the norm, it was still greatly appreciated.

Maria Rodriguez, my business partner at Vanguard Communications, has patiently and uncomplainingly awaited the end of this project so that I could get back to doing my share of the work at our consulting firm. She's been a terrific source of support and a wonderful friend.

Finally, my deepest appreciation goes to my husband, Dick Munson. Thanks to his patience, encouragement, and endless hours at the playground with Daniel, I met the deadline that made this book possible.

SAVE

750 EVERYDAY WAYS YOU CAN HELP

OUR

CLEAN UP THE EARTH

PLANET

INTRODUCTION: THE PLANET IN PERIL

*T*he *Exxon Valdez*. Alar-treated apples. Love Canal. Bhopal. Three Mile Island. Chernobyl. The list of individual examples of environmental degradation could fill this book. But none of these calamities should be thought of as isolated incidents. Cumulatively, they add up to the worst state of environmental affairs since the dawn of civilization. And they've contributed to a fraternity of staggering problems whose scientific jargon has become the common language for consumers as well as scientists: global warming and the deterioration of the ozone layer, acid rain and urban smog, deforestation, toxic waste, garbage overload, water pollution.

But as ominous as these phrases sound, it is not too late to reckon with them—at least not yet. As a first step, we can educate ourselves about the predicaments that have given rise to the words and their consequences for the earth.

1

WATER

Clean water is our most precious resource. But as much as a fourth of the world's reliable water supply could be rendered unsafe for use by the year 2000.

The human body is composed of more than 65 percent water. An Indian mystic purportedly once fasted for more than eighty days without food, yet no one can survive more than a few days without water. We rely upon it to quench our thirst, brush our teeth, take a bath, and wash our groceries. When we turn on the tap, we expect clean water to come flowing out, and we'd be shocked if it didn't—if it dripped out thick as mud or smelling like rotten eggs.

But in fact, how safe and plentiful is our water supply? In terms of both quality and quantity, clean water is one resource we should not take for granted.

Consider this:

◐ Between 1971 and 1985, over 100,000 cases of disease in the United States were attributed to drinking water, representing more outbreaks than in any fifteen-year period since 1920.

◐ During the same period, traces of about 2,100 different chemical contaminants, including brain-damaging lead, were discovered in public water systems.

◐ Underground reservoirs of fresh water, known as aquifers, contain nearly fifty times as much water as do lakes and rivers and constitute 96 percent of all the fresh water in the United States. But within the last few years, thousands of wells that tap aquifers have been closed in California, 2,600 in Long Island, 700 in Connecticut, 500 in New Jersey, and 250 in Massachusetts. In 1984 alone, 4,400 well-contamination incidents were reported by twenty-one states.

◐ Meanwhile, the famous Ogallala Aquifer, which has lain under vast sections of the arid Great Plains since the Pleistocene era, now has a life expectancy of about forty years. When it is gone, it will take thousands of years to replenish itself.

◐ Even the mighty Colorado River no longer runs out to the sea; all its water is used up before it gets there.

Most of us get our water from one of two sources: surface waters such as lakes and rivers, or the deep underground aquifers. But both of these sources are being threatened by the pollution that has become part of our everyday lives, because almost everything we put on the ground ends up in the water: lawn fertilizer and bug killers, the changed car oil, hazardous chemicals stored in dump sites and municipal landfills, even the salts used to de-ice highways.

This pollution pours indiscriminately into rivers and streams simply when rain or irrigation water washes across the surface of the land, sweeping up toxic substances as it goes along. Runoff from agriculture and urban areas now constitutes the major American water pollution problem, along with groundwater contamination from toxic waste sites and the leaking underground storage tanks used to contain chemicals and petroleum products. Virtually every state has experienced water quality problems from "runoff" water pollution.

Not only is the quality of our water on the decline, so is the amount of it available for us to tap. In locations where lakes and rivers are inadequate, groundwater often supplements surface water supplies. Indeed, fully one-half of the U.S. population relies on groundwater for drinking water. But in many areas this reserve is being depleted at a break-neck pace. In Florida, for example, rapid population growth has placed unreasonable demands on available drinking water, which comes almost exclusively from groundwater. Although the area has high rainfall, it's not nearly enough to replenish the levels at which the groundwater is being drained, and aquifers are beginning to fill up with salt water instead. Irrigation imposes another significant drain on water supply: Often more than 70 percent of the water used for irrigation never reaches the crops it's intended to sustain.

New Water?

Scientists and engineers have frequently heralded the advent of "new" water sources to augment surface and underground reserves. In earlier decades, desalinization, cloud seeding, and other innovative technologies were widely ballyhooed as ways to expand the supply

of drinking water. Some even suggested towing huge icebergs to Los Angeles, Houston, or Miami, where they could be melted and converted into fresh water! But once economic reality set in, these technologies fizzled. Clearly, to have clean abundant water we are going to have to change the way we use it.

Industry uses more water than any other sector of society, primarily to generate electricity and to cool or clean off equipment after the manufacturing process. Although more than 80 percent of this water is returned to its souce, it is often polluted with manufacturing by-products, effectively preventing it or the creatures that live in it from being consumed.

When power companies draw water from the sea or a river or lake for cooling their equipment, they too return the water back to its source, but at a much warmer temperature than when it came out. As its temperature increases, water can hold less and less oxygen. Even though nothing has been added to the water but heat, the change in temperature can dramatically alter the ecological balance of a stream or river. Moreover, many aquatic animals and plants need cool water to survive or reproduce, and heat pollution can affect them severely.

On forest land, precipitation is absorbed and filtered by the soil, gradually releasing high quality water suitable for drinking, fisheries, and recreation. But if the forests are chopped down, this natural filtration process grinds to a halt. In at least thirty-eight states, the cultivation, production, and harvesting of timber produce sediment, pesticides, and other organic materials that pollute the water.

In addition to the lakes, streams, and aquifers that we tap for drinking water, we also rely on other important bodies of water for food, commerce, and protection from the forces of nature. Estuaries, which form where rivers meet oceans, serve as a spawning or nursery ground for many species, particularly shellfish. Many estuaries, especially the Chesapeake Bay and Puget Sound, are clouded by sediments and pollutants carried from streams and rivers many miles upstream.

Wetlands, the areas between land and water, keep water clean by filtering out sediment and trapping many harmful chemicals; they also help cushion coasts from the full force of storms and control floods by temporarily storing water that runs off the land after a storm. And wetlands provide a breeding ground for birds as well as for many of the fish that we eat.

But wetlands are under siege, losing ground at an estimated national rate of about 300,000 acres per year, thanks to development, roadway construction, mining operations, agricultural practices, and dredging and filling.

Nearly a third of Louisiana's oyster beds are routinely closed because of pollution, and half the shellfish beds in Galveston Bay, Texas, are off limits to fishermen.

A Sea of Sewage—and Transparent Traps

Then there are the beaches. From Staten Island to San Francisco, beaches have been shut down by the arrival of potentially hazardous medical wastes: sutures, hypodermic needles, catheter bags, and vials of blood.

The primary cause of coastal pollution is human sewage, the wastes flushed down toilets and drains in homes, office buildings, commercial establishments, and other places where people work or play. Some of this sewage drains directly into our oceans through pipes called ocean outfalls. More than 189 million tons of solid waste are legally dumped off the Atlantic, Pacific, and Gulf coasts every year.

Plastics are another insidious enemy of the water. Lightweight plastic enables fishermen to use nets that may extend over twenty miles across the ocean, and plastic is rapidly replacing steel as strapping used to bind crates. But when discarded, much of this plastic ends up in the water. As if that weren't enough, plastic litter disposed of on land is washed into marine areas via rivers and sewer systems, while other plastic is blown into the water from landfills. Because it's buoyant and resembles jellyfish and other prey when afloat, plastic is often eaten by birds, fish, and other sea creatures, leading to death from choking, malnutrition or even starvation. Plastics are the most common people-made objects sighted at sea. In one survey, 86 percent of

WHAT ENDS UP IN THE WATER BESIDES WATER?

- ◐ 2,100 kinds of chemicals
- ◐ Gasoline and other petroleum products
- ◐ Lawn and agricultural fertilizer
- ◐ Insecticides, herbicides, fungicides, rodenticides
- ◐ Animal wastes from agriculture, pets, and stray animals
- ◐ Construction debris
- ◐ Paints and solvents
- ◐ Changed car oil
- ◐ Salts that de-ice highways
- ◐ Sediment
- ◐ Plastic six-pack rings
- ◐ Plastic bags
- ◐ Fishing line
- ◐ Hypodermic needles
- ◐ Tampons
- ◐ Industrial pollutants

the trash observed floating in the northern Pacific Ocean was plastic. Even in remote areas of Antarctica researchers find plastic bottles, bags, and sheeting.

When not overburdened, nature can do its job: Bacteria naturally present in the water can break down many pollutants into materials more easily used by aquatic animals and plants. But today's levels and types of pollution demand more: immediate assistance from the human populations responsible for it all.

TOXICS

Enough hazardous waste is generated in one year to fill the New Orleans Superdome 1,500 times over.

The dimensions of the toxics problem are so vast that they are almost incomprehensible. According to the EPA, hazardous waste is

produced in this country at the rate of 700,000 tons per day. That's 250 million tons per year. Or think of it this way: Approximately 240 million people live in the United States. Try to imagine a ton of hazardous waste—an amount equal to the weight of your car—piled next to each of us. Each and every year, add another ton.

Where does it all come from? Primarily from the manufacture, use, and disposal of chemicals.

More than 7 million chemicals are now known, and thousands of new ones are developed each year. As many as 80,000 chemicals are in common use today, often precisely because they are extremely toxic, as with pesticides, herbicides, and fumigants.

Though industry makes toxics, consumers often use them or the products made with them. We may not think of it this way, but almost every household cleaner we buy, every bug spray we use contains toxic chemicals. In fact, every year, Americans ply their gardens, lawns, trees, and parks with 270 million pounds of pesticides. What doesn't remain as residue from spraying these chemicals into the air can still invade the environment when the containers they came in are tossed into a landfill or incinerator.

The first major international scare relating to toxic chemicals occurred late in the 1950s, when large numbers of people around Minamata Bay in Japan began to contract an unusual disease. Research revealed that they were suffering from mercury poisoning, victims of wastes discharged into waterways and ingested by fish. The fish concentrated the chemical, with disastrous consequences when eaten by humans.

Since that time, literally thousands of toxic tragedies have occurred:

◗ Love Canal, a neighborhood in Niagara, New York, had to be evacuated after hazardous waste buried over a twenty-five-year period contaminated the neighborhood's ground water.

◗ Times Beach, Missouri, was transformed into a ghoulish national sensation when it was learned that oil contaminated with dioxin, perhaps the most poisonous toxin of them all, had tainted the soil and water in this eastern Missouri community.

◗ In the state of New York, at least 992 toxic chemical accidents

occurred in a nine-month period in 1987, injuring 148 people and forcing more than 1,200 to evacuate their homes or workplaces.

◗ In October 1987, 4,000 residents of Texas City, Texas, fled a five-square-mile area when a ruptured tank at the Marathon Oil Company plant spilled 35,000 gallons of hydrofluoric acid. The toxic plume arising from the spill sent over 1,000 victims to area hospitals.

◗ Barely a month later, a storage tank at the Ashland Oil Company in Pennsylvania collapsed, pouring an estimated 1 million gallons of diesel fuel into the Monongahela River. Water supplies from Pittsburgh all the way to Wheeling, West Virginia, were threatened, and more than 500,000 people had to forego using their tap water.

◗ In 1988, there were two evacuations from chemical spills involving more than 20,000 people in Massachusetts and southern California.

◗ And in March of 1989, the *Exxon Valdez,* a supertanker loaded with crude oil, crashed into a reef in the pristine waters of Alaska's Prince William Sound, spewing 11 million gallons of oil into the environment at tremendous cost to wildlife and a flourishing commercial fishing industry.

There are approximately 12,000 major chemical manufacturing plants and 400,000 primary chemical storage facilities in this country; 180,000 shipments of very hazardous substances—ranging from nuclear weapons to gasoline—occur each day. Every day, in every state in America, toxic accidents are waiting to happen over and over and over again.

But it's not just the transportation of these poisons that poses the threat. Thousands of abandoned or inactive dump sites containing hazardous waste have been identified nationwide. Many of these sites are located in environmentally sensitive areas, such as flood plains or wetlands. Rain and melting snow seep through the sites, contaminating underground waters and nearby streams and lakes. At some sites the air is also contaminated, as toxic vapors rise from evaporating liquid wastes or from uncontrolled chemical reactions. In the Great Lakes alone, five different toxins have been found for every species of fish that swims there. The National Wildlife Federation reported in June 1989 that a person who eats just seven meals of lake trout over a lifetime is taking a 1 in 1,000,000 risk of getting cancer, a threshold sometimes used by government agencies in setting pollution controls.

When the federal Superfund Law was enacted in 1980, many people hoped that the federal cleanup program could be a short-term, one-time effort. It now appears that the task of cleaning up hazardous waste sites will haunt us well into the twenty-first century.

Not only is it taking longer to clean up sites, but new sites continue to be discovered. Over 300,000 locations now contain hazardous substances, and the number

is growing at a pace that far outstrips the rate of cleanup. The price of cleaning up only the 1,175 highest priority Superfund sites will exceed $30 billion—triple the entire budget of America's space program.

Faced with the rising costs of safe waste disposal in the United States, many chemical firms prefer to pass their waste problems on to other countries, particularly developing ones, where waste disposal laws are often less strict and less vigorously enforced. Exporting pollution is big business for those who can get away with it, and many do. It's easy. Improperly labeled containers of hazardous wastes are shipped to developing countries, which set up waste disposal facilities of their own on the assumption that such plants will attract money and create jobs.

Pesticides

Since 1970, increasing herbicide use has created a jungle of at least forty-eight "super weeds" that are resistant to chemicals.

"Pesticide" is the general term that describes the insecticides, herbicides, rodenticides, and fungicides used to eradicate bugs, weeds, rats and voles, and fungus that plague plants and cut into farming profits. Unlike most industrial compounds, pesticides were created specifically to alter or kill living organisms.

The Environmental Protection Agency has ranked pesticide residues as the third most important environmental problem in the

United States in terms of cancer risk, after exposure to indoor radon pollution and farm worker exposure to pesticides. In fact, between 1982 and 1985, federal and state monitoring programs detected more than 110 different pesticides on commonly eaten fruit and vegetables.

The National Academy of Sciences concluded in 1987 that pesticide contamination of our food supply may be responsible for up to 20,000 cancer cases each year. Birth defects, mutations, or damage to the kidneys, liver, nervous system, or the immune system have also been linked to pesticide contamination. A report by the Natural Resources Defense Council in February 1989 noted that the problem may be greatest for children, who consume larger quantities of pesticide-laden fruit than do adults but for whom tolerance standards have never specifically been established by the EPA.

Why should we be surprised? Pesticide use in agriculture nearly tripled between 1965 and 1985. And in 1989, the U.S. Department of Agriculture projected that farmers would apply 463 million pounds of pesticides to the nation's ten major crops, an average of almost 2 pounds for every acre planted. Today, roughly 70 percent of all American cropland receives some dosage of pesticides. The applications in fruit orchards could be higher.

But even if we weren't getting these pesticide doses from our own crops, we'd be getting them from the foods we import. The U.S. Food and Drug Administration found pesticide residues in 49 percent of the imported fruit samples it tested, in 45 percent of the imported vegetables, and in 26 percent of the imported grains and grain products.

Pesticides also show up in places other than on the food we eat. They have seriously contaminated our groundwater. In the United States, routine agricultural practices have contaminated groundwater with at least forty-six different pesticides in at least twenty-six states. The two most widely used herbicides, atrazine and alachlor, are frequently detected. (Alachlor has caused cancer in laboratory animals, making it a probable human carcinogen.) The risk is particularly acute in rural areas, where millions of people get their drinking water from private wells that are rarely treated or monitored. Though the federal government regulates public water suppliers, its drinking water standards cover only six pesticides, none of which are among the forty-six that the Environmental Protection Agency reports have contaminated groundwater.

The great tragedy of all this contamination and pollution is that it doesn't kill bugs. In response to heavier pesticide use, insects have evolved mechanisms of detoxifying and resisting the chemicals designed to kill them. In 1938, scientists knew of just seven insect and mite species resistant to pesticides. By 1984, that figure had climbed to 447, and included most of the world's major pests as well as the beneficial insects that have served for centuries as their natural predators. According to the National Coalition Against the Misuse of Pesticides, there has been an elevenfold increase in insecticide use over the last thirty years, while crop loss due to insect resistance has doubled.

As for weeds, chemical resistance was virtually nonexistent before 1970. But since then, increasing herbicide use has created "super weeds" that are resistant to chemicals.

Thousands of other compounds not routinely monitored, including PCBs, heavy metals, and other toxins, also make their way into the food chain and are often found in meat, poultry, fish, and shellfish. According to estimates from the Food and Drug Administration, Americans suffer 20 to 90 million cases of illness due to food contamination each year.

Joel Hirschhorn, of the Congressional Office of Technology Assessment, remarks, "Producing as much toxic waste and other forms of environmental pollutants as we now do is not inevitable, nor is it demanded by science and engineers. . . . Up to 50 percent of all environmental pollutants and hazardous waste—across air, water, and land environmental media in which they are managed or disposed—could be eliminated with existing technology in the next few years."

GARBAGE OVERLOAD

In 1987, Americans generated almost enough trash to fill a twenty-four-lane highway one foot deep from Boston to Los Angeles.

Each year, Americans throw away 18 billion disposable diapers, 1.7 billion pens, 2 billion razors and blades, and 220 million tires. Enough aluminum is discarded to rebuild the entire U.S. commercial airline fleet every three months. But it doesn't stop there. Predictions are that by the year 2000, each American will generate 6 pounds of junk a day. Where in the world are we going to put all that garbage?

Eighty percent of America's solid waste is being dumped into 6,000 landfills, spread across every state in the country. But that option is shrinking fast: In the past five years, 3,000 dumps have been closed, and by 1993, some 2,000 more will be jammed to capacity—and closed. In just four years, Chicago's landfills will be full; dumps in Los Angeles should reach capacity by 1995.

Plastic is a particular bane of the shrinking landfill. It doesn't degrade and can't easily be recycled. Plus, it's derived from petroleum, a dwindling and nonrenewable resource. In 1986 alone, more than 20 billion plastic bottles and nearly 1 billion pounds of plastic trash bags were manufactured, occupying fully a third of available landfill space in America.

Many cities already ship their trash somewhere else. Towns in

New England run trucks twenty-four hours a day to Pennsylvania and Ohio, and communities on Long Island ship as far west as Michigan. In New York City, the Fresh Kills landfill on Staten Island is already 150 feet high, but it may reach a peak of 500 feet by the time it closes a decade from now. (It can't go any higher because it's in the flight path of Newark International Airport.) And who can forget the infamous "garbage barge" from Long Island that roamed up and down the East Coast for months looking for a harbor willing to take its trash?

Even if there were room for it all, dumped garbage and industrial waste can become a lethal potion when corrosive acids, chemicals, and discarded metals leach out of landfills and into groundwater supplies, contaminating drinking water and polluting agricultural land. It's estimated that the Fresh Kills landfill leaks 4 million gallons of toxic liquids a day into nearby streams. And that's just one landfill. What about the other 5,999?

One alternative to dumping garbage is burning it. But incinerating wastes at a high temperature for a set period of time turns garbage into gaseous emissions (which can include lead and dioxin) and toxic ash. Scrubbing exhaust gases to prevent air contamination leaves behind hazardous waste water, while improperly storing ash could pollute groundwater and even cause fires or explosions. If some mechanical problem arises at the incineration facility, and wastes begin to pile up,

incompatible chemicals could mix, brewing a poisonous cloud.

DEFORESTATION

One-quarter of the medicinal drugs prescribed in the United States today are derived from natural compounds, many of which are found only in tropical rain forests.

Fifty acres of rain forest are destroyed each minute. That's almost 27 million acres a year, an area equal in size to the state of Pennsylvania. At no time in history has the rate of deforestation approached what we are seeing as we enter the 1990s.

Two-fifths of the world's original rain forest cover has been decimated, mostly in the last fifty years. Wrote Nicholas Guppy in "Tropical Deforestation: A Global View" in *Foreign Affairs,* "Unless we can halt this destruction, straight line projection gives a date seventy-three years ahead (2057) for the final demise of this currently still vast, irreplaceable sector of our planet."

Half of all plant and animal species in the world live in the rain forests. And yet it has been said that we know more about some areas of the moon than we do about tropical rain forests. If deforestation continues unabated, the ecological riches of these unique ecosystems will soon be lost forever.

The Source of Modern Medicine

As we've noted, many of the medicinal drugs prescribed in the United States today contain a natu-

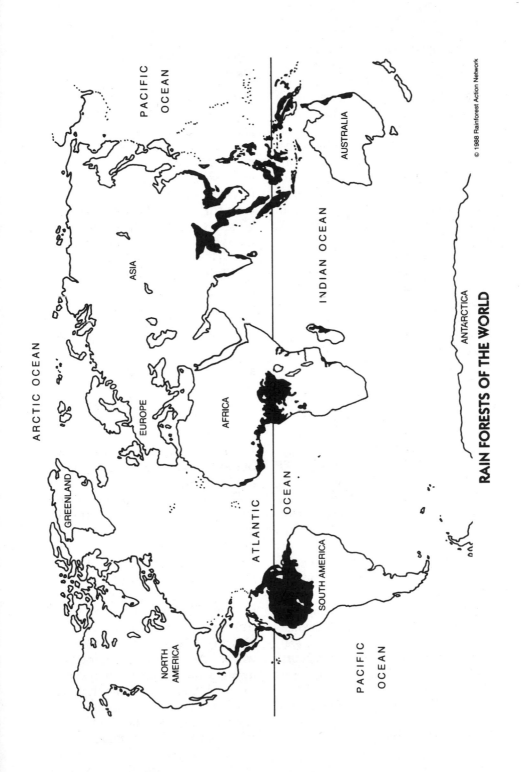

RAIN FORESTS OF THE WORLD

© 1988 Rainforest Action Network

ral compound derived from the rain forest. Curare, used by certain Indian tribes in arrow poison, has become a modern anesthesia. Until recently, diosgenin, derived from a tropical yam, was a key component of the birth control pill. Ipecacuanha roots, found in Brazilian rain forests, are the source of emetine, used to treat amoebic dysentery. The snakeroot plant that grows in India's forests yields alkaloid reserpine, the base of many tranquilizers. The corkwood tree of eastern Australia provides scopolamine, used to treat schizophrenia. And the list goes on. Seventy-three percent of the 3,000 plants identified by the National Cancer Institute as having properties that fight cancer come from the rain forest.

The rain forest is also home to more kinds of plants and animals than any other ecosystem on Earth. In a typical four-square-mile patch of rain forest, the National Academy of Sciences found as many as 1,500 species of flowering plants and as many as 750 species of trees, plus hundreds of different species of mammals, birds, reptiles, amphibians, and butterflies.

Deforestation is taking a heavy toll on these life forms. According to the international organization Friends of the Earth, currently at least one species a day becomes extinct in a tropical rain forest, and that could soon rise to one an hour. Within fifteen years, we may have killed off up to one-quarter of all the world's wildlife—by destroying their habitats as well as through illegal wildlife trade.

What's Happening to These Trees?

The rain forests are disappearing because people are poor and greedy, not because they're ignorant or stupid. Most attempts to grow plants and animals in the tropics have been geared to producing food for subsistence and commodities for cash. Trees have been gleaned for foreign exchange as though they were abundant minerals. They're burned in increasing quantities for fuel and cut up for building materials. Mahogany and other rare tropical hardwoods are recast as living room furniture, while teak ends up on the patio. Plus, forests are decimated to clear acres for cattle ranching. In the last two decades alone, over 40 percent of Central American rain forests have been converted into pastures for beef production, 90 percent of which is exported to the United States primarily for use in the fast food market or in pet food.

Deforestation is not only a problem in the tropics. Long-term planning for forestry in the United States has not always been practiced, either. Development of the American frontier saw a period of reckless logging that severely eroded hillsides and wasted tons of topsoil. Today, very little old-growth "virgin" forest is left anywhere. And many of America's remaining timberlands are being cut to build houses for the Japanese, costing America jobs as well as our environment. In the past decade alone, an amount of timber equivalent to a 600,000-acre forest was shipped overseas; and in 1988, exports, mostly to Japan, consumed one in four logs cut on the West Coast and in Alaska.

In the world's drier tropical regions, deforestation can spur deserts to expand. In fact, desertification commonly follows deforestation, because water runs off the bare hills too quickly, carrying much of the topsoil with it and disturbing the water balance. As crops fail, domestic animals die, water sources dry up, and fuel wood becomes more and more difficult to obtain, prospects for survival by person or beast dwindle. Thirty-five million people in Africa alone have been threatened by drought.

Nature's Regulators

In addition to preserving life-giving species and protecting millions of living creatures, rain forests regulate the flow of water on earth. Like a gigantic sponge, they soak up water from heavy tropical rainfalls, then release it slowly and steadily, providing a constant supply for people and farmers living hundreds, even thousands of miles away.

Tropical forests also play a crucial role in the global recycling of carbon, a process that has been linked to the twentieth-century phenomenon known as global warming. Trees absorb carbon dioxide in the process of growing. But when trees are cleared or harvested, the carbon they contain, as well as some of the carbon in the underlying soil,

is released back into the air, adding to a carbon dioxide buildup that is weaving a blistering atmospheric blanket around the entire globe. According to the Environmental Defense Fund, the latest scientific data show that the burning of tropical forests is responsible for one-tenth or more of this "greenhouse effect."

GLOBAL WARMING

Burning coal, oil, and natural gas is turning the earth into a planetary hothouse, changing climates worldwide.

Climate profoundly affects the way we live. When and where we farm, how much we heat and cool our homes, and how we obtain our water all depend on the weather around us. But the energy-intensive activities of modern society are modifying the atmosphere to such an extent that the climate of future generations may be virtually unrecognizable to those of us closing out the end of the twentieth century.

The four hottest years of the last century occurred during the 1980s, with the first five months of 1988 the warmest on record. The planet seems to be heating up, and the implications are profound: Rainfall and soil moisture patterns could shift dramatically, skewing agricultural productivity worldwide; sea levels could rise from one to four feet, swamping coastal cities; ocean currents could shift, further altering climate and disrupting fisheries; whole populations of plants and animals could move north or south; and record heat waves and other weather anomalies could harm people, crops, and forests.

What's Going On?

Burning fossil fuels, deforestation, and the production of certain synthetic chemicals are releasing large quantities of heat-trapping gases into the atmosphere. These gases absorb the earth's infrared radiation, preventing it from escaping back into space. Trapping heat close to the surface of the planet raises global temperatures, giving rise to what is becoming popularly known as the "greenhouse effect."

Carbon dioxide (CO_2) is the main offender in the global warming crisis. Like a one-way filter, CO_2 lets energy from the sun pass through it but absorbs the longer wavelength radiation emitted from the earth, creating an atmospheric greenhouse around the planet.

Under normal conditions, greenhouse gases play a very useful role. If none were present in the atmosphere, the earth's average temperature would be about 54 degrees colder than it is now, making life as we know it impossible to maintain. But the buildup of these gases is now so great that excessive amounts of heat are being trapped, turning the earth into a planetary hothouse.

About 6 billion tons of carbon dioxide are spewed into the atmosphere each year, accounting for about half of the greenhouse warming. Generating and using energy accounts for the lion's share of carbon dioxide emissions: In the United States, electric utilities emit the most CO_2, followed by transpor-

HOW THE "GREENHOUSE EFFECT" WORKS

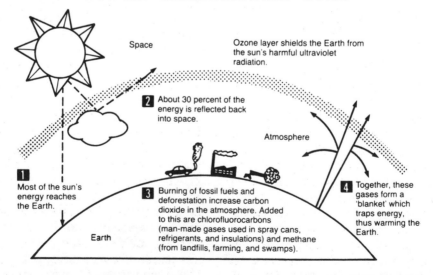

SOURCE: World Resources Institute

tation—cars, buses, trucks—industry, and residential uses. Together deforestation and the combustion of fossil fuels have raised the level of carbon dioxide in the atmosphere 25 percent since the beginning of the Industrial Revolution. The United Nations Environment Programme believes CO_2 levels could increase an additional 30 percent in the next fifty years if we ignore the problem today.

Among fossil fuels, coal—the most plentiful and cheapest—is the greatest malefactor. Coal releases twice as much CO_2 as natural gas, and almost a quarter more than oil. So clearly, a major solution to the global warming crisis involves burning less—and less damaging—fossil fuels. Ultimately, the United States must wean itself completely from oil, coal, and natural gas.

Nuclear power can't substitute for fossil fuels, since it is fraught with so many difficulties itself, including the routine emission of low-level radioactivity, the risk of catastrophic accidents, storage or disposal of radioactive waste, and the potential to divert plutonium and uranium for nuclear weapons.

Clearly, the essential ingredient in the global warming solution is to make a complete transition to renewable sources of energy—those that derive their power from the sun. Already, active and passive solar collectors, wind turbines, hydropower, and geothermal and biomass facilities provide more energy than do nuclear reactors. And many exciting innovations are taking place in industry and business, with solar-powered cars racing across continents even as hydrogen-derived fuels are being developed to power them.

But the most immediate way to curtail carbon dioxide emissions is by reducing the total amount of energy used. More efficient appliances and lights, better insulated buildings, energy-saving heating and cooling systems for buildings, greater use of public transportation, and more efficient modes of private transportation are essential if we are to cool the globe and keep it cool.

The Ozone Layer

In addition to carbon dioxide, there are other greenhouse gases consisting of chlorine, fluorine, and carbon atoms. Because these "chlorofluorocarbons" (CFCs) vaporize at low temperatures, they have become the essential ingredients in refrigerator and air conditioner coolants (marketed by the Du Pont Company as Freon) and as the propellant gases for aerosol spray cans. CFCs also make good insulators in a solid form, because the lightweight, closed-cell bubbles they form (marketed as Styrofoam by Dow Chemical) are poor conductors of both heat and cold. Even the computer revolution is aided by CFCs—they are used to remove the smallest contaminants on microchips and other components of electronic equipment.

When CFCs escape into the atmosphere, they trap heat. In fact, CFCs and halons, which release ozone-depleting bromine, are estimated to account for 15 to 20 percent of global warming. Because they are synthetic chemicals for which substitutes can be developed, they are the easiest greenhouse gases to control.

But concern about the greenhouse effect is not the only reason to curtail use of chlorofluorocarbons.

Ozone, a pure form of oxygen found in the stratosphere ten to thirty miles above the earth's surface, acts like a big umbrella to protect the earth from the dangerous ultraviolet rays of the sun. It is the only gas in the atmosphere that limits the amount of harmful solar ultraviolet radiation reaching the earth.

If all the stratospheric ozone were collected at the earth's surface, it would form a layer not much thicker than the sole of your shoe. Because there is so little of it, and because it is so important, small changes in ozone concentrations could have dramatic effects on life on earth. Algae are particularly sensitive to ultraviolet radiation, raising fears that damage to the ozone layer could upset marine ecology and lower fish populations. For people, ultraviolet rays cause sunburn and have been linked to skin cancer, cataracts, and weakened immune systems. The EPA predicts that over the next eighty years more than 150 million more people will get skin cancer in the United States alone if nothing is done to save the ozone layer. Moreover, reduced crop yields could lead to losses

costing billions of dollars, and the climate could be altered.

Since the early 1970s, scientists have warned that emissions of chlorofluorocarbons (CFCs) and other chemicals that convert protective ozone molecules into less useful oxygen molecules may ultimately deplete this essential ozone layer. In 1978, the EPA banned the use in this country of CFCs in nonessential aerosol propellants, at that time the largest source of CFC emissions. Emissions of CFCs from other sources, however, such as refrigerants, air conditioners, and various solvents, have continued to increase. Worldwide, CFC emissions also have increased, in part because many countries still use CFCs in aerosol sprays and spray products.

In 1985, a "hole" was found eating its way across the sky above Antarctica. It is now believed that this hole is as deep as Mount Everest is tall and as wide as the United States. Most scientific researchers are convinced that global CFC emissions must be reduced substantially, if not completely, to avoid a catastrophic depletion of the stratospheric ozone layer. Though twenty-four countries, including the United States, signed a protocol in Montreal in 1987 to cut CFC production by 50 percent over the next ten years, this agreement is inadequate. CFC production should be banned completely, worldwide, within the next five years.

ACID RAIN

Dead lakes, dying forests, and a growing population of children and adults with breathing disorders have become the legacy of energy use in America, the fallout of intense air pollution, and the deleterious phenomenon known as acid rain.

Acid rain is caused by emissions of sulfur dioxide and nitrogen oxides. Each year, almost 25 million tons of sulfur dioxide are pumped into the sky, primarily from furnaces run by coal-burning utilities and nonferrous metal smelters. Nitrogen oxides, formed when fuel is burned at high temperatures, come principally from motor vehicle exhaust and stationary sources such as electric utilities and industrial boilers that burn coal or oil.

Once released into the atmosphere, these compounds can be carried long distances by prevailing winds until they return to earth as acidic rain, snow, fog, or dust. When the environment cannot neutralize the acid, damage occurs. Fish and wildlife are harmed, lakes and forests ruined, the productivity of crops reduced, and buildings and statues deteriorate. The human toll is even more devastating.

Together, sulfur dioxide and nitrogen oxides wreak havoc on the natural environment. At least 1,734 large lakes have been damaged due to acid rain, at substantial cost to the tourism, fishing, and lumber industries. And thousands of acres of woodlands have been chemically stripped on hills and mountaintops stretching from Maine to Georgia, from the Rocky Mountains to the Sierra Nevadas, leaving behind a swath of ghostly forests spiked by withering trees.

But as we have seen with other environmental problems, human health is once again a victim of pollution. Droplets of highly concentrated sulfuric acid can penetrate deep into the lungs, carrying with them toxic chemicals and gases. According to researchers at Harvard University, these "acid aerosols" may be responsible for 100,000 deaths every year, amounting to 5 percent of total mortalities in the United States. And nitrogen oxides are known to narrow airways and irritate the lungs, contributing to pneumonia and bronchitis and weakening the body's immune system. Such diseases are a high price to pay for maintaining dependency on nonrenewable energy resources that are fraught with so many environmental disadvantages.

In addition to acid rain, an unconscionable number of other pollutants are making it an act of courage for many people to take a breath of "fresh" air:

◑ Ozone, the same substance that acts as a protective shield in the stratosphere, becomes a dangerous pollutant at ground level. Ground-level ozone, the main component of smog, is formed when sunlight combines with nitrogen dioxide and hydrocarbons. It retards crop and tree growth and limits visibility. Ozone levels at just half the current allowable standard can send asthmatics into a coughing, wheezing, or simple breathing frenzy.

Many more Americans live in areas with unhealthy levels of ozone than any of the other major pollutants, and levels far in excess of health standards occur regularly in many heavily populated areas, including some that have instituted control measures.

⦿ Carbon monoxide is a colorless, odorless, poisonous gas that poses the greatest risk for heart patients. Emissions from cars contribute more than two-thirds of all emissions nationwide, though combustion in industrial processes produces it as well. Carbon monoxide reduces the amount of oxygen available to the body tissues and weakens heart contractions, reducing the flow of blood through the body.

⦿ Nonferrous smelters, battery plants, and lead additives in gasoline are the major sources of lead emissions to the atmosphere. Of these, leaded gasoline historically has been the most significant source. Lead affects the kidneys, nervous system, and blood-forming organs. Ingesting excessive amounts of lead may cause seizures, mental retardation, and/or behavioral disorders. Infants and children are particularly susceptible to lead pollution.

Emissions of lead have been cut 96 percent since 1970, thanks in part to the serendipitous discovery that the catalytic converter (designed to reduce emissions of hydrocarbons, carbon monoxide, and nitrogen oxides) functions only on unleaded gasoline. Since 1975, all new cars have been equipped with catalytic converters. Though agricultural equipment, old cars, and incinerators still use leaded fuel, the EPA has banned all lead in gasoline beginning in the 1990s.

⦿ Particles of airborne toxic chemicals are also hovering over our heads. Congressman Henry Waxman of California has said, "The magnitude of this problem far exceeds our worst fears." According to a Congressional report, at least 2.4 billion pounds of dangerous pollutants are released into the air each year—and they're coming from every state. The largest single source of air toxics, releasing more than four times the amount from any other source, is the chemical industry, which reportedly released some 886.5 million pounds of toxics into our air supply in 1986 alone. Though the total health impact of being exposed to so many pollutants at once is not fully understood, we do know that millions of pounds of carcinogens, mutagens, and neurotoxins are clogging our air supply, and those who live near chemical plants show higher cancer rates than people who don't.

In addition to polluting our air, airborne toxics are poisoning our fresh water, maiming our fish and wildlife, and endangering our children. Each year Vulcan Chemical in Kansas emits 69,000 pounds of the poison gas phosgene, which killed thousands of soldiers in World War I. Indiana air is getting 143,097 pounds of methyl isocyanate annually, the same poison that killed over 3,000 Indians in Bhopal. At least 80 percent of the toxic pollution in Lake Superior and up to 50 percent of the toxic pollution in

Lake Michigan and Lake Huron comes from the atmosphere. Over 800 toxic chemicals, some from as far away as Central America and Asia, have been found in the water, fish, and wildlife of the Great Lakes.

Some sixty U.S. counties, including much of the urban Midwest and East, violate minimal air quality standards, spewing more pollution into the air than is legally permitted under the federal Clean Air Act. The American Lung Association believes that about 115 million Americans are being exposed to treacherous air pollution levels; the American Academy of Pediatrics believes that as many as 28 million children have been put at risk because the air is too dirty to breathe safely.

FOR THE CHILDREN

In many ways, all of the environmental problems listed above have the gravest consequences for children. Not only are their immature immune systems less capable of handling toxics and contaminants, but a lifetime of pollution awaits them—and *their* children—unless we act now to save the planet.

Paradoxically, one way we can begin is by having fewer children ourselves. World population, now over 5.2 billion people, is growing at a much faster rate than expected and could easily reach 10 billion by the middle of the next century. The implications for the fate of the earth are staggering.

The earth has a limited "carrying capacity," or ability to provide people and other forms of life with adequate food, shelter, and the resources to maintain an acceptable quality of life without itself being degraded. But the world's ballooning human population is unquestionably straining the earth's carrying capacity today. Overfishing has caused the collapse of many oceanic fisheries; farmers move onto ever more marginal land, aggravating an already serious soil erosion problem; and overgrazing is worsening the spread of deserts, which is occurring on 12 percent of the surface of the earth.

As Judith Jacobson observed in *U.S. Carrying Capacity: An Introduction,* the United States is not immune to these stresses. The U.S. commercial fish catch has fallen; overgrazing is desertifying an area the size of the thirteen original states; and soil erosion is more widespread than ever. Population growth throughout the United States causes the loss of enough farmland to provide millions of people with a minimum diet.

And the demands expected to converge on U.S. natural systems in the next few decades are expected to be even more intense: The Bureau of the Census projects that U.S. population, currently 243 million, could reach 300 million by the year 2030.

Though Americans constitute only 5 percent of the earth's population, we consume approximately 25 percent of the earth's resources. One immediate way we can help conserve these resources is by having only one or two children, rather than three or more. Do such choices really make a difference? Compare two families: After four generations, a family with a three-child tradition will consume 160 percent more resources (including fish, meat, wood, and vegetable products) than a two-child-per-generation family.

Notes Zero Population Growth, the national organization devoted to establishing sound population policies for the United States, "A child's best chance for a happy life flows from a combination of things: parental love; adequate food, water, and space; and the security that comes from finding, as he or she grows older, that the *next* generation will have these resources. Two commitments can protect such a legacy for the world's children: responsible parenting and caring for the environment."

Let's begin today.

1 IN YOUR HOME

Put this book down and take a walk through your house. Ignore the fingerprints smudging the walls, the hole in the rug, the lampshade that doesn't quite seem to fit anymore.

Instead, walk past the windows. Do you feel a draft? Peek under your kitchen counter. Is it crowded with bottles of toxic cleaning agents? Go into the bathroom. Is the hot-water faucet slowly—but unmistakably—dripping into the tub?

Now take a stroll outside. How many garbage cans do you put by the curb for pickup each week? Are they already filled to capacity (even though pickup is still three days away)? Is the garage full of pesticides and other poisons? Take a look at your car. Is it one of those nice fuel-efficient models? Or have you taken to driving a gas guzzler again?

Every day, "little" things like these—the drafty windows, a leaky faucet, the stuff that keeps the roses bug-free—directly impact the health of the environment. Why? Because they cause us to use more energy, spread unnecessary toxic chemicals, produce garbage overload, and generally continue to eat away at a planet that's reached its limit of assault and abuse.

Fortunately, there's good news, too. In many communities, people have finally decided "enough is enough" and are taking matters into their own hands to turn the environment around.

○ Residents of Osage, Iowa, adopted a model conservation program that saved this town of 3,600 an estimated $1.2 million in energy costs in 1988—just by plugging leaky windows, replacing inefficient furnaces, and wrapping hot-water heaters in blanket insulation.

○ City officials in Seattle, Washington, have set up a door-to-door recycling program that offers financial incentives to individuals and businesses to reduce their output of garbage. Their goal: to reduce waste by 60 percent over the next eight years.

○ The American Forestry Association, the nation's oldest citizens' conservation organization, has launched a nationwide campaign to stop global warming. Their goal: to get 100 million trees planted in America's cities and towns by 1992.

○ And hundreds of millions of individuals, community organizations, national governments, and world leaders are gearing up to launch an "International Decade of the Environment" when they commemorate the twentieth anniversary of Earth Day on April 22, 1990.

The message is simple: All of us, individually as well as collectively, can make a major contribution to cleaning up the earth—with consequences that will improve our own health and leave the planet in better shape than we found it for our children and theirs. Though it may mean we do things differently, in no case are we talking about sacrificing anything more than an unnecessary, polluting power plant or a batch of toxic chemicals.

Let's begin now, by taking some simple, practical steps in our own home.

IN ALL LIVING AREAS

As much energy leaks through American windows every year as flows through the Alaskan pipeline.

If your house is like most homes in America, it loses furnace heat through the roof or attic; through walls, joints, and cracks; out the doors and windows; and even through electrical outlets and switches.

Though you waste several hundred dollars a year if your house leaks like a sieve, the environmental consequences are even more astonishing, because *every energy-wasting situation in your home not only costs you money, but promotes air pollution, acid rain, and global warming at the same time.* For example, heating one home with oil for a year creates 6.5 tons of carbon dioxide (CO_2), the primary culprit behind global warming. You could use 50 percent less oil—and generate that much less CO_2—just by weatherizing your house.

When the Heat Is On . . .

No matter how much you insulate, at some point you will still need to turn on the heat. You can

TEN WAYS TO WEATHERIZE YOUR HOUSE

1. Ask your local utility to perform an "energy audit" of your house. At no or low cost, a specially trained auditor will examine your home and explain what inexpensive and free energy conservation actions you can take to save money and energy immediately. The auditor can also help you determine the potential your home has for using active and passive solar energy systems to reduce your reliance on nonrenewable energy provided by polluting coal, oil, or nuclear power plants. In most cases, you'll receive a written report of the estimated energy and dollar savings you could realize by implementing the auditor's recommendations, along with an estimate of the do-it-yourself and contractor cost of making the recommended changes. Some utilities will even take an infrared photograph of your house (a "thermogram") to pinpoint exactly where heat is being lost.

2. Test your windows and doors for leaks. Move a lighted candle around the frames and sashes of your windows and doors. If the flame "dances," the frames are leaking. You should close the gaps by caulking or weather-stripping. The materials for the average twelve-window, two-door house could cost about $25, but savings in annual energy costs could amount to 10 percent or more of your yearly heating bill. According to the Department of Energy, if every gas-heated home were properly caulked and weather-stripped, we'd save enough natural gas each year to heat almost 4 million more homes.

3. Insulate windows with thick curtains or blinds to reduce heat loss. Thermal draperies, made with a thick, fiber-filled backing to fit snugly against the entire window frame, can reduce heat loss by as much as 50 percent and save you $15 per window each winter. But even simple heavy drapes attached to the window with a valance can save about $10 per window each winter.

4. Install storm windows and doors. Combination screen and storm windows and doors are the most convenient and energy efficient because they can be opened easily when there is no need to run heating or cooling equipment. For windows, alternatives range from a heavy-duty, clear plastic sheet on a frame to clear plastic film that can be taped tightly to the inside of the window frames. Savings in reduced space-heating costs as a result of any of these types of protection can amount to as much as 15 percent a year, or $10 to $15 per window. When storm doors are added, you could save as much as $170.

5. Add insulation. No matter how you heat or cool your home, you can reduce your energy needs by as much as 20 to 30 percent—and save about four months' worth of household energy—by investing in insulation. For guidance in installing or repairing insulation, consult with a reputable insulation dealer in your community or with your local building inspector or county agent.

6. Find out about "R-values" before you buy your insulation materials. Then buy the thickness of insulation that will give you the R-value you should have. (See Heating Zone Map on page 26.) R-values or numbers indicate the resistance of an insulation material to winter heat loss or summer heat gain. The higher the R-value, the greater the insulating capability. The numbers should appear on packages of all insulation materials.

7. Insulate your attic floor or top floor ceiling. If you have 3 inches or less of old insulation in your attic, no matter where you live, the Department of Energy recommends that you bring the insulation level up to a minimum of R-26. And treat doors to attics as you would exterior doors by installing weather stripping and door sweeps. Lift-up hatches and fold-down attic stairs should be sealed with weather stripping around the perimeter and insulated on top, and fiberglass batts can be stapled to the backside of the fold-down hatch. Though overall investment costs could range from $100 to $1,000, heating and cooling savings could be as much as 30 percent of your energy bill if your attic isn't insulated at all right now.

8. To avoid fires, don't insulate over eave vents or on top of recessed lighting fixtures or other heat-producing equipment on the attic floor. Also, keep insulation at least 3 inches away from the sides of these types of fixtures.

9. Consider insulating exterior walls. This is an expensive measure that requires the services of a contractor, but it may be worth the cost if you live in a very hot or very cold climate.

10. Insulate floors over unheated spaces such as crawl spaces and garages. Again, check the heating zone map for the R-value appropriate for where you live. At the very least, carpet cold or leaky floors to prevent cold air from seeping into your living areas from cold basements or crawl spaces below.

make each unit of energy you use go farther by taking the following steps:

◑ Keep your heating equipment in top operating condition. Have your equipment maintained periodically by a professional serviceman. When the time comes, replace your old furnace with a new, energy-efficient model.

◑ Consider a heat pump. The heat pump uses thermal energy from outside air for both heating and cooling. Costs for heat pumps run from about $2,000 for a whole-house unit to about $425 for room size. But they can cut your use of electricity for heating by 30 to 40 percent and might provide some savings in cooling costs as well.

◑ Lower your thermostat to about 65 degrees F during the day and 60 degrees at night. If every household in the United States lowered its average heating temperatures 6 degrees over a twenty-four-hour period, nationwide we would save the equivalent of more than 570,000 barrels of oil per day.

◑ Keep windows near your thermostat tightly closed. Otherwise, the thermostat will keep your furnace working after the rest of the room has reached a comfortable temperature.

❍ **Install a clock thermostat for your heating system.** The clock thermostat will turn the heat down for you automatically at a regular hour before you retire and turn it up again before you wake, making saving energy a convenience rather than a chore. Though the thermostat could cost you a one-time "investment" price of $40 to $60, it could save you as much as 20 percent of your heating bill every year.

❍ **Buy a proper size gas furnace that incorporates an automatic stack damper or induced draft fan, or an oil furnace with a flame-retention head burner.** These devices reduce the loss of heat when the furnace is off; your gas utility or oil supplier will be able to give you guidance on the right furnace to buy.

❍ **Lessen heat loss if you use your fireplace when the furnace is on.**

• Lower the thermostat setting to between 50 and 55 degrees. Some warmed air will still be lost, but the furnace won't have

to use as much fuel to heat the rest of the house to these temperatures as it would to raise the heat to 65 degrees.

• Close all doors and warm-air ducts entering the room with the fireplace, and open a window near the fireplace about ½ to 1 inch. Air needed by the fire will be provided through the open window, and the amount of heated air drawn from the rest of the house will be reduced. If the fireplace has an outside supply of air, opening a window is not needed.

• If you have a simple open masonry fireplace, install a glass screen, a convective grate, a combination convective grate with glass screen, a radiant grate, or a fireplace insert. Some of these devices will cut down on the loss of warm air through the fireplace chimney. Many of these accessories will considerably improve heat recovery from the fire.

❍ **Have your oil furnace serviced at least once a year.** If you do this in the summer, you'll get cheaper, off-season rates. The

---

BODY HEAT

You might be surprised at how much energy you can save by dressing more warmly to retain your own natural body heat. For women, slacks are warmer than skirts. For men and women, long-sleeved sweaters can add between 2 and 4 degrees in added warmth; and two lightweight sweaters add about 5 degrees in warmth because the air between them serves as insulation to keep in more body heat. During the summer, save on air conditioning in the same way: Wear short-sleeved shirts and blouses, skirts and shorts, and light fabrics.

HEATING ZONE MAP

Recommended R-Values

Heating Zone	Attic Floors*	Exterior Walls	Ceilings Over Unheated Crawl Space or Basement
1	R-26	R-Value of full wall	R-11
2	R-26	insulation, which is	R-13
3	R-30	3½" thick, will depend	R-19
4	R-33	on material used.	R-22
5	R-38	Range is R-11 to R-13.	R-22

*If you already have R-11 or R-19 insulation on your attic floor, carefully evaluate the cost and potential energy savings of added insulation to determine whether it will be cost effective.

R-Values Chart

	Batts, Blankets, Boards		**Loose Fill (Poured In)		
	glass fiber	rock wool	glass fiber	rock wool	cellulosic fiber
R-11	3½"-4"	3"	5"	4"	3"
R-13	4"	4½"	6"	4½"	3½"
R-19	6"-6½"	5¼"	8"-9"	6"-7"	5"
R-22	6½"	6"	10"	7"-8"	6"
R-26	8"	8½"	12"	9"	7"-7½"
R-30	9½"-10½"	9"	13"-14"	10"-11"	8"
R-33	11"	10"	15"	11"-12"	9"
R-38	12"-13"	10½"	17"-18"	13"-14"	10"-11"

**R-value of rigid foamed boards is 5.2 per inch when new.

simple precaution could save you 10 percent in fuel consumption.

○ **Clean or replace the filter in your forced-air heating system each month.**

○ **Dust or vacuum radiator surfaces frequently.** Dust and grime impede the flow of heat, so keep radiator surfaces clean. And if the radiators need painting, use flat paint, preferably black. It radiates heat better than glossy.

Keeping It Cool with Air Conditioning

With global warming on the rise, we'll probably be demanding more, not less, air conditioning as the years go by. Still, we can conserve energy while keeping cool by treating our air conditioners the same way we treat other energy-demanding appliances: by using them wisely and keeping them running efficiently.

○ **Buy an energy-efficient air conditioner.** New air conditioners come labeled with an Energy Efficiency Rating (EER), a standard that lets you calculate how much electricity the air conditioner will consume. The higher the EER, the less it will cost you to operate the appliance to achieve the same level of cooling. See page 50 for more information.

○ **Avoid overcooling.** Don't use or buy more cooling equipment capacity than you actually need. If you decide on central air conditioning, select the most energy-efficient unit that will cool the size space you have. Bigger is not bet-

ter. A larger unit than you need will cost more to run and may not remove enough humidity from the air, the feature that some consumers like most about air conditioners.

○ **Keep your cooling system well tuned.** Have it professionally maintained, and ask how the energy efficiency of the system may be increased.

○ **Make sure the ducts in your air-conditioning system are properly sealed and insulated,** especially those that pass through the attic or other uncooled spaces.

○ **Keep your air conditioner itself cool.** According to the American Forestry Association, one or two trees shading your outdoor air-conditioning units can increase their operating efficiency by as much as 10 percent.

○ **Consider using individual window or through-the-wall air conditioner units.** Room-size air conditioners cost less to operate than central units because cooling is "zoned," meaning that you cool only one or two rooms, not the entire house. Thus, where it might cost $200 a year to run two room-size units, a much larger central air conditioner could cost about $500 to operate for the season—without keeping your living space twice as cool.

○ **Install a whole-house ventilating fan.** This can be put in your attic or in an upstairs window to cool the house, even if you have central air conditioning. Though they only cost $200 to $400, installation and such accessories as lou-

BRIGHT IDEA

If you often forget to turn your air conditioner off when you leave your home, consider using a timer to control your unit the same way an energy-saving thermostat regulates your furnace, and reap the same benefits in lower fuel bills and energy consumption.

Though several devices are available, *Consumer Reports* has highlighted the Hunter Energy Monitor for its effectiveness and simplicity. The device plugs directly into a wall socket and accepts the plug from the air conditioner. To program the Energy Monitor, you push buttons similar to those on some microwave ovens. An instruction manual walks you through the steps required.

You can program up to four temperature changes a day on weekdays, two on weekends. For example, you may want to have the air conditioner hold the room at 85 degrees while you're at work; but you can have it brought down to 75 degrees just before you get home, and allow the temperature to rise to 80 degrees during the night. After 500 hours of air-conditioner use, the Monitor flashes a reminder to clean the filter, though *Consumer Reports* recommends checking the filter every two weeks. The list price is $45, though you may be able to find it for less; it's carried in home centers and appliance stores.

vers, shutters, and remote switches can easily double this initial cost. On the other hand, according to *Consumer Reports,* a big fan working under the right conditions can cool and ventilate an entire house for about the energy cost of running an air conditioner in one room.

⊙ **Set your thermostat as high as possible** (78 degrees F is often recommended as a reasonably comfortable and energy-efficient indoor temperature). The higher the setting and the less difference between indoor and outdoor temperature, the less outdoor hot air will flow into the building. According to the Department of Energy, if everyone raised air-conditioning temperatures 6 degrees, we'd save the equivalent of 190,000 barrels of oil every day.

⊙ **Don't set your thermostat at a cooler setting than normal when you turn your air conditioner on.** It will not cool faster. It will cool to a lower temperature than you need and use more energy to do so.

⊙ **Clean or replace air-conditioning filters at least once a month.** When the filter is dirty, the fan has to run longer to move the same amount of air, using more electricity.

○ **Turn off the window air conditioner when you leave a room for several hours.** You'll use less energy cooling the room down later than if you had left the unit running.

○ **Use a fan with your window air conditioner.** Use the air conditioner to cool one room, then put the fan to work blowing that cooled air into an adjacent room or hallway. You'll use less energy than if you had turned window air conditioners on in both rooms.

○ **Don't place lamps or TV sets near your air-conditioning thermostat.** Heat from these appliances is sensed by the thermostat and could make the air conditioner run longer than necessary.

With or Without
Air Conditioning . . .

○ **Keep your house itself cool.** Planting three trees around your house can block incoming sunlight by as much as 70 percent and reduce air-conditioning cost by 10

to 50 percent. Awnings, overhangs, and shutters mounted on the south, east, and west sides of your house can be installed for as little as $250 to $300, but you'll save $100 to $150 each year thereafter in cooling costs.

○ **Keep daytime lights low or off.** Electric lights generate heat and add to the load on your air conditioner, so use daylight instead.

○ **Do your cooking and use other heat-generating appliances in the early morning and late evening hours whenever possible.**

○ **Open the windows instead of using your air conditioner or electric fan on cooler days and during cooler hours.**

○ **If you have no air conditioning, be sure to keep windows and outside doors closed during the hottest hours of the day.**

○ **Use vents and exhaust fans to pull heat and moisture from the attic, kitchen, and laundry directly to the outside.**

OURCE

○ The U.S. Department of Energy has prepared an easy-to-read booklet brimming with energy conservation suggestions. For your free copy, write: *Tips for Energy Savers,* DOE Conservation and Renewable Energy Inquiry and Referral Service, P.O. Box 8900, Silver Spring, MD 20907; or call 800-523-2929 or 800-233-3071 in Alaska and Hawaii.

○ For a complete analysis of air conditioners on the market today, as well as alternatives for cooling your house, see "Cool Aid," *Consumer Reports,* July 1989, pages 431–440.

Building or Buying a Home

You can avoid making energy-wasting mistakes in advance if you consider climate, local building codes, and energy-efficient construction when you build or buy a home.

Ⓞ **Site your house to take maximum advantage of the climate, available sunlight, and wind patterns.** An exposed location near the top of a hill will be windier than most nearby locations but will help ventilate in hot, humid seasons. On the other hand, cool air flows toward valley bottoms and other low-lying areas, desirable locations for nighttime cooling in hot, arid climates. Choose the right site to maximize the seasonal benefits a site offers and minimize the seasonal liabilities.

Ⓞ **Design a square floor plan.** It is usually more energy efficient than a rectangular plan.

Ⓞ **Insulate walls, roof, and floors to the highest specifications recommended for your area** (see heating zone map).

Ⓞ **If the base of a house is exposed, as in the case of a mobile home, build an insulating "skirt" around it to keep cold air from seeping into the house through the floor.**

Ⓞ **Install louvered panels or wind-powered roof ventilators** rather than motor-driven fans to ventilate the attic.

Ⓞ **Install windows you can open** so you can use natural or fan-forced ventilation in moderate weather.

Ⓞ **Use double-pane glass throughout the house.** Windows with double-pane heat-reflecting or heat-absorbing glass provide additional energy savings, especially in south and west exposures.

Ⓞ **In a warm climate, roof your house with light-colored**

BRIGHT IDEA

Unlike coal, oil, or nuclear power, the supply of solar energy is unlimited. Every day, the earth receives enough solar energy—free—to heat every home in the world for one year. Consider the possibilities in your home.

Sunlight can be used to heat space and water in two ways: with "active" systems that employ photovoltaic cells or solar collectors to heat liquid or air, and with "passive" systems that rely on architectural features—glass, awnings that keep out sun during the summer, and south-facing solar greenhouses that circulate warmed air into the rest of the house—for heating, cooling, and lighting. A well-designed passive solar home can reduce energy bills by 75 percent. And because it doesn't rely on power generated by coal or oil, you can live in a solar home and produce almost no greenhouse gases or air pollution.

ƒOURCE

For more information about the potential to heat your home with power from the sun, contact the Solar Energy Industries Association, Suite 610, 1730 North Lynn Street, Arlington, VA 22209-2009; telephone: 703-524-6100.

shingles to keep your house cooler.

◐ **When buying a home, ask the sellers how much energy the building uses.** Relevant information would include the amount of insulation in the house and how efficiently space heating, air-conditioning, and water heating systems work. Ask to see the utility bills from the previous year. You may want to compare the bills of all the houses you're thinking of buying for a sense of which uses less energy.

Turn the Lights On—and the Energy Off!

◐ It takes approximately 394 pounds of coal to keep a single 100-watt incandescent light bulb burning for twelve hours each day for one year.

◐ Burning the coal to produce the energy to light the bulb creates about 936 pounds of acid rain–causing carbon dioxide and 7.8 pounds of sulfur dioxide.

◐ Lighting the bulb during daylight hours uses an additional 438 kilowatt hours of electricity.

Twenty-five percent of the electricity generated in America is used to keep the lights on. But according to the Lawrence Berkeley Laboratories in California, forty large U.S. power plants—a primary source of the sulfur dioxide and nitrogen oxides that cause acid rain, and of the carbon dioxide behind the green-

---

SUN POWER

◐ Solar energy systems at work today supply enough energy to power 58 million American homes for a year.

◐ Active solar hot-water and space heating systems can save 5 to 40 percent of the energy a building otherwise uses.

◐ There are 100,000 passive solar homes in the United States; one million U.S. buildings employ some aspect of passive solar design, and another million benefit from active solar heating.

◐ One family in one year can eliminate almost three-quarters of a ton of atmospheric CO_2 emissions by using a solar hot-water heater as their primary heating source.

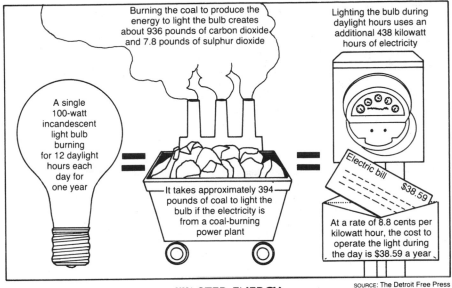

WASTED ENERGY

SOURCE: The Detroit Free Press

Labels in figure:
Burning the coal to produce the energy to light the bulb creates about 936 pounds of carbon dioxide and 7.8 pounds of sulphur dioxide

Lighting the bulb during daylight hours uses an additional 438 kilowatt hours of electricity

A single 100-watt incandescent light bulb burning for 12 daylight hours each day for one year

It takes approximately 394 pounds of coal to light the bulb if the electricity is from a coal-burning power plant

Electric bill $38.59

At a rate of 8.8 cents per kilowatt hour, the cost to operate the light during the day is $38.59 a year

house effect—could be given early retirement by fully using fluorescent bulbs and other new, cost-effective lighting technologies.

Though you may equate "fluorescent" with long, skinny tubes that emanate an eerie light, new technological advances have developed a small fluorescent fixture capable of fitting into any standard light bulb socket. Southern California Edison has given away 450,000 such bulbs to low-income ratepayers, displacing 8 megawatts of generating capacity. The cost per saved kilowatt hour is less than it costs to produce a kilowatt hour of electricity at the nuclear power plant at San Onofre.

Each time an incandescent bulb burns out, replace it with a fluorescent one. In the meantime, take these other light-saving steps:

○ **Use daylight whenever possible.** Many tasks—reading, writing, studying, sewing—can be done quite comfortably by the light of a window. And using daylight offers twin benefits: It's free and doesn't pollute!

○ **Replace fixtures that use two or more low-wattage bulbs with one that uses only one bulb.** A single 100-watt bulb gives off 20 percent more light than two 60-watt bulbs, and it uses less power. (Just don't exceed the acceptable wattage for a particular fixture.)

○ **Don't overlight an area.** Experiment with less powerful bulbs in hallways and lamps until you find the minimum wattage bulb needed to meet your lighting requirements. Higher wattage bulbs

WHY SWITCH TO FLUORESCENT LIGHT BULBS?

○ One 18-watt fluorescent bulb provides the light of a 75-watt incandescent bulb and lasts ten times as long.

○ Even though the purchase price is higher, over its useful life an 18-watt fluorescent light bulb keeps more than eighty pounds of coal in the ground.

○ Substituting just one fluorescent light for a traditional bulb can keep about 250 pounds of carbon dioxide out of the atmosphere.

○ Fluorescent lights are three to four times more efficient than incandescent bulbs.

can be used in lamps that concentrate light on your work area, reducing the need for overhead lighting.

○ **Use dimmers.** Dimmers save energy by making it easy to reduce light intensity.

○ **Dust light fixtures and bulbs.** Regular cleaning around light bulbs and fixtures will get rid of light-absorbing dirt.

LIGHT BULB ALTERNATIVES

○ Fluorescent lights.

○ Frosted bulbs—they generate more light than a soft-white bulb of the same wattage.

○ Reflector bulbs—a 50-watt reflector bulb can concentrate as much illumination as a 100-watt standard bulb (even though it costs only half as much to operate).

○ "Energy Miser" or "Supersaver" type incandescent bulbs—though they cost slightly more than other incandescents, they use 5 to 13 percent less electricity than ordinary bulbs.

DON'T LEAVE THE LIGHTS ON!

When a sixty-year-old Michigan man cruises the streets of Detroit and its environs on any given day, he always seems to find what he's looking for—and that doesn't make him happy. His "quarry": outside lights that are left on during the day, forcing the Detroit Edison Company to burn that much more coal—and dump that much more carbon dioxide into the atmosphere. At five-foot-one, gray-bearded Tom Anderson has gone after Detroit's Department of Public Works, the AAA Michigan offices in Dearborn, the Michigan Department of Transportation, private hotels and local businesses, all in the fight against global warming and acid rain. If he sees a light burning outside during daylight hours, he'll track down the building or lighting superintendent and ask that person to turn off the lights. Usually, he does. That's one way to cool the globe.

ᛉOURCE

For hundreds of ways to save energy on electricity, see *Cut Your Electric Bills in Half* by Ralph J. Herbert, Ph.D. If you can't find the book in your local bookstore, order it from Rodale Press, 33 East Minor Street, Emmaus, PA 18098.

○ Short-life bulbs—they actually are more energy efficient than the so-called long-life models.

As for That Coffee Table . . .

There's no sense in chucking your mahogany furniture if that's what's already in your living room. But when the time comes to replace it, think globally and act locally. Chances are, the mahogany table or teak chair you consider buying played a role in tropical deforestation.

Tropical hardwoods like mahogany and teak are valued for both esthetic and practical reasons: Many are resistant to decay and attack from termites and other wood-boring insects. Others are appreciated for their exotic beauty. The United States imports more tropical hardwoods than any other nation in the world except Japan. In fact, Americans spend at least $2 billion a year on tropical wood products that include furniture, pulp, wood chips, matches, and even feedstocks for chopsticks.

But this market may not be open to America much longer. A combination of slash-and-burn agriculture, logging, and cattle ranching is

YOU CAN'T SEE THE FORESTS OR THE TREES

○ Between 50 and 100 acres of tropical rain forest—an area the size of ten city blocks—are destroyed every minute.
○ An area the size of New York's Central Park is destroyed every sixteen minutes.
○ Every hour 3,000 acres are demolished.
○ Every day, an area the size of Philadelphia (74,000 acres) is lost.
○ Every year, an area the size of Pennsylvania (27 million acres) is ruined.
○ Every ten years, we lose an area the size of the northeastern United States.
○ Every fifty years, we lose an area the size of the United States east of the Rocky Mountains.
○ At the current rate of deforestation, there will be no intact tropical forest left within one hundred years.

For more information, write: Rainforest Alliance, 270 Lafayette Street, Room 512, New York, NY 10012; telephone: 212-941-1900.

chewing up tropical forests with stupefying velocity. Though a variety of projections have been made about the rate of deforestation, they all reach the same conclusion: Unless the rampant destruction of these priceless forests is stopped, some day in the very near future, they will be gone.

There are several steps you can take to help prevent deforestation:

◦ Don't buy tropical wood products. Skip the teak, mahogany, rosewood, ebony, iroko, or other tropical timbers; instead, favor oak, pine, cherry, birch, or maple.

◦ If you're a carpenter or building contractor, don't buy plywood made from timber clearcut from rain forests.

◦ Don't buy animals or plants taken illegally from the wild. Native species help maintain fragile rain forest ecosystems. Favor pothos, philodendron, and amaryllis over rare orchids and bromeliads. If you decide to get a pet, stick with a cat, dog, rabbit, goldfish, or canary. More unusual animals, such as those listed here, may be endangered.

Macaws
Cockatoos
Monkeys
Marmosets
Pythons
Boa constrictors
Iguanas
Red-footed tortoises
Poison arrow frogs
Jaguars
Ocelots
Margays

The World Wildlife Fund monitors the global trade in wildlife and wildlife products. For more information, see the Vacations chapter of this book. Or contact TRAFFIC (U.S.A.), World Wildlife Fund, 1250 24th Street, NW, Washington, DC 20037; telephone: 202-293-4800.

Does the Nose Know?

Before leaving your living room, do one more thing. Take a deep whiff. Smell anything? Even if you don't, that may not be good news. Many indoor pollutants, including radon gas, give off no odor whatsoever. Yet they can have deadly or serious effects on your health.

Indoor air pollution differs from the other environmental problems addressed in this book in that eliminating it doesn't necessarily do much to restore the earth's ecological balance. But it's a major part of this chapter because, according to the U.S. Environmental Protection Agency, the air within homes and other buildings can be more seriously polluted than the outdoor air in even the largest and most industrialized cities.

Research indicates that people spend approximately 90 percent of their time indoors. Thus, for most people, the risks to health may be greater due to exposure to air pollution indoors than outdoors. The good news is that, unlike so many other forms of pollution, indoor air pollution is relatively easy to correct.

While pollutants commonly found in indoor air can be responsible for many harmful illnesses, there is considerable uncertainty about what concentrations or periods of exposure are necessary to produce specific health effects. To play it safe, take the precautions recommended here.

RADON

Radon is a colorless, odorless gas that occurs naturally and is found everywhere at very low levels. But when radon becomes trapped in buildings and concentrations build up in indoor air, exposure to radon, which causes lung cancer, raises concern. The most common source of indoor radon is uranium in the soil or rock on which homes are built. As uranium naturally breaks down, it releases radon gas. The gas enters homes through dirt floors, cracks in concrete walls and floors, floor drains, and sump pumps.

A second entry route for radon in some areas of the country is through well or even tap water. And in some unusual situations, houses are made of radon-containing con-

BRIGHT IDEA

Homeowners have begun using air-to-air heat exchangers to combat radon and the buildup of other toxic gases in their houses. The exchanger extracts heat from air it expels from the house and transfers this heat to fresh air it draws in from outside. Stale air is removed from the house with minimal heat loss. House-size exchangers generally cost $300 to $800.

struction materials; in such cases, those materials can release radon into the indoor air.

According to the EPA, as many as 10 percent of all American homes—about 8 million homes—may have elevated levels of radon, and the percentage may be higher in geographic areas with certain soils and bedrock formations. Radon can be detected only by mea-surement instruments called radon detectors.

In addition to radon, several other sources of indoor air pollution should concern you, including to-bacco smoke, biological contami-nants, pollution from stoves, heat-ers, fireplaces and chimneys, household chemicals, and pollutants emitted from building materials and furniture.

REDUCING EXPOSURE TO RADON IN YOUR HOME

Ⓞ Measure radon levels in your home. Two types of radon detectors are most commonly used in homes: charcoal canisters that are exposed for two to seven days; and alpha track detectors that are exposed for one month or longer. Your state radiation protection office can provide you with information on the availability of reliable detection devices or services.

Ⓞ Refer to EPA guidelines in deciding whether and how quickly to take action based on your test results. The higher the radon level in your home, the faster you should take action to reduce your exposure.

Ⓞ Control the sources of radon pollution in your home. Seal cracks and other openings in basement floors, ventilate crawl spaces, install sub-slab or basement ventilation, or install air-to-air heat exchangers.

Ⓞ Avoid drawing larger amounts of radon into the house. In homes with elevated concentrations of radon, using fans to dissipate radon gas may actually draw even larger amounts of radon into the home from the foundation. You can get the benefits of increased ventilation without increasing radon exposure by opening windows evenly on all sides of your home. Opening windows is particularly important when you are using outdoor-vented exhaust fans.

Ⓞ Select a qualified contractor to draw up and implement a radon mitigation plan. EPA suggests that all but the most experienced do-it-yourselfer get professional help in selecting and installing radon reduction measures. The EPA booklet *Radon Reduction Methods: A Homeowner's Guide* (see Source note on page 40) offers advice on how to select a contractor and how to evaluate proposals for radon mitigation. EPA does not certify contractor competency for planning or executing radon mitigation measures.

Ⓞ Stop smoking and discourage smoking in your home. Scientific evidence indicates that smoking may increase the risk of cancer associ-ated with exposure to radon.

TOBACCO SMOKE

The smoke that comes from the burning end of a cigar, cigarette, or pipe, as well as the smoke that is exhaled by the smoker, is a complex mixture of over 4,700 compounds. According to reports by the U.S. Surgeon General, tobacco smoke may increase the risk of lung cancer by an average of 30 percent in nonsmokers who are regularly exposed to it. Very young children exposed to smoking at home are more likely to be hospitalized for bronchitis and pneumonia.

The EPA estimates that 467,000 tons of tobacco are burned indoors each year. "Passive" smoke, that inhaled by nonsmokers, is one of the largest sources of indoor air pollution because it diffuses rapidly through buildings and persists long after the cigarette has been snubbed out. But smoking is also one of the easiest sources of indoor air pollution to deal with.

○ **Give up smoking and discourage smoking in your home.**

○ **Ask smokers to smoke outdoors.**

○ **Ventilate rooms in which smoking is taking place.**

BIOLOGICAL CONTAMINANTS

Bacteria, mold and mildew, viruses, animal dander and cat saliva, mites, cockroaches, and pollen are among the biological contaminants you might find in your house. Some trigger allergic reactions, including asthma. Some transmit infectious illnesses, such as influenza, measles, and chicken pox. And others release disease-causing toxins. Symptoms of health problems caused by biological pollutants range from sneezing, watery eyes, coughing and shortness of breath to dizziness, lethargy, fever, and digestive problems.

○ **Install and use exhaust fans that are vented to the outdoors in kitchens and bathrooms, and vent clothes dryers outdoors.** Many biological pollutants thrive in moist conditions. Fans will eliminate much of the moisture that builds up from everyday activities.

○ **Ventilate the attic and crawl spaces to prevent moisture buildup.** Keeping humidity levels in these areas between 30 and 50 percent can prevent water condensation on building materials.

○ **Thoroughly dry and clean water-damaged carpets and building materials (within twenty-four hours if possible) to prevent mold and mildew from growing.** If health problems persist after you have tried to dry these materials, you may have to replace them.

○ **If you are building a new home, choose building materials and furnishings that will keep indoor air pollution to a minimum.** To date, studies of pollutants emitted by building materials have been restricted to wood and pressed-wood products. Results have led the EPA to recommend the use of solid wood whenever possible. Exterior-grade pressed-wood products made with phenol-formaldehyde, which emits very low levels of formaldehyde, are also recommended for floors, cabinetry, and wall surfaces. Do not permanently adhere carpets directly to cement floors, because cement floors tend to be cold and moisture condenses on the carpet, providing a place for mold and dust mites to grow. Instead, build a plywood subfloor to lay padding and carpet on.

CONTAMINANTS FROM STOVES, HEATERS, FIREPLACES, AND CHIMNEYS

The major pollutants released from these sources are carbon monoxide, which can cause fatigue, headaches, dizziness, nausea, and disorientation; nitrogen dioxide, which can cause shortness of breath and increase the risk of respiratory infection; and particles, which can lodge in the lungs and irritate or damage lung tissues. Clear the air by keeping gas appliances properly adjusted, venting stoves outside, and keeping the flue open if you use a gas fireplace. Each year, have a

trained professional inspect, clean, and tune up your central heating system.

FORMALDEHYDE

Formaldehyde is an invisible, pungent-smelling gas that can cause watery eyes, burning sensations in the eyes and throat, nausea, and difficult breathing. If you have asthma, high concentrations may trigger an attack. Formaldehyde has also been shown to cause cancer in animals and may cause cancer in humans.

In homes, formaldehyde can seep out of pressed wood products that contain high-emitting urea-formaldehyde (as opposed to phenol-formaldehyde) resins—particleboard, plywood paneling, and fiberboard. You can find it in subflooring and shelving as well as in some cabinetry and furniture. Protect yourself by asking about the formaldehyde content of building materials, cabinetry, and furniture *before* you purchase them. Keep temperature and humidity levels inside your house moderate, since cabinets and furniture are more likely to release

SOURCE

The U.S. Environmental Protection Agency has prepared three helpful booklets to help you maintain the quality of the air inside your home and office. These are: *The Inside Story: A Guide to Indoor Air Quality; A Citizen's Guide to Radon;* and *Radon Reduction Methods: A Homeowner's Guide.* All three booklets are available free of charge from the U.S. Environmental Protection Agency, Office of Public Affairs, Washington, DC 20460.

formaldehyde in a hotter, more humid room. Buy solid wood or nonwood products whenever possible.

LEAD

Children who eat paint chips containing lead risk suffering nerve and brain damage and some blood disorders. It has been estimated that lead paint was used in about two-thirds of the houses built before 1940, one-third of the houses built from 1940 to 1960, and some housing built since 1960.

◐ If you suspect that paint in your home contains lead, have it tested. Consult your state health or housing department to find a private laboratory or public agency to do the test.

◐ Leave lead-based paint undisturbed if it is in good condition. By trying to remove it, you may create more hazards than it's worth.

◐ Do not sand or burn off paint that may contain lead. If paint is cracked or peeling, cover it with wallpaper or some other building material. Consider having painted woodwork such as doors and molding taken out of the house and sent off-site for chemical removal. If lead-based paint must be removed in the house, everyone not involved should leave the house while removal takes place.

In the Kitchen

Your kitchen is the environmental "hot spot" of your house. It's where you use significant amounts of energy (in cooking, refrigeration, food processing, microwaving, and dishwashing), where you create the most garbage (remember the mess of plastic and paper left after you unpacked last week's groceries?), and where you probably store toxic chemicals (cleaners, polishes, bug sprays, etc.). Virtually everything you do in the kitchen affects the environment one way or the other with, in some cases, significant impacts on your own health.

How Safe Is Your Drinking Water?

The Center for Science in the Public Interest raised the following question: Suppose all the water on earth could fit in a gallon jug. If you poured out the portion that was nondrinkable, too salty, polluted, or hard to get, you'd end up with one single drop. Is that drop safe to drink?

In many areas of the United States, the answer is yes. But for tens of millions of us, drinking water is contaminated. A disturbing number of health-related drinking problems have cropped up in the last twenty years, and it pays to be sure that your drinking water is as pure as it possibly can be. Here's how:

◐ Look at the color. High levels of iron in the ground, from rusting pipes, or from landfills can give water an orange or red hue that may indicate contamination.

◐ Smell the water. Sulfur, decaying bacteria, and other contaminants will make the water smell like rotten eggs. Organic chemicals give

SOURCE

The Environmental Hazards Management Institute in Durham, New Hampshire, has produced a Water Sense Wheel, which provides commonsense approaches to investigating home water quality. It includes a guide to water quality standards set by the U.S. Environmental Protection Agency, potential health effects associated with specific contaminants, and ways to reduce water contamination. The wheel lists clues to help you identify water problems (such as "salty, brackish taste" or "musty, earthy smell"), suggests possible causes and contaminants, describes the federal standard for the content of possible chemical contaminants in water, and lists health effects and treatment options. A similar wheel has been produced identifying household hazardous wastes. It lists waste categories, chemical products, hazardous ingredients, alternatives, and waste management. Both wheels can be obtained from Environmental Hazards Management Institute, 10 Newmarket Road, P.O. Box 932, Durham, NH 03824 for $2.75 each, and bulk rates are available.

off a sweet candy-like smell, while gasoline or fuel oil from leaking underground gas tanks smell predictably oily.

○ **Does the water make you tingle or burn?** Tingling or burning sensations while showering or bathing, or rashes on your hands and arms and other parts of the body, may mean that your water has a problem.

WHAT ABOUT BOTTLED WATER?

Bottled water is not necessarily better. It can come from a spring, a well, a river, or even a tap. It may have been processed in some way—or not at all. Bottled water is supposed to meet EPA water quality standards for only twenty-two contaminants—eight *fewer* than for tap water. Americans spent $1.5 billion

on an estimated 1.25 billion gallons of bottled water in 1987, and one out of six households now uses bottled water as its primary source of drinking water. But a 1987 state survey revealed that thirteen of fifteen brands of mineral water sold in Massachusetts were considered polluted according to federal and state standards. And a New York survey found traces of toluene, carbon tetrachloride, and other dangerous solvents in forty-eight of ninety-three bottled waters sampled in that state in 1988.

After extensive surveys, *Consumer Reports* concluded that there is little evidence that bottled water is any healthier than tap water. Indeed, bottlers are not allowed to claim any health benefits for their products. "Only if the local tap water were seriously polluted would

IS YOUR WATER CONTAMINATED?

If you have any reason to believe your drinking water is contaminated, take these precautions:

❍ **Contact your local water company.** Ask for the most recent analysis of the compounds and chemicals found in your water and for records of all violations of the Safe Drinking Water Act or state rules in the last four years. Note: Lead contamination often is not detected by the water utility because lead leaches from pipes under the streets or in homes. You must test for lead in your home to be sure you have no problems. A lead test generally costs $10 to $35.

❍ **If necessary, obtain your own water analysis.** Use the telephone book to locate a state-certified laboratory. Or contact your regional EPA office (address and phone number can be found in the Resources section of this book) for suggestions and referrals.

❍ **Compare the results of your analysis with the national limits set by the Environmental Protection Agency.** If your water deviates from EPA standards, notify your local water quality board and your local EPA regional office immediately. Ask your water quality board to recheck the water supply and to locate the source of harmful water contaminants. Depending on the seriousness of the problem, you may need to organize your neighborhood into a community-wide effort to restore safety to your drinking water supply. (See also "Hunt the Dump," pages 159–161 in chapter 7, for suggestions.)

❍ **If you suspect that your water may be contaminated by lead, take two steps:**

First, do not consume water that has lain in your home's plumbing for more than six hours, such as overnight or during your workday, since the longer water is exposed to lead pipes or lead solder, the greater the possible lead contamination. Before using water for drinking or cooking, "flush" the pipes by allowing the cold water faucet to run until the water has become as cold as it will get. You must do this for each drinking water faucet—taking a shower will not flush your kitchen tap. Once you have flushed a tap, fill one or two bottles with water and put them in the refrigerator for use later that day. (To conserve water, use the one or two gallons that were flushed for nondrinking purposes such as washing dishes.)

Second, never cook with or consume water from the hot-water tap. Hot water dissolves lead more quickly than cold water and should not be used for cooking or drinking.

SOURCE

When should you put a filter on your drinking water faucet? Most filters cannot remove lead, but certain legitimate filters can reduce some other toxic chemicals found in drinking water. Filters can be useful when there is no alternative water supply or when you are trying to provide an extra measure of safety for your family. There are nine basic types of water purifiers available for home use: For a complete rundown on each system, see *Is Your Water Safe to Drink?* (1988) by Consumer Reports Books.

For more information about lead contamination, get a free copy of *Lead and Your Drinking Water* from the U.S. Environmental Protection Agency, Office of Public Affairs, Washington, DC 20046. For general information about drinking water contamination, request the *Citizens Guide to Drinking Water* and *Danger on Tap* from the National Wildlife Federation, 1400 16th Street NW, Washington, DC 20036. Single copies are free.

bottled water be better for your health," advised *Consumer Reports*.

What Can You Do to Save Water?

All drinking water begins life as precipitation, trickling into streams, draining into rivers, seeping down through the ground into vast hidden reservoirs. But rain doesn't fall endlessly, and even if it did, it is doubtful that the heavens could keep up with society's ever growing water demands.

❍ Factories consume huge quantities of fresh water to make consumer products. Authors John Seymour and Herbert Girardet calculated in *Blueprint for a Green Planet* (Prentice Hall, 1987) that up to 120,000 gallons of water can be used just to wash, cool, and process the components that make up a car.

❍ Up to a fifth of our water is lost before it reaches the tap, leaking away through fractured pipes and badly fitting seals.

❍ Domestic consumption accounts for between 10 and 40 percent of all treated water. Of this only a tiny fraction is used for our biological needs; the rest is used by household appliances and in washing and flushing the toilet.

❍ By the time a river has passed through heavily built-up areas, it has probably been contaminated by runoff from garbage dumps, salt from roads, and dissolved chemicals, some of which are next to impossible to remove.

The greatest potential to save water is in the bathroom, where we consume more water—flushing toilets, brushing teeth, taking showers, and shaving—than we do anywhere else in the house. (See "Bath" section later in this chapter for suggestions on how to conserve water there.) But you can also save water in the kitchen by adopting a few simple practices:

❍ Don't leave the water running. A full gallon of water can run out of your kitchen faucet in less than sixty seconds! You can end up using 10 to 15 gallons of water just to wash one load of dishes or peel a couple pounds of potatoes if you leave the water running the whole time. If you are washing dishes by hand, fill up a pot with soapy water and scrub each utensil separately, keeping the faucet turned off until you're ready to rinse the dishes off. When you do rinse, you'll use half as much water by turning the faucet on only halfway. Rarely is it necessary to turn the faucet all the way on to rinse off your dishes.

In like fashion, to peel and clean fruits, vegetables, and other foods, fill up a large bowl of cold water, and dunk the peeled or trimmed food into it. You can also set aside the food in a colander or bowl until you've finished preparing it, then wash all of it at once. By doing so, you may be able to save 10 gallons of water for each gallon you use.

❍ Buy and use a water-saving dishwasher. Washing dishes by hand instead of in a fully loaded machine requires about 6 extra gallons of water. So use a dishwasher—but use it wisely. Newer model dishwashers now come with several water-saving options that might read "pot scrubber," "normal wash," or "light wash." Whenever possible, choose the "light wash" option; this will usually get your dishes quite clean while using as much as 20 percent less water than the "normal" or "pot scrubber" mode. But ignore the "rinse and hold" option if your machine has one; if you don't plan to wash the dishes right away, wipe them off with a wet sponge before you load them into the dishwasher to remove stubborn food particles. Finally, it should go without saying that you should only run your dishwasher when it is full.

Keeping the Water Clean

Everything you dump down your kitchen drain ends up at a water treatment plant, where it will be cleaned and purified and may be sent right back to your tap. Though normal kitchen garbage doesn't contaminate water, toxics do. So don't use your kitchen sink as a toxic waste dump. Whenever possible, avoid using toxic chemicals in and around your home. But if you do use them, don't pour leftover cleaning agents, paint, solvents, or other chemicals down the drain. Close their lids tightly and store on an out-of-the-way shelf in your garage or basement until you can take them to your local household hazardous waste collection facility. (Call the public works department in your city for the one closest to you.) Or help your neighborhood organize a "Clean Sweep" program to make it easier for you and your neighbors to dispose of toxic chemicals. (See chapter 7 for details on how to organize a "Clean Sweep" in your neighborhood.)

Energy Savings and Kitchen Appliances

DISHWASHERS

An efficient automatic dishwasher, when used properly, can consume less hot water than washing dishes by hand, especially if you only use the dishwasher once a day. According to the American Council for an Energy Efficient Economy, the most efficient dishwasher now on the market costs nearly half as much to run as the most inefficient model. You can make your dishwasher stretch the amount of energy it uses by taking the following steps.

◐ Buy a model with a booster heater. Dishwashers use energy to heat water as well as to actually run the dishwasher. Dishwashers need water heated to about 140 degrees F to clean greasy dishes. But setting your water heater this high wastes a lot of energy in excessive heat loss through the hot-water storage tank and pipes. A booster heater in your dishwasher raises the temperature of water entering the dishwasher to 140 degrees F, while allowing you to keep your main water heater set 20 or 30 degrees lower. A booster heater typically adds just $30 to a dishwasher's cost, but you'll save that much in water heating energy savings in about one year if you reduce your household water heater temperature from 110 to 120 degrees F.

◐ Favor models with short cycled selections and an "air dry" selector. Short cycle selections use less hot water and are suitable for times when dishes are not very dirty. An "air dry" selector automatically shuts off the heat during the drying cycle, cutting electricity use by up to 20 percent.

◐ Install your dishwasher away from your refrigerator or freezer. Dishwashers produce moisture and heat, which will make your refrigerator or freezer use more energy. If you must install your dishwasher close to your refrigerator, slide a layer of fiberglass or other insulation between the two appliances.

REFRIGERATORS

Our nation's refrigerators consume the yearly energy output of about twenty-five large power plants, about 7 percent of the nation's total electric consumption and over 50 percent of the power generated by nuclear power plants. According to the American Council for an Energy Efficient Economy, if all the households in the United States installed the most efficient refrigerators currently available, the electricity savings would eliminate the need for about twelve large power plants.

◐ Choose an energy-efficient refrigerator. In most size classes, the most inefficient refrigerator/freezer on the market today may use as much as 50 percent more energy than the most efficient models available. Side-by-side refrigerator/freezers typically use about 35 percent more energy than models with the freezer on top, which means new side-by-side models typically cost $30 more to run each year. Compare Energy Guide Labels (see page 50) so that you can buy the most efficient appliance for the size and price you have in mind.

⊙ **Set temperatures at appropriate settings.** The refrigerator compartment should be between 38 degrees and 42 degrees F, the freezer about 0 degrees to 5 degrees. If the temperature is outside these ranges, adjust the temperature control: You could cut your energy use as much as 25 percent by raising the temperature 10 degrees.

⊙ **Periodically clean condenser coils.** Found in the back of most refrigerators, condenser coils should be cleaned with a vacuum or brush. Dust on the coils can make it more difficult for the coils to cool down. Make sure you unplug the refrigerator when cleaning the coils.

⊙ **Defrost regularly if you have a manual defrost model.** Leaving more than one-quarter inch of frost on a freezer's walls makes the motor run longer to maintain cool temperatures inside. Follow manufacturer's recommendations for defrosting your refrigerator.

FREEZERS

⊙ **Choose a manual defrost freezer.** Automatic defrost models typically consume about 40 percent more electricity than equivalent size and style manual defrost models.

⊙ **Consider a chest freezer.** Chest or top-loading freezers are typically 10 to 15 percent more efficient than upright models, because they are better insulated and because cold air doesn't spill out when chest freezers are opened.

STOVES

Kitchen stoves consume either electricity or gas: Electric stoves use less energy than those fueled by gas but usually cost more to operate due to the high cost of electricity. Stoves that rely on natural gas have one added benefit: Natural gas emits only half the carbon of coal, none of the sulfur, and less nitrogen, so using a natural gas stove instead of one powered by coal-fired electricity does not add significantly to acid rain or global warming.

When buying a stove, look for these energy-efficient features:

⊙ **If choosing a gas range, choose a unit with an electric ignition.** Electric ignition replaces the pilot light, cutting gas consumption by about 40 percent and saving $25 to $30 per year.

⊙ **Choose a convection oven.** Convection ovens contain a fan that circulates air evenly through the oven, eliminating hot and cold spots. Cooking temperatures can be lowered and cooking times can be shortened if a convection oven is used.

⊙ **Use alternatives when cooking small quantities of food.** It generally pays to use microwave ovens, toaster ovens, and slow cookers when cooking small- to medium-size meals. Microwave ovens typically consume one-third to one-half as much electricity as conventional ovens for cooking the same food item. And a pressure cooker will cut cooking time—and energy use—by about two-thirds.

○ **Preheat the oven the shortest amount of time possible.** Often preheating is unnecessary, especially when you're cooking roasts or casseroles.

○ **Don't peek into the oven when something is cooking.** A lot of heat escapes each time you open the oven door, so it takes longer for food to cook, and browning and baking results may be affected. Use timers and the oven door window instead.

○ **Put lids on pots.** Lids help keep heat in and speed up cooking times.

○ **Match the size of the pot to the size of the burner.** Why put a 6-inch pot on an 8-inch burner when the 6- or even 4-inch burner would work just as well?

SOME OF THE MOST ENERGY-EFFICIENT APPLIANCES

Refrigerators

Single-door manual defrost
     Kenmore Model 86611*0: 11.6 cubic feet, 489 kwh/yr.
Top freezer automatic defrost
     White-Westinghouse Model RT1742C*1: 16.6 cubic feet, 767 kwh/yr.
Side-by-side freezer automatic defrost
     Whirlpool Model EF19Mk*S: 18.7 cubic feet, 1156 kwh/yr.

Freezers

Upright manual defrost
     Frigidaire UFE16D-L*3: 16.1 cubic feet, 610 kwh/yr.
Upright automatic defrost
     Amana ESUF160: 16.2 cubic feet, 872 kwh/yr.
Chest manual defrost
     Panasonic NR 1705 FC: 16.8 cubic feet, 434 kwh/yr.

Dishwashers

     Roper 8515-L80: 574 kwh/yr.
     Peerless DWI80-*: 574 kwh/yr.

Clothes washers

Front-loading
     Gibson WS27M6WTMA: 451 kwh/yr.
Top-loading
     Montgomery Ward LnC6*05A: 651 kwy/yr.

Room air conditioners

5,000–6,999 BTU/hr.
   Sharp AF-607m: 6,300 BTU/hr.
9,000–10,999 BUT/hr.
   Friedrich SM10H10C: 10,100 BTU/hr.
17,000–19,999 BUT/hr.
   Friedrich SL19H30: 19,000 BTU/hr.

Water heaters

Gas
   Amana EGWH0040X-A: .83 efficiency (if only used with Amana
   EGHW gas furnace)
   Bradford-White M-111-403T5C*-7: .65 efficency
Oil
   Bock 32PP: .63 efficency

Electric resistance heat

   Sears 2203*300: .97 efficiency

Heat pump

   ThermaStore TS-HP-52-HR: 3.5 efficiency

Gas furnace

   Clare Brothers HEGB 80S: 96.0 efficiency

Oil furnaces

   Yukon

   Though you may not be able to find exactly these models when you
go appliance shopping, other comparable models and brands are available that will surely meet your energy requirements.

SOURCE

For a complete listing, write for a copy of "The Most Energy-Efficient
Appliances" ($3.00), American Council for an Energy Efficient Economy,
Suite 535, 1001 Connecticut Avenue, NW, Washington, DC 20036. "Saving
Energy and Money with Home Appliances," a 34-page guide to the pur-
chase and use of energy-efficient appliances, is also available from ACEEE
for $3.00.

ENERGY GUIDE LABELS

Federal law requires that Energy Guide Labels be placed on all new refrigerators, refrigerator/freezers, freezers, water heaters, clothes washers, dishwashers, and room air conditioners. These seven appliances were chosen for labeling because their energy costs can vary greatly, depending on how they are built. The labels provide specific information on yearly energy costs.

Each label shows the following information:

A. The manufacturer, model number, type of appliance, and capacity are listed at the top of the label.

B. The large number shown on the label gives the yearly energy cost in dollars. This is based on estimated hours of use per year and a standard energy price. This standard price is the average for the entire country and changes over time as energy prices increase. The labels you see in stores may have been printed at different times and thus may use different standard energy prices. Also, the standard energy price may be different from the price in your area. Therefore, it is best to find out the actual energy price for your area and use the yearly cost table (see D below).

For room air conditioners, the large number is not dollars but the Energy Efficiency Rating (EER). This tells you how much cooling the air conditioner provides for the amount of electricity that it uses. The higher the EER rating the better. An EER of 8 is good, and 10 or more is excellent.

C. The line scale shows how the appliance compares in energy-efficiency with other models on the market of comparable size and type. You will see a range of lowest to highest costs and where the model you are considering fits into this scale. The label does not tell you who makes the more efficient models or whether they are available locally. To find out about the most efficient models, a guide listing the top-rated models on the market is published by ACEEE (see "For More Information").

D. The yearly cost table allows you to estimate the yearly operating cost based on your local electric or gas rates. Ask the salesperson, or check your latest utility bills to see how much you pay per kilowatt hour of electricity or therms of natural gas (divide the total amount of the bill by the total amount of kilowatt hours or therms used). In the Northeastern United States, for example, energy prices are generally above the national average, so you should use this table to figure energy costs, rather than relying on national average energy cost figures described in B.

For dishwashers and clothes washers, the table shows what the costs are depending on whether you heat your water with gas or electricity and how many loads you do per week. A typical household of four runs about six dishwasher loads each week and about seven clothes washer loads each week.

For room air conditioners, the table shows what the energy costs are for different numbers of hours of use. In the Northeast, an air conditioner will typically run for 250 to 500 hours each year, while 500 to 1,000 hours per year is more typical in hotter regions.

Labels on furnaces and central air conditioners only provide general information and some simple tips on keeping energy consumption down. For more specific information on these appliances, ask a salesperson for the manufacturer's fact sheets.

Energy Guide Labels are not required on kitchen ranges, microwave ovens, clothes dryers, heating equipment other than furnaces, demand-type water heaters, portable space heaters, and lights. With these appliances, look for the energy-conserving features discussed in the rest of this chapter.

Protecting the Ozone Layer

Once you stop thinking about the energy your refrigerator uses, think about its impact on the ozone layer. Chlorofluorocarbons, the compounds that eat away the earth's protective ozone shield (and cause about 20 percent of the greenhouse effect) make up the refrigerant that cools both your refrigerator and freezer. CFCs are also used to manufacture the foam insulation in the refrigerator. Unfortunately, all refrigerators on the market today contain CFCs, so for the moment, the best you can do to control their release into the atmosphere is to keep your unit in top working order until CFC-free models become available (which should be within the next five years). If your refrigerator does wear out, try to find a salvager (identified through your local utility or telephone book) who can both cart the appliance out of your house and recover and recycle the CFCs prior to dismantling the refrigerator.

You can help protect the ozone layer from damaging CFCs found elsewhere in your home by taking the following steps:

○ **Avoid building insulation made with CFCs.** Use fiberglass, cellulose, or other materials that do not contain chlorofluorocarbons. Though they may have to be thicker to achieve the same level of insulation, if you have the space, you can use them without losing energy efficiency.

○ **Don't buy halon fire extinguishers.** Halons also deplete the ozone layer. Even if you never have a fire, the halons can leak out of the extinguisher and into the air. A traditional fire extinguisher using dry chemicals will do the job.

○ **Avoid aerosols that contain CFCs.** Such products include cans that spray strings of plastic confetti, aerosol dust removers used by photographers, boat horns, and cleaning sprays for sewing machines, VCRs, and electronic equipment.

○ **Support legislation that will make CFC labeling mandatory** so you'll know what items not to buy.

SOURCE

The National Toxics Campaign has prepared an excellent brochure to help you avoid purchasing products that contain CFCs and other ozone-depleting chemicals. For your copy of *A Consumer's Guide to Protecting the Ozone,* write National Toxics Campaign, 29 Temple Place, 5th floor, Boston, MA 02111 ($1.50).

THE BATHROOM

You do something in the bathroom that you never talk about and probably never think about: use water.

In fact, if you are like most Americans, you probably consume more water in your bathroom than anywhere else in your house.

DAILY WATER USE FOR A TYPICAL FAMILY OF FOUR

Activity	Water use (gallons)
Toilet flushing	100
Shower and bathing	80
Laundry	35
Dishwashing	15
Bathroom sink	8
Utility sink	5
Total	243

(Source: U.S. Environmental Protection Agency)

A shower alone uses up to 4 gallons of water per minute; brushing your teeth can take 10 gallons, and shaving 20 gallons if you leave the water running while you're cleaning up. Even a leaky faucet can lose 50 to 100 gallons of water a day—and nobody has to be around to notice.

But the "king" of water waste is your toilet. A quarter of all the domestic water consumed in most countries goes straight down the commode. In the United States that means that every time you flush, you pollute another 5 gallons of pure water. Not even if we had an unlimited supply of clean, fresh water (which we don't) would it make sense to do this as often as an average American family of four does: 16 to 20 times a day, seven days a week. For just one person, the typical 5-gallon flush contaminates about 7,500 gallons of fresh water each year to move a mere 165 gallons of body waste.

While no one is suggesting you flush the toilet only once a day, shower only once a month, or give up shaving, it is time to think about conserving water the way you conserve energy—by using bathroom "appliances" like the shower and the toilet more efficiently to make every gallon of water go as far as possible, and by installing permanent water conservation devices that will help you save water day in and day out with no inconvenience or worry.

Where to Save Water

TOILETS

◉ Put a bottle in your toilet tank to use less water per flush. You can save up to 15 percent of the water you use to flush your toilet by installing weighted plastic bottles in the toilet tank. The water saved will equal the volume of the bottles used: A quart bottle will save a quart of water and so on. More bottles may be added based on how well the toilet flushes with the bottles in place. (While some people put bricks into their tanks, left-over one-quart plastic milk jugs are better, as bricks may disintegrate and clog plumbing.) Flat, rectangular bottles or liquid soap and detergent containers will also work. If you prefer a brick, use a ceramic model that won't corrode.

"Toilet dams" are also available from several manufacturers. Toilet dams are made of flexible plastic and metal that can be wedged into the tank on either side of the flush valve, holding back a reservoir of water at each flush. Adjustable float assemblies are another water-saving device allowing the water level in the tank to be reduced as desired.

◉ Check your toilet for leaks. Add a few drops of food coloring to the tank water. If there is a leak, colored water will show up in the bowl within a few minutes. A worn or poorly seated tank ball or a defective toilet tank valve can silently leak many hundreds of gallons of water a day. Although most toilet leaks are not expensive to fix, at some point you may find it more economical to buy a new toilet.

◉ When buying a new toilet, select a water-saving model. These toilets are designed to use 1.6 gallons of water per flush and are available from most U.S. plumbing manufacturers.

SHOWERS

◉ Sing shorter songs. No kidding.

◉ Install a water-saving shower head. Several different brands of inexpensive water-saving shower heads on the market today limit shower flow rates to 2 gallons per minute—as opposed to 4—with no sacrifice of a forceful, pleasing shower. You could end up using 30 to 60 percent less water by installing a low-flow shower head. (The actual amount of savings will depend upon the type of shower head that is replaced and the water pressure.) In most places, the money you save as a result of energy savings (you use less hot water) will pay for these shower heads—which can cost from $7.95 to $15.95—in one to three months.

To save the most water, the EPA recommends water-saving shower heads over the many types of cheap flow restrictors that can be purchased for insertion between the shower head and the shower arm, both because the water-saving shower head gives a more pleasing shower, and because most flow restrictors don't actually limit flow substantially.

SOURCE

If you can't find a low-flow shower head in your hardware or plumbing supply store, you can order one from a list of manufacturers compiled by the National Wildlife Federation, 1400 16th Street, NW, Washington, DC 20036. Or contact either of the following two companies directly.

❍ Lovo Products Division, Vanderburgh Enterprises, Inc., P.O. Box 138, Southport, CT 06490

❍ Con-Serv Inc., 7745 Reinhold Drive, Cincinnati, OH 45237

❍ **Take a shower instead of a bath.** A shower uses one-third the amount of water a bath does.

FAUCETS

❍ **Install a flow-control aerator.** Water flow from all faucets in the house adds up to a significant portion of household water use, especially when you consider that about 4 gallons of water per minute pass through the average faucet. Though flow rates vary depending on whether the faucet is new or old, for most faucet uses, flow rates of 0.5 to 1.0 gallons per minute (gpm) are not only adequate but a great energy saver.

Of the faucet flow-control restrictors available, aerators which use only 0.5 to 1.0 gallons per minute of water are the simplest to install. (They are designed to fit faucets with threaded or unthreaded spouts. An adaptor may be required for installation involving unthreaded faucet spouts.) Installation is relatively simple: You remove the old aerator by turning it counter-clock-wise with a large pair of pliers, then install the flow-control aerator by turning it clockwise onto the spout with the pliers.

At $4.00 to $7.00 per aerator, these devices are a bargain.

In addition to installing faucet aerators, you can practice other simple, water-saving measures:

❍ **Wash hands in the basin instead of under a running faucet.**

❍ **Turn off the water when brushing your teeth.** That will save 1 to 2 gallons of water each time you brush.

❍ **Fix leaks promptly.** Up to 100 gallons a day can drip from a single leaky faucet down the drain. Frequently, the hot-water faucet leaks first, because the heat accelerates the wear on the washer. Tighten the washers on all leaky faucets to reduce drips to zero.

Personal Hygiene

The overpackaged, throwaway nature of many of the "personal care" products flooding the market

SOURCE

If you can't find flow-control aerators locally, they can be ordered from:
- Chicago Faucet Company, 2100 South Nuclear Drive, Des Plaines, IL 60018
- Omni Products, 55666-B Yucca Trail, Yucca Valley, CA 92284

HOW MUCH MONEY DO THEY COST?

Toilet dam—free, if you use recycled bottles	
Two 2-gpm shower heads ($7.95 each)	$15.90
Three flow-control faucet aerators ($4.00 each)	<u>12.00</u>
Total	$27.90

How Much Money Do They Save?

(expected life: 15 years)

Material cost	$27.90
Labor cost	0
Cost per year ($27.90 ÷ 15 years)	1.86
Maintenance and power cost/year	0
Cost of water and sewage saved per year	26.28
Cost of power saved per year ($10.00 per 1,000 gallons of water heated electrically, at 4 cents per kwhr.)	<u>$69.35</u>
Total savings per year	*$95.63*
Net savings per year	*$93.77*
Water saved per day: 48 gallons	

(Source: Environmental Protection Agency)

today makes them environmentally irresponsible and a considerable waste of money.

- **Avoid throwaway contact lenses.** Even though the lenses themselves are quite small and innocuous, the plastic-wrapped paper box they come in represents the worst in garbage overload. Throwaway lenses are also a rip-off. Ac-cording to a report in the Business section of the *New York Times,* instead of $24 for a pair of soft lenses that most patients keep for a year or two, manufacturers will get $60 for a three-month supply of twenty-four disposable lenses, or $240 a year. With the doctor's markup, the lenses alone cost many patients $480 a year, and fittings and checkups bring it up to the $600 level. If you are one of the 15 million to 17 million wearers of soft lenses (the target market for this product), resist the marketing ploys to get you to try disposables! Work with your optometrist to find a comfortable pair of long-lasting soft or hard contact lenses.

◑ **Don't use disposable razors and blades.** Each year, Americans throw away 2 billion disposable razors and blades, enough to shave every man in America fifty times over. Since the razors are made of plastic, not only do they consume high quantities of energy and toxic chemicals during their manufacture, but they don't degrade in a landfill, and incinerating them creates noxious air pollutants. Instead of using the one-use plastic razor, switch to a heavy-duty, long-lasting metal razor, and buy blades that will last for a month. Or change to an electric razor. The amount of power the electric shave will use is negligible compared to the energy needed to manufacture plastic disposable razors, then to landfill or burn them when they're thrown away.

◑ **Buy the largest possible shampoo container you can find,** and use it to refill a small container that you keep in the shower. You'll save money buying the larger size, and you'll throw out fewer empty containers each week.

◑ **Use biodegradable feminine hygiene products.** Tampons and tampon applicators show up on beaches, and nonbiodegradable sanitary napkins are not much better

for their impact on shrinking landfill space. To minimize the ecological impact of both these products, select items that are biodegradable (made of paper instead of plastic) and that come wrapped in the minimum amount of packaging. A plastic-coated tampon packaged in its own plastic, then put in a box and wrapped in cellophane, is not the most resource-efficient option.

◑ **Think twice before you buy deodorants and douches, particularly the aerosol kind.** Demand for these products has been totally fabricated by the advertising and manufacturing industries; using them is not only environmentally unsound but can create unwanted health problems. If you feel you need a feminine deodorant, check with your doctor to see if you have a more serious health problem.

◑ **Where possible, favor cream mousses and gels over hair sprays.** Hair sprays and aerosol mousses are worrisome because they are usually used in close quarters—bathrooms and beauty parlors—where you can easily inhale the fine particles meant for your hair. If you must use an aerosol, open windows or doors to ventilate the room.

The Medicine Cabinet

Most of the medical waste that's washing upon our beaches comes from improper disposal of hypodermic needles, sutures, and other items from hospitals. But casual home disposal of some of these items can cause problems, too. Often, home medical waste is simply thrown in the regular trash. One particular concern involves the 1 billion disposable needles that diabetics are believed to discard each year.

○ Don't toss unused or discarded needles, drugs, aspirators, or other waste into your trash. Keep them in a sealed bag or a jar with a tight-fitting lid. Try returning them to the pharmacy on your next trip. Many pharmacists will then dispose of them in sealed containers with the rest of their pharmaceutical debris.

○ When it comes to buying medicine cabinets, toilet seats, and other accessories, stick to the traditional metal and porcelain varieties. If you must have wood, don't use tropical hardwoods like mahogany. Favor pine, oak, or another domestic wood that is easily available.

LAUNDRY

You can save energy, water, and money in the laundry as well as the bathroom by following these tips:

○ Buy a front-loading washing machine. Front-loaders will use up to 40 percent less water than a comparable top-loading model. A suds-saver option is also a good idea. In all cases, always wash full loads.

○ Use a "solar" clothes dryer. Hanging your clothes on a clothesline to dry outside saves you 100 percent of the energy you would use in any other kind of clothes dryer. Even if you only use a clothesline six months out of the year, you'll reduce the amount of energy you use for drying clothes by 50 percent.

○ For drying small loads of laundry, use an indoor drying rack. Instead of tossing a few socks or underwear into the dryer, hang them over the rack. It can be set up in your bathtub or shower, where it will be out of the way.

○ Use a gas, rather than an electric dryer. You can save as much as two-thirds on your energy bill by converting to an energy-efficient gas dryer with electronic ignition. A $320 model should pay for itself in about four years.

○ Use your dryer efficiently. Dry only full loads, but don't overload the machine. Keep your exhaust outlet and lint screen clean. And set your automatic dry cycle so that it does not run longer than necessary—you can always start the dryer again if clothes do not come out dry the first time around. You should also dry loads consecutively to take advantage of the built-up heat, and separating loads into heavy and light items will also help you save drying time.

○ When buying a new dryer, look for energy-efficient features such as a moisture sensor control, which will automatically turn the dryer off as soon as the clothes are dry. A moisture sensor typically cuts energy use by about 10 to 15 percent; they're much more effective than timers or temperature sensor controls.

Is Cleaning Your Clothes Ruining the Water?

Phosphates are frequently added to powdered laundry soaps to soften the water. But they're banned around the Great Lakes, the Chesapeake Bay, and Florida because excessive phosphorus "loading" in fresh water is one of the greatest contributors to the decline in water quality and the loss of living water resources. Excess amounts of phosphorus can cause abnormally high algal growth. When the algae decay, oxygen is depleted from the water faster than it can be supplied, and fish, crabs, and other aquatic life can die as a result. Removing phosphorus at sewage treatment plants can be done, but it's expensive and can take years to implement if a plant isn't currently equipped to handle it.

O **Always use low-phosphate or phosphate-free cleaning products in clothes washers and dishwashers—in fact, whenever using a detergent.** Or use a liquid laundry soap—none of them contain phosphates.

O **Use chlorine bleach sparingly, or switch to a non-chlorine bleach like borax.** Chlorine bleach is a powerful chemical—otherwise it wouldn't get out all the dirt. But if it ends up in streams, rivers, or lakes, it can kill fish and other aquatic life.

THE NURSERY

Every year, parents and babysitters throw away about 18 billion "one-use" diapers, plastic-wrapped bundles of urine and feces that take as much as 500 years to decompose. Though they represent the ultimate in short-term modern convenience, plastic diapers have created an everlasting ecological nightmare. Flushing them down the toilet clogs sewer lines and creates 43,000 tons of extra sludge each year. Throwing them in the trash burdens landfills with 84 million pounds of raw fecal matter, creating an immediate public health hazard. Flies and other insects drawn to them can disseminate viruses they may harbor. Dr. Jonas Salk, developer of the oral polio vaccine, has warned that a vaccinated infant can eliminate live polio virus for several weeks, and that the virus may survive for weeks after that to contaminate landfills and water supplies.

HOW MANY DISPOSABLE DIAPERS DO WE THROW AWAY EACH YEAR?

O Enough to construct a trail stretching from the earth to the moon 240,000 miles away and back again—several times.

O Enough to fill a barge half a city block long—every six hours of every day.

Using throwaway diapers in the United States alone wastes nearly 100,000 tons of plastic and 800,000 tons of tree pulp. Just one child can use 8,000 to 10,000 diapers before becoming fully toilet trained. As taxpayers, we all pay an average of $350 million annually to get rid of disposable diapers, even if we don't have any kids.

None of the 800 million pounds of paper used each year to make the $3.3 billion worth of throwaway diapers sold each year is recyclable.

One alternative being touted is the so-called biodegradable diaper. Made of cornstarch-based plastic, biodegradable elastic, tissue, wood pulp, and rayon, these chemical-free items take only two to five years to decompose—in the laboratory. But due to the compaction of garbage and the lack of sunlight, water, and oxygen in landfills, studies have raised doubts about how quickly biodegradable plastic actually breaks down. And even if the diaper itself does decompose, it leaves behind the urine and feces, as well as minute particles of plastic whose toxicity has yet to be determined. Unless biodegradable diapers are deposited in a sewage treatment plant, they don't offer much of an alternative to the regular plastic diapers. (Nevertheless, a Nebraska law will ban sales of nondegradable diapers beginning in 1993. Other states may follow suit.)

Choose Cloth Diapers

● Each cloth diaper can be used anywhere from 80 to 200 times.

● When the cloth diaper finally gets to the landfill (if it hasn't been recycled into a cleaning rag), it only takes six months to decompose.

● According to *Consumer Reports,* you can save $12 to $50 a month by switching to a diaper service or washing and drying your own cloth diapers—a saving of as much as $1,200 by the time your child turns two!

● It takes the pulp from one tree to make 500 disposable diapers. At that rate, you can save 20 trees by using cloth diapers instead of disposables for every child you diaper.

Many people who favor cloth diapers but don't have the time or inclination to wash them themselves rely on a diaper service to do the job for them. Diaper services usually cost about the same as buying stocks of disposables, and they'll deliver the diapers right to your door each week when they pick up the dirty diapers. The primary drawback with diaper services is that some of them use enormous quantities of chemicals, including chlorine bleach and other polluting agents, to get the diapers "white as snow." If you use a diaper service, ask your supplier to minimize the amount of chemicals used to clean your diapers, or to use a nonchlorine bleach.

The bottom line is this: If you have a child, don't use disposables. If possible, wash your own cloth diapers at home. Or check your telephone book for the name of a reliable diaper service.

TO WASH DIAPERS AT HOME

If you wash your diapers at home, follow this prescription:

1. Rinse out diapers in the toilet bowl, then toss them into a plastic diaper pail in a solution of cold water, a half cup of borax, and three capfuls of nonchlorine bleach. This will help control odors and at the same time will begin sterilizing the diapers.

2. When ready to wash, drain the excess solution into the toilet. For optimum cleanliness, wash only twenty-four diapers in an average wash load. First, use the spin cycle to drain dirty water.

3. Put in soap the way you normally do, then use the hot wash and warm rinse selectors to wash the clothes. Rinse the diapers twice to remove detergent or soap residues.

4. Drying diapers in the sunlight is probably the most effective way to kill any remaining bacteria on the diapers. Otherwise, dry in a dryer on high heat for forty-five minutes.

BRIGHT IDEA

If you like the idea of cloth diapers but hate the thought of plastic pants and pins, try the alternatives: breathable coverings with Velcro fasteners that minimize diaper rash and let you change your baby in twenty seconds. Several varieties are available from these mail-order companies:

❍ Biobottoms, P.O. Box 6009, 3820 Bodega Avenue, Petaluma, CA 94953—offers soft wool diaper covers with Velcro-like fasteners and a cotton diaper liner.

❍ Baby Bunz & Co., P.O. Box 1717, Sebastopol, CA 94573—offers Nikky's, cotton velour, terry, and 100 percent cotton waterproof diaper covers with Velcro fasteners.

❍ R. Duck Company, 953 W Carillo Street, Santa Barbara, CA 93101 (or call toll-free: 1-800-422-DUCK)—offers less expensive diaper covers.

CLEANING UP ALL AROUND THE HOUSE

Cleaning Up . . . with Toxics?

What does a typical Saturday morning hold for you? If it involves cleaning the house, in all likelihood you'll be turning to your own little reservoir of toxic chemicals to get the job done.

Keeping one place clean often means just shifting pollution from one location to another. The floor wax, furniture polish, window cleaner, copper scrub, tile disinfectant, and air fresheners you use each week may leave your house spic and span, but they also make a pernicious contribution to the hazardous waste problem in America. Vast quantities of detergents, bleaches, and polishes are manufactured from toxic chemicals like hydrochloric acid, sulfuric acid, and benzene. The atmospheric and aquatic pollution that these chemicals produce has grown rapidly over recent years. Just disposing of the "empty" container these chemicals come in can send them right to the landfill, where the toxins leach into groundwater—possibly to end up back in the kitchen, coming out of the tap.

The Alternatives

❍ **Avoid unnecessary use of toxic household cleaners.** Your household cleaning needs can largely be met with six simple ingredients: vinegar, soap, baking soda, washing soda, borax, and ammonia. Various combinations of these simple substances can accomplish most household cleaning jobs cheaply and safely.

Try the following recipe for an all-purpose cleaner:

1 gallon hot water
¼ cup sudsy ammonia
¼ cup vinegar
1 tablespoon baking soda.

This solution is safe for all surfaces, can be rinsed away with water, and is very effective for most jobs. For a stronger cleaner or wax stripper, double the amounts of all ingredients except water. Use gloves, and do not mix with other compounds, especially chlorine bleach. (*Never mix ammonia and bleach.* Doing so produces an extremely toxic gas.)

❍ **Don't use deodorizers that**

SOURCE

Two detailed consumer guides suggest hundreds of recipes for nontoxic cleaning agents you can make yourself that will effectively remove dirt, grease, grime, and stains without leaving behind toxic residues. You can mix them up in used glass or plastic bottles that you would otherwise have thrown away, so you'll be reducing garbage overload at the same time. See:

❍ *Nontoxic and Natural: How to Avoid Dangerous Everyday Products and Buy or Make Safe Ones,* by Debra Lynn Dadd, 289 pages, Jeremy P. Tarcher, Inc., Los Angeles/St. Martin's Press, New York

❍ *Cheaper and Better: Homemade Alternatives to Storebought Goods,* by Nancy Birnes, 423 pages, Harper and Row, New York

In addition, Greenpeace has published an excellent 8-page guide that is full of practical ways to "detox" your home. For a free copy of *Toxics: Stepping Lightly on the Earth: Everyone's Guide to Toxics in the Home,* write Greenpeace, 1436 U Street, NW, Washington, DC 20009.

NONTOXIC ALTERNATIVES TO CHEMICAL CLEANERS

Traditional cleansers based on natural products will usually clean just as effectively as harmful, fast-acting chemicals. Here are some suggested alternatives to the cleaning agents you may have stocked under your kitchen sink.

Product	*Natural Alternative*
Furniture and floor polish	Several commercial products are available that contain lemon oil and beeswax in a mineral oil base.
Toilet bowl cleaner	A strong solution of a natural acid, such as vinegar, will remove most limescale without polluting water.
Glass cleaners	First of all, don't wash the windows when the sun is shining directly on them; the cleaning solution will dry too fast and streak. To cut dirt, mix 2 tablespoons borax or washing soda in 3 cups water and spray onto the glass using a pump sprayer. If you use a "squeegee," similar to the kind used in gas stations to clean windshields, your windows won't streak.
Laundry detergent	Soak in cool water any particularly dirty items before you throw them into the washing machine to avoid using harsh chlorine bleaches that could pollute the water. For hand-washing, use a bar of soap and small amounts of washing soda dissolved in hot water. For washing machines, use phosphate-free powders.
Drain cleaners	To keep your drains open, clean, and odor-free, never pour liquid grease down a drain, and always use the drain sieve. Once a week, mix 1 cup baking soda, 1 cup salt, and ¼ cup cream of tartar. Pour ¼ cup of this mixture into the drain, followed by a pot of boiling water. Your drain should remain open and odor-free. (In the event a drain becomes clogged, pour in ¼ cup baking soda, followed by ½ cup vinegar. Close the drain until the fizzing stops, and flush with boiling water. As a last resort, use a plumber's snake, available at most hardware stores, but be aware it can damage pipes.)
Air fresheners	Open the window or use an exhaust fan as a natural air freshener. Or simmer a small amount of cinnamon, orange peel, and cloves on the stove or in a small ceramic saucer over a candle to give your home a pleasant fragrance. Several "potpourri" candles are commercially available. Fresh cut flowers will also pleasantly scent your home. An open box of baking soda will help absorb odors in the refrigerator; sprinkling baking soda in the garbage can or diaper pail will do the same.

RIGHT IDEA

If it's just too much trouble for you to make your own safe cleansers, you may want to try dishwashing liquid, floor soap, cream cleaner for tub and tile, and laundry powder made from a pure biodegradable coconut base and milk whey and sea salt for cleaning power. If you can't find such products on your grocery store shelves, check a natural foods store or food co-op.

Or order directly from the Compassionate Consumer catalog, 141–44 25th Avenue, Whitestone, NY 11357, or the EccoBella catalog, 125 Pompton Plains Crossroad, Wayne, NJ 07470.

contain **paradichlorobenzene (PDCB)** (found in solid cakes used to deodorize toilets and urinals). Continued exposure to PDCB can lead to liver ailments, cataracts, headaches, and, in the worst cases, seizures and hallucinations. If you're looking for something just to make your clothes smell good, try sachet or cedar chips.

NONTOXIC CONTROL OF INDOOR PESTS

A variety of nontoxic methods will help you control indoor insects.

○ **To control ants,** sprinkle barriers of talcum powder, chalk, bone meal, or boric acid across their trails.

○ **To control cockroaches,** plug or caulk small cracks along baseboards, wall shelves, and cupboards and around pipes, sinks, and bathtub fixtures. A light dusting of borax around the fridge, stove, and ductwork will further help control cockroaches. For a trap, lightly grease the inner neck of a bottle and put a little stale beer or a raw potato inside. You can also combine sugar, flour, and boric acid into a powder that cockroaches will take back to their nests and poison other insects with.

○ **To control flies,** close windows before the sun hits them. Flies usually enter homes through sunny windows.

○ **To control moths,** keep woolens and other clothes dry and well aired. In the summer, store woolens in cedar chests or closets or in tightly sealed plastic bags.

○ **To control ticks and fleas,** wash your pets well with soap and warm water, dry them thoroughly, and use an herbal rinse made by adding one-half cup of fresh or dried rosemary to a quart of boiling water. (Steep twenty minutes, strain, and allow to cool.) Spray or sponge the herbal rinse evenly onto your pet and allow it to air dry. Do *not* towel down, as this will remove the residue. Make sure pets are dry before letting them outside.

❍ **Prevent pests from getting in.** Avoid slow-release insecticides (like dangling fly traps), which can fill rooms with dangerous biocides you could inhale and which easily find their way onto food. And the production of all household pesticides creates massive quantities of toxic and potentially carcinogenic chemicals that can end up in our air or water supply. Bypass these chemical killers by repairing holes in walls and window screens. Since many wood-damaging pests are attracted by excessively damp conditions, it also helps to reduce moisture by repairing leaks, cleaning gutters, and maintaining good soil drainage. Caulk cracks and crevices, and fill or screen holes in walls. Add weather stripping to windows and doors and vapor barriers beneath buildings to block insect paths.

❍ **Use low toxicity chemicals.** These include boric acid, silica aerogel, and diatomaceous earth. All are effective against indoor crawling insects like roaches, ants, silverfish, and termites.

❍ **Protect natural fibers from moths.** Susceptible clothing includes wool, fur, hair, feathers, and to a lesser extent cotton, rayon, paper, and straw. If items are not stored, periodically shake, brush, and air them outdoors in the sun. Pay special attention to hidden areas such as the reverse side of cuffs, the inside of pockets, and the underside of collars.

So Much Garbage, So Little Space

Each week, you probably throw away two to three cans of garbage. If you had to keep all this trash in your own yard, it wouldn't take long before even the mailman might have a hard time finding your address ("Neither snow, nor sleet, nor rain, nor garbage . . . !").

But you don't need to trash so much trash. You can easily cut the amount of garbage you generate in half or even by two-thirds by making a few wise shopping decisions, reusing as much as you can, and recycling the rest. Of all the environmental problems you have to contend with, you can probably have the most immediate impact on garbage overload just by creating less waste in your own home.

FOOD AND OTHER ORGANIC MATERIAL

Every day, Americans jettison food, from potato peelings and apple skins to the leftovers after supper or the last piece of crust in a loaf of bread. For every ten pounds of garbage the average household throws out each week, from one to three pounds are food that could be fully recycled. Here are a few suggestions for keeping the treasure out of the trash:

❍ **Separate your food waste and other organic material from the rest of your garbage.** Even if you live in a high-rise apartment building, you can keep your food scraps separate from the trash; and if you dispose of them in a paper bag, rather than plastic, they'll decompose more quickly in the landfill and make room for more garbage. To prevent the bag from leaking, put some newspaper in the bottom of the bag, or wrap juicy waste in newspaper before you toss it out.

◐ Compost. If you live in a house, townhouse, or apartment that is on or adjacent to some parcel of land, you should not only separate your organic waste from the rest of your garbage but compost it as well.

Compost is nothing more than decayed organic matter. In many ways, it is the perfect form of recycling, not only because it converts organic wastes into rich fertilizer and thereby helps restore the soil, but because it's easy. Once the compost bin itself is built, it is just as quick to take your food scraps out to the compost pile as to your garbage can. (For a complete explanation of how to build a compost pile, see pages 76–78 in chapter 2.)

◐ Reduce the amount of organic garbage you produce. Instead of tossing leftovers out, freeze them for later use in soups and stews. Or, if that doesn't suit your cooking style, try to cook more accurate portions so that you only prepare as much food as you're going to eat. And don't go out to a restaurant when you have a refrigerator full of food at home; eat what's in the fridge first, and save dining out for a better time.

NEWSPAPERS

If you're like many people, you get at least one newspaper deliv- ered to your home every day. When you add up the special sections— comics, want ads, and TV program guides, that amounts to 1,000 pounds of newsprint over the course of a year, enough to fill a living room 18 feet long and 15 feet wide from floor to ceiling every three years. And that's *per person!*

Recycling newspapers rather than discarding them reduces acid rain and the carbon dioxide buildup that causes global warming by using 30 percent less energy than what is needed to make paper from scratch. Recycling also saves trees: Recycling the print run of just one *New York Times* Sunday edition would leave 75,000 trees standing. Plus, recycling just one ton of newspapers conserves 7,000 gallons of water. (For ideas on organizing a recycling program, see page 00 in chapter 7.)

Packaging Waste

In addition to food waste and newspapers, packaging creates an unholy amount of trash. Fully one-tenth of the average weekly shopping bill is spent on packaging alone. To minimize this rubbish:

◐ Use cloth napkins and dish towels instead of paper. Keep old towels, stained napkins, and cloth diapers around to use as rags for mopping up spills.

◐ Bring home groceries in the fewest number of bags possible. Ask for paper bags and remember, the fewer bags you bring home, the fewer you'll have to throw away. Try to reuse the bags you do bring home by taking them

---

WATCH OUT FOR PLASTIC

The packaging industry is the single largest user of plastics today. But that's nothing to be proud of, says a report in *Environmental Action* magazine (July/August 1988), because the plastics revolution in packaging has had a devastating impact on the environment.

"At the front end, many of the chemicals used in the production and processing of plastics are highly toxic, resulting in hazardous wastes, toxic air emissions, and discharges of toxic effluents into waterways. At the back end, once the short lifetimes of throwaway plastic packages and products are over, this "post-consumer" plastic trash litters our streets, oceans, and wilderness areas, and contributes to the nation's solid waste crisis.

"People don't think of plastic products as toxic, because by the time they get to supermarket shelves, they're not. But ingredients in plastic production have dangerous properties for those who work with them or live near plastic factories," said the report.

In 1986, EPA ranked the twenty chemicals whose production generates the most hazardous waste. Five of the top six were chemicals commonly used by the plastics industry.

---

back to the store the next time you shop, using them as garbage bags, or storing your newspapers in them for recycling.

◊ **Buy food and other products wrapped in the least amount of packaging possible.** Skip prepackaged produce in favor of bulk fruits and vegetables you can bag yourself, and ask your grocery store to stock paper, not plastic, produce bags.

◊ **Use glass dishes and cups and metal silverware instead of plastic.** In fact, avoid buying anything that's plastic unless it's extremely durable, you can use it many times over, and you have no other option.

◊ **Recycle glass and aluminum.** If you can, buy the largest size glass bottle of the product you want, and reuse the bottle at home for iced tea, juice, or other foods.

SOURCE

For a complete analysis of the use of plastics in packaging, see *Wrapped in Plastics: The Environmental Case for Reduced Plastics Packaging,* available from Environmental Action Foundation, 1525 New Hampshire Avenue, NW, Washington, DC 20036; telephone: 202-745-4870. (The cost is $10.00 for individuals, $20.00 for government and educational institutions, $30.00 for industry.)

No matter how many bottles you reuse, though, you'll reach a point where you'll either have to start throwing them out or recycling them, along with your aluminum cans. If you're already recycling your newspapers, ask your recycling center if it will also accept aluminum and glass. If not, try to find one that does.

For more suggestions on how to reduce packaging waste, see "Pick the Best Package" on page 120 in chapter 4.

BAN FOAM PLASTICS

Polystyrene foam plastics such as Styrofoam seem to be everywhere: in the food trays we get in fast food restaurants, in the coffee cups we buy for a picnic, in the packaging pellets that surround our mail order purchases. They are a consumer's dream (basically, they keep hot liquids hot and cold liquids cold and are very lightweight) and a manufacturer's windfall (they are very cheap to manufacture). But they have become a scourge on the environment.

Polystyrene plastic does not degrade. It remains in the environment forever, taking up valuable landfill space and creating a major litter problem.

When polystyrene, the main ingredient in foam plastics, is burned, it can release as many as fifty-seven chemicals, including some that have caused cancer in laboratory animals.

Because foam plastic is a petroleum-based product, manufacturing it depletes the earth's limited supply of oil resources.

The earth does not need foam plastic. And if you, and thousands of people like you, stop buying it, the earth won't have to contend with it in the future. Starting immediately, take these actions:

◐ Refuse to buy food that is served in or on polystyrene plastic. Keep a travel mug in your car for stops at fast food restaurants and have them fill that up instead of a foam plastic cup.

◐ If you are having a party or picnic, use nondisposable cups and plates. If you feel you must use throwaway items, use heavy-duty paper products instead of foam plastic. The paper will ultimately degrade in a landfill with fewer harmful side effects.

◐ Use newspapers or straw for packing materials when shipping fragile items. Never buy foam pellets for shipping.

◐ Buy eggs in cardboard cartons, not foam plastic ones.

◐ When given the choice between a product packaged in foam plastic and one that's not, choose the alternative item.

What Should You Do with Your Old Batteries?

According to *Sierra* magazine, each year Americans throw away 2.5 billion pounds of household batteries containing mercury, cadmium, lead, lithium, manganese dioxide, silver, nickel, and zinc. Though there is currently no evidence that these metals are leach-ing into landfills, scientists worry that burning them in incinerators releases toxic chemicals into the air. The U.S. Environmental Protection Agency requires that businesses dispose of them as hazardous waste; however, no regulations exist for batteries used at home. Several communities, notably Vermont and New Hampshire, collect used batteries, sell the expensive metals such as mercury, silver, nickel, and cadmium, and bury scrap materials and alkaline batteries in a hazardous waste landfill.

⊙ **If you must buy batteries, buy the nickel-cadmium rechargeable type.** They're three times as expensive as common alkaline batteries, but can be recharged up to a hundred times. In the long run, by using rechargeable batteries you'll save money and keep more toxic metals out of your local landfill or incinerator.

⊙ **Rather than throwing used batteries in with the rest of your trash, store them in a small box on a shelf in the garage or basement, and donate them to your neighborhood's "Clean Sweep" the next time one is organized.** (For information about "Clean Sweep" efforts, see chapter 7.)

HOME FOR THE HOLIDAYS

Holidays should not be a celebration of the packaging industry. But in many homes, that's what they've become. Birthdays, Halloween, Christmas, Hanukkah, graduations, weddings, and many other social, cultural, or religious occasions, as wonderful as they are, leave behind $300 million worth of trash a year. Most of this garbage is not reusable and, depending on your community's solid waste management system, it may not even be recyclable.

The winter holiday season has got to be the most egregious from an ecological point of view. During one holiday season alone, an incalculable amount of wrapping paper, bows, ribbons, and tape is consumed. On Christmas Day, all of this material ends up in yet another package—the one that's used to cart it out to your garbage can.

You can clean up your act without being a Scrooge!

⊙ **Recycle used ribbons, bows, and decorative wrappings.** If you take care when you're unwrapping your presents, you can reuse the wraps at least one time, at least for family members. Store used paper and accessories in a convenient place so that you can use them for the next holiday occasion.

⊙ **Find alternatives to store-bought wrapping paper.** Leftover fabric or lightweight wallpaper work as well as wrapping paper; and kids will be just as pleased with a toy wrapped in a page from the Sunday comics as they will with one wrapped in the stuff that comes from the store.

HOUSEHOLD HAZARDOUS WASTE CHART

The following chart prepard by the Water Pollution Control Federation will help you establish the most effective means of disposing of typical hazardous wastes used around your home or garden.

Bullets (●) indicate products that can be poured down the drain with plenty of water. If you have a septic tank, additional caution should be exercised when dumping these items down the drain. In fact, there are certain chemical substances that cannot be used with a septic tank. Read the labels to determine if a product could damage the septic tank.

Diamonds (♦) indicate materials that cannot be poured down the drain but can be disposed of safely in a sanitary landfill. Be certain the material is properly contained before it is put out for collection or carried to the landfill.

The squares (■) indicate hazardous wastes that should be saved for a community-wide collection day or given to a licensed hazardous wastes contractor. (Even the empty containers should be taken to a licensed contractor if one is available.)

Checks (✔) in the fourth column indicate recyclable material. If there is a recycling program in your area, take the materials there. If not, encourage local officials to start such a program.

For more information on the safest way to dispose of these and other products contact your state's solid and hazardous waste department or the United States Environmental Protection Agency. We suggest that you note here these important phone numbers in your local area:

Hazardous Waste Management Agency: _____
Poison Control Center: _____

Type of Waste	●	♦	■	✔
KITCHEN				
Aerosol cans (empty)		♦		
Aluminum cleaners	●			
Ammonia based cleaners	●			
Bug sprays			■	
Drain cleaners	●			
Floor care products			■	
Furniture polish			■	
Metal polish with solvent			■	
Window cleaner	●			
Oven cleaner (lye base)		♦		

Type of Waste	●	◆	■	✔
BATHROOM				
Alcohol based lotions (aftershaves, perfumes, etc.)	●			
Bathroom cleaners	●			
Depilatories	●			
Disinfectants	●			
Permanent lotions	●			
Hair relaxers	●			
Medicine (expired)	●			
Toilet bowl cleaner	●			
Tub and tile cleaners	●			
GARAGE				
Antifreeze	●			
Automatic transmission fluid			■	✔
Auto body repair products		◆		
Battery acid (or battery)			■	✔
Brake fluid			■	
Car wax with solvent			■	
Diesel fuel			■	✔
Fuel oil			■	✔
Gasoline			■	✔
Kerosene			■	✔
Metal polish with solvent			■	
Motor oil			■	✔
Other oils			■	
Windshield washer solution	●			
WORKSHOP				
Paint brush cleaner with solvent			■	✔
Paint brush cleaner with TSP	●			
Aerosol cans (empty)		◆		
Cutting oil			■	
Glue (solvent based)			■	
Glue (water based)	●			
Paint—latex		◆		
Paint—oil based			■	
Paint—auto			■	
Paint—model			■	
Paint thinner			■	✔
Paint stripper			■	

Type of Waste	●	◆	■	✔
Paint stripper (lye base)	●			
Primer			■	
Rust remover (with phosphoric acid)	●			
Turpentine			■	✔
Varnish			■	
Wood preservative			■	

GARDEN

Fungicide			■	
Herbicide			■	
Insecticide			■	
Rat poison			■	
Weed killer			■	

MISCELLANEOUS

Ammunition			■	
Artists' paints, mediums			■	
Dry cleaning solvents			■	✔
Fiberglass epoxy			■	
Gun cleaning solvents			■	✔
Lighter fluid			■	
Mercury batteries			■	
Moth balls			■	
Old fire alarms			■	
Photographic chemicals (unmixed)			■	
Photographic chemicals (mixed and properly diluted)	●			
Swimming pool acid			■	

This chart is based on information from the United States Environmental Protection Agency's Hazardous Waste regulations. Copyright © 1987, Water Pollution Control Federation.

● **Buy a live holiday tree.** A "live" tree (as opposed to a "cut" tree) is one that actually is still living. It comes with its roots bound in burlap and can be kept alive by generously watering it until you plant it in the ground. Keep the tree outside on your porch, decorated, until right before Christmas. Once indoors, it will survive nicely for about a week with ample watering and a somewhat cool air temperature. Afterward, transplant it outside, to a spot you have already prepared. The hole for the tree should be deeper and larger than the tree's own root ball, and it should contain well-rotted compost of soil mixed with horse or cow manure. Water the tree regularly for two weeks, and let Nature do the rest.

○ If a live tree isn't an option, think of using an artificial one. Advocating an artificial tree in a book like this may sound like heresy, but it's not. Whether it's made of fireproof plastic or coated paper, an artificial tree will last almost indefinitely with proper care and storage. It will require no fertilizers year after year, no irrigation water, no chopping down, and no transportation to a tree lot. And you can still get that great "Christmas" smell in your house by decorating with pine wreaths and holly and simmering a potpourri of cinnamon, cloves, and orange rind on the stove.

○ Recycle your tree when the holidays are over. If you do buy a cut tree, at least try to recycle it when the holidays are over. Put the tree in your backyard, where it will have a chance to dry out. Trim off the branches and use them, needles and all, as mulch under acid-loving bushes and shrubs. Chop the tree trunk into firewood, or donate the tree to a charity that can use the wood at its own discretion.

○ Give the gifts that keep on giving. Ignore the advertising hysteria that precedes holidays in America. Be creative, and give gifts that are memorable more for what they mean to the recipient than for the attractive packaging they come in or how much they cost.

THE SAVE OUR PLANET HOLIDAY LIST

Next holiday season, instead of an over-packaged, plasticized "thing," give:

An experience (how about a ride in a hot air balloon?)
Season tickets to a sporting event
A recording or compact disc
A subscription to *Organic Gardening* magazine
Membership to a museum
Membership in your favorite nonprofit organization
Theater tickets
A house plant
Homemade confections or gourmet foods
Cloth napkins and napkin rings
Cloth dish towels
Books like *Save Our Planet*
Donations to the needy
Photographs
Low-flow shower head
Toilet dam
A set of biodegradable, no-phosphate cleansers
A solar watch or calculator
An energy-saving fluorescent light fixture
For friends with children, five hours of free babysitting
A day trip on a train
A tree

2 IN YOUR GARDEN

*I*t doesn't matter if you plant food or flowers, a lawn or a grove of trees. The experience you'll have working with Nature to make something grow and prosper will satisfy you long after you've put the hoe back in the shed. That's the personal reward. The planetary one is more magnanimous. Through gardening, you can actually help restore the earth in many, many ways. By favoring ivy or grass over concrete and asphalt, you replenish underground aquifers every time it rains. Because they absorb carbon dioxide, which causes global warming, every tree you plant will help cool the globe. And maintaining a green landscape provides a safe haven for wildlife, especially the hundreds of thousands of birds whose breeding grounds are being destroyed by deforestation.

The most "benign" way you can garden is organically. To many this means "without insecticides"—period. But organic gardening is really much more than that. It's a way of building and rebuilding the soil and encouraging populations of desirable insects and birds to sustain plantings year after year. In 1988 alone, over 200,000 people began gardening organically.

Organic gardening "works" just as well on trees and flowers as on fruits and vegetables, but the need for organic approaches to food production, in particular, could not be more critical. Both the groundwater we tap for drinking supplies and our own personal health have been put at great and unnecessary risk from the application of excessive quantities of pesticides by the agriculture industry.

But we can't lay all the blame on the agriculture system. According to the Ringer Corporation, a manufacturer of organic lawn and garden products, each year American homeowners apply half a billion pounds of chemical fertilizers to their lawns, vegetable gardens, and shrubbery—at a cost of well over $1 billion. They use an additional 20 to 30 million pounds of active chemical ingredients in the form of pesticides to "protect" everything from the tomatoes to the rosebushes.

Whether you're a farmer, a homeowner, or someone who gardens a community plot, organic gardening lets you get the most out of your labor by causing the least amount of damage to the environment. If you currently rely on pesticides and synthetic fertilizers, now is the time to begin the transition to chemical-free gardening. It will probably require an "investment" of two or three years to revive your soil and start attracting the desirable bugs and birds that will control insects naturally. But as with any sound investment, the payoff will only multiply in the years to come as the bounty of your garden increases—and your bills for synthetic fertilizers and other chemicals evaporate. Even if you can't give up all your chemicals, perhaps you can use less of them. At the very least, try some of the simple, chemical-free preventive techniques, such as mulching. You have nothing to lose, not even a plant.

HOW TO GROW AN ORGANIC GARDEN

○ **Start small.** Don't try to garden more than you can handle. Choose a few familiar vegetables, such as lettuce, peas, carrots, squash, cucumbers, tomatoes, and herbs. You can always expand the garden next year.

○ **Get the soil ready.** Work your soil with a hoe or, if you have a big garden, a garden tiller, so that it's loose and airy and all the big dirt clods are reduced to a fine seedbed. Vegetable roots need a loose soil structure to develop properly. If the soil is too dense, the roots won't penetrate freely and growth may be stunted.

○ **Feed the soil.** Here is the secret of organic fertilization: The bacteria in the soil digest decaying plant and animal matter, producing acids that dissolve plant nutrients from rocks and soil particles and feed them to the plant as they are needed. So you need to feed the bacteria as well as the plants (which is all that synthetic fertilizers do). Bacteria thrive on compost, but if you haven't made any yet, you can blend together an organic fertilizer yourself using 4 parts blood meal, 2 parts bone meal, and 1 part kelp, green sand, or ground rock phosphate, all of which can be obtained at your local garden center or nursery. A soil test, done through your state agricultural school, county extension service, or with a do-it-yourself kit, will tell you which major elements your soil may be lacking and whether you need to adjust the acid/alkaline balance (the pH). To boost the level of organic matter in your soil, add peat moss, peat humus, horse manure, or decomposed leaves.

○ **Start composting.** (See the directions that follow below.)

○ **Plant.** You can sow seeds directly in the garden, or transplant small seedlings.

○ **Mulch.** Once seedlings and sprouts are about 3 inches tall or so, apply a thick layer of undecayed plant matter, such as grass clippings, decomposed leaves, or old alfalfa hay. In addition to controlling weeds, mulch soaks up rain and holds moisture like a sponge, so you'll water less frequently and protect your plants during drought. And at the end of the growing season you can work the organic matter back into the soil. Mulch will save you the most work in the garden. (NOTE: Some gardeners use wide strips or sheets of black plastic, with holes cut around each plant to allow water to seep into the ground, to smother unwanted weeds. If you must use plastic, an energy-intensive and nonbiodegradable material, make sure it is sturdy enough so that you can use it for several seasons.)

○ **Water.** Water deeply during dry weather, giving the soil the equivalent of 1 inch of rain once a week. Many gardeners use drip irrigation or soaker hoses, which make watering more efficient and increase yields.

○ **Control the bugs.** But first, don't worry about them. You can lose up to a third of the leaf area of many vegetables without hurting yields. Expect some damage and plant a little more for compensation. When possible, pick bugs off by hand. Or lay boards between the rows and go out early in the morning and turn the boards over, killing any bugs you find beneath. You can also lay spun-bonded polyester material over plants as a barrier to flea beetles, leaf miners, and cucumber beetles. If you find you must spray, use insecticidal soap or biological controls such as *Bacillus thuringiensis* and milky spore disease.

○ **Keep records.** Identify when various insects appear, when they do their damage, and other data you may need to help you combat pests. And draw a map of what you planted where, since you will need to rotate your crops to different locations each year.

○ **Harvest and clean up.** Remove all remaining plant debris or, if it's not diseased, till it into the soil. Then cover your garden with mulch or plant a cover crop like annual rye to begin rebuilding the soil for next spring's garden.

How to Compost

Healthy soil is the basis of the organic system. To produce vigorous growth, a plot of land needs

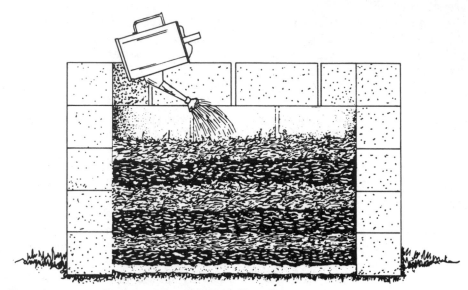

Illustration on page 76 reprinted from *Rodale's Guide to Composting* © 1979 by Rodale Press, Inc. Permission granted by Rodale Press, Inc; Emmaus, PA 18098.

adequate nutrients, helpful bacteria and animal and plant organisms, and a good structure to allow it to "breathe" and absorb moisture.

Synthetic fertilizers sacrifice the long-term texture and flavor of your vegetables for short-term, rapid growth and produce size. Besides, many synthetic fertilizers are derived from dwindling petroleum resources and themselves consume excessive energy during production. And the concentrated nitrates and other substances in synthetic fertilizers cannot be used completely by plants; excess chemicals leach out of the soil to pollute waters and drive away or destroy earthworms and other helpful soil organisms.

SOURCE

Organic Gardening magazine provides simple, easy-to-follow information on chemical-free gardening techniques every month. Subscriptions are available for $14.97 from Organic Gardening, 33 East Minor Street, Emmaus, PA 18098. Also ask for a list of reprints and source lists that include "Quick Ways to Better Soil" and "Five Steps to Quick Compost," available for $.50 each.

The single most effective way you can build up your soil is by composting. Composting is a simple way of reducing organic wastes to humus. Not only does compost feed microorganisms that aid plants in growing, but it improves the structure of soil—breaking up clay, holding sand together, and making the soil easier to cultivate and for plant roots to penetrate. And by darkening its color, compost helps soil warm up in the spring, making it possible to plant earlier.

Composting is also the cheapest, most practical way of disposing of kitchen garbage as well as of tree branches, dead leaves, weeds, and other garden refuse. Almost 20 percent of the solid waste stream

---

THE ORGANIC GARDENER'S RECIPE FOR QUICK COMPOST

1. **Pick a level, well-drained spot in full sun for the compost pile.** To save some work, build the pile in the middle of your garden, where collection of raw materials is easiest.

2. **Build a compost bin out of easily available materials: scrap lumber, chicken wire, bricks, or concrete blocks.** Or just build free-standing piles, and cover them with tarps to protect them against the wind. Make sure the bin has enough openings to allow air to penetrate the pile so that the bacteria and fungi that do the composting can get enough oxygen.

3. **Feed it.** Compost works best with a mixture of coarse and fine materials, layered together in 6- to 8-inch layers. Lay down a bottom layer of twigs, cornstalks, hay, wood chips, or other coarse material. Follow with a layer of high-nitrogen material like manure or grass clippings. You can add a layer of garden soil, then more rough materials, more clippings, and so on. Sprinkle the materials with water as you build the pile. Repeat the sequence until the pile is 4 or 5 feet high, and keep everything covered until the pile is built up.

4. **Keep it going.** As you build the pile, make sure it's at least 3 feet square and 3 feet high, the minimum size needed to sustain the required biological reactions. But don't let the pile get over 5 feet high—the mass may pack down and squeeze out air and slow down decomposition. Turn the pile every three or four days to move the fully composted material out of the hot center of the pile, where the most intense decomposition is going on, and replace it with the partially composted material on the sides. (Turning the compost also helps prevent strong smells from building up.) Remoisten the material as you turn it.

5. **Dig it in.** Compost may be ready as early as twelve days after you begin the process, though most well-managed piles will produce usable compost in four to eight weeks. You can apply the compost to your vegetable garden; around shrubs, bushes, and trees; in window boxes and potted plants; or, sifted, as a luxuriant bed for seeds.

BRIGHT IDEA

Grass clippings and yard wastes can be recycled into compost along with your kitchen scraps to make a valuable—and cheap—mulch and fertilizer. Over the next four years, Wisconsin, Illinois, Florida, and Minnesota will enforce statewide bans prohibiting landfills from accepting leaves, brush, and grass clippings, which make up about a fifth of the garbage in most municipal landfills. The first statewide ban, in Illinois, takes effect January 1, 1990. New Jersey has already banned leaves but not grass clippings from its landfills. Pennsylvania and Connecticut are preparing to do the same.

could be reduced if every American who gardens also composted, throwing in yard waste, lawn clippings, tree limbs, and leaves in the process.

Three Simple Techniques to Reduce Your Dependence on Chemicals

If you can't bear to give up synthetic chemicals altogether, you can still use less of them.

◐ Adopt a program of integrated pest management. Integrated pest management, or IPM, draws on biological controls such as natural predators of pests, planting patterns, pest-resistant crop varieties, and minimum use of chemicals to stabilize crop production while minimizing hazards to health and the environment. The goal is not to eradicate insects and weeds but to keep them below the threshold at which they do too much damage. Chemicals are used selectively and only when necessary, not as a first and primary line of attack.

What's the payoff? On a grand scale, in the United States in 1987, IPM programs practiced on nine crops from fifteen different states yielded farmers collectively $579 million more in profits than they would otherwise have earned. In Texas alone, cotton farmers using IPM earned an average of $282 more per hectare than other cotton farmers. Though no figures are available on what you as a backyard gardener could save by practicing IPM, clearly, the fewer chemicals you buy, the less gardening is going to cost you—both in terms of dollars spent and the pollution of the environment.

◐ Use intercropping to help control bugs and weeds. For example, growing a nitrogen-fixing legume, such as beans or peas, between rows of other plants helps reduce the need to apply artificial fertilizers and keeps weeds in check at the same time. Interplanting herbs with vegetables won't protect the vegetables per se, but they will attract insects that prey on pests.

WHAT TO PLANT TO KEEP THE BUGS YOU LIKE AROUND THE HOUSE

○ Herbs belonging to the mint family: lemon balm, pennyroyal, thyme
○ Plants belonging to the carrot family: dill, parsley
○ Vegetables belonging to the cabbage family: radishes, mustard, and broccoli that have been allowed to bolt
○ Queen Anne's lace, also known as wild carrot, one of the most important nectar plants for native parasitic wasps
○ Poppies, black medick, ivy, red campion: to attract butterflies and bees

○ **Rotate your crops.** This helps, too. Ten years ago in Minnesota, farmers began rotating corn with other crops instead of growing it continuously. In addition to using less fuel and fertilizer, over the last decade soil insecticide use on Minnesota's corn crop dropped 45 percent. On a smaller scale, hundreds of home gardeners apply the same procedure, dividing their gardens into thirds or quarters and resting portion each planting season.

None of these techniques gets rid of every single bug on every single plant. But they don't have to. For effective insect control, pest populations need not be eradicated, just reduced to an acceptably low level. If pests aren't gnawing on the part of the plant you plan to eat, then you may be able to tolerate a greater amount of damage. More than half of the foliage of potatoes and turnips can be chewed up before yields start to decline.

What Else Can You Do to Reduce Use of Toxics?

○ **Identify the pests in your garden.** You can't eliminate a pest organically unless you know what it is. Use picture guides available from your library or county extension service, or take specimens of the pest or evidence of its damage to your county extension agent. Many county offices will let you mail the specimens to them to save you time.

○ **Try the least toxic solution first.** If you can't wash the pests off the plants by spraying them forcefully with a water hose, use a diluted spray of liquid soap and water, or nicotine spray (made by soaking cigarette butts in water). If that fails, try one of the insecticidal soaps available in many hardware stores and nurseries. If you must use toxic chemicals, aim to do so when the pests are about to emerge. Call your local county extension agent for advice on how to keep track of insect pests.

○ **Keep garden areas free of insect-attracting debris.** Properly store and dispose of garbage. Remove weeds promptly to prevent their scattering seeds. Fallen fruit and vegetables should be picked up, and all diseased plants or parts of plants should be removed and destroyed to prevent the spread of disease.

○ **Attract native predatory insects and mites.** In every area of the country, thousands of native bugs consume other insect pests. For example, aphids are the main course for many valuable insects, including ladybugs, tiny parasitic wasps, and the sluglike larvae of flower flies. And fireflies feed mostly on snails, slugs, and insect larvae.

○ **Keep plants properly watered and organically fertilized.** Water should not be allowed to form pools, which can stress plants and where mosquitoes breed.

○ **Use your garden hose.** A direct stream of water from a garden hose can knock out many insect and mite pests in the garden.

○ **Plant resilient varieties.** Resistance to pests should be the primary consideration when choosing what to plant in your garden or yard. Bug- and disease-resistant varieties of virtually every vegetable you'd want are available for the vegetable garden. (For example, sweet corn with "good husk cover" resists corn earworm; red cabbage is preferable to white because cabbage butterflies prefer white or yellow plants.)

○ **Shift planting dates.** For example, in most northern regions, cabbage root maggots have two generations each year, the first in April–May, the second in August. Cabbages planted after May are too big to be seriously harmed by the time the late summer brood hatches; midseason radishes avoid the problem altogether. Consult gardening guides or your county extension service for more details about planting dates in your region.

○ **Use physical barriers.** "Collars" made of 2-inch-wide strips of light cardboard, taped or stapled into a ring around the stem of a plant and set half above and half below the soil line, protect transplanted seedlings in early spring. Early cabbage seedlings can be protected from root maggots by plant-

---

A NOTE ABOUT "FOSSIL FLOWERS"

Diatomaceous earth is a soft white powder mined from geological deposits of fossilized marine organisms. When crushed, the fragments break into microscopic, sharp pieces that scratch the protective waxy layer that encases insects, causing them to dehydrate and die. It's an excellent, safe pesticide for use in stored grain, on pets to kill fleas, and in houses to control insect infestations. But because it will kill any insect, never use it in a garden.

ing the seedlings through a cut in a square of heavy paper. (Press flat against the soil and as tight to the stem as possible to prevent flies from laying their eggs around the roots.) Covering seedlings with a fine mesh cloth works just as well if not better. The spun polypropylene fabric lets in sun and rain and acts as a minigreenhouse by raising temperatures under the covering as well as reducing evaporation.

◊ **Design your garden so that it contains perennial beds or areas that remain undisturbed each year.** If possible, garden in permanent beds with sod or mulched paths between them that are not cultivated. Perennial beds and paths provide refuge for animals and insects that will eat your pests while providing a stable habitat from year to year so populations of the beneficial animals and insects can build up.

◊ **Plant flowering plants.** Small flowers, rich in nectar, attract many beneficial flies and wasps to the garden. Once they are well fed, these insects will lay a maximum number of eggs, which will hatch into pest-eating larvae.

◊ **Build a "bird bath" for insects.** Aphid-loving honeybees and parasitic wasps will drop in for a drink. Providing drinking water for female aphid midges causes them to lay nearly twice as many eggs as they do when they have ample food but no water.

◊ **Don't buy bugs.** Ladybugs are usually collected from a warmer climate and probably won't stick around your yard anyway. Praying mantids eat any insect they catch, beneficial or not. Since nine out of ten insects are not pests, the indiscriminate feasting of praying mantids makes them hooligans in any garden.

"SAFE" PESTICIDES

◊ **Insecticidal soap.** Postassium salt–based, it effectively controls aphids, whitefly, red spider mites, scale insects, and mealy bugs. It must hit the insect directly.

◊ **Soft soap** like Ivory Liquid Soap. It controls aphids and red spider mite but will only kill insects it touches.

◊ **Quassia.** Derived from the bark of the *Picrasma quassidoes* tree, it is effective against aphids, some caterpillars, sawfly, and leaf miners.

◊ **Pyrethrum.** Derived from the chrysanthemum plant, pyrethrum is effective against most insects, especially aphids. But beneficial insects will also succumb. If possible, spray directly on the pest.

◊ **Copper fungicide.** Several varieties are available to control mildews and blights. (It is sometimes sold as copper sulfate.) It coats leaves and stays active for several weeks.

RIGHT IDEA

Forget toxic insecticides. If you need to clean up your strawberries, just get out the vacuum cleaner and go to work.

Farmers in California who are beginning to make the switch to organic gardening have begun using a giant vacuum cleaner to suck up lygus bugs and other insects right off their strawberry plants. Using it during the growing season greatly reduces the use of dangerous insecticides on one of America's favorite berries.

Obviously, this machine is not your standard, everyday Hoover. The "BugVac" is at least 15 feet wide, with two huge suction hoses flanking each side of the engine. Driven by a tractor, each hose glides over one row of strawberries, gently sucking insects off the top. Bug populations are kept to a minimum, some chemicals are eliminated, and the soil is having a chance to rebuild its strength for ultimate conversion to all-organic growing. The BugVac was invented by engineers for Driscoll Strawberries in Watsonville, California. The first one made its debut in 1986; by 1989, there were at least fifty sucking up bugs on other California strawberry fields. (For more information, call Driscoll Strawberries at 408-722-7126.)

Banquets for Birds

The best way to attract birds and keep them coming back is to grow natural plantings that offer food, shelter, and cover. The National Audubon Society recommends the following:

◑ Create irregular-shaped borders and plant hardy, native fruit- and seed-bearing bushes.

◑ Establish a spot for a brush pile of old leaves, stumps, and brambles to provide cover for birds as well as habitat for the insects, worms, and crustaceans upon which many birds thrive.

◑ When it is safe to do so, leave dead tree limbs in place

OURCE

Rodale Press has published a series of straightforward books and guides to organic gardening, including *How to Grow Vegetables Organically* and *The Encyclopedia of Natural Insect and Disease Control.* For these and other helpful Rodale publications, check your local bookstore. Or write to Rodale Press at 33 East Minor Street, Emmaus, PA 18098.

![SOURCE]

S̸OURCE

For a more complete description of what to feed birds to keep them in your backyard, get a copy of *Banquets for Birds,* National Audubon Society, 950 Third Avenue, New York, NY 10022, or *Invite Wildlife to Your Backyard,* National Wildlife Federation, 1400 16th Street, NW, Washington, DC 20036.

to provide nesting cavities for owls and food for woodpeckers, nuthatches, and creepers.

○ **Allow annuals and perennials to go to seed** before pruning them, to provide additional food, shelter, and cover.

○ **Provide different kinds of bird seeds and bird feeders** to encourage a diverse population of bird species.

Watering the Garden

You could use half the water you currently do to keep your gardens growing by taking the following steps to water wisely.

○ **Plant plants that do well in drought conditions.**

- Native shrubs: bayberries, butterfly weed, Joe Pye weed, coreopsis, calliopsis, and rudbeckias.
- Plants with gray foliage, many of which originated in dry climates: lavender, lamb's ears, mini artemisias and achilleas, and silver leafed salvia. (Gardeners who are surrounded by shade, however, do not have this gray option—these plants require lots of sunshine to thrive.)

- The common yucca, which is hardy in most of the United States, capable of withstanding torrid summers, frigid winters, and months without rainfall.
- Plants with succulent leaves: sedums and sempervivums.
- Plants with waxy leaves: the Madagascar periwinkle *(Catharanthus roseus).*
- Clover: It will remain green weeks after unwatered turf grass browns off.

○ **Mulch.** Use wood chips, cocoa hulls, salt hay, pine needles, or whatever else can be found to cover the ground and reduce evaporation and keep roots as cool as possible. (Don't use peat moss. Once it dries out, it prevents moisture from reaching the soil when rainfall does come.)

○ **Throw away your sprinklers.** Sprinklers waste a good bit of water through evaporation. Instead, use rubber soaker hoses. They leak moisture to the soil at slow rates, enabling the water to be absorbed rather than running off. Such hoses can be put under mulch or placed a couple of inches below ground level. Alternatively, invest a little more time and put in a drip irrigation system (see below).

๐ Try a new invention, horticultural polymers. These form a transparent gel when mixed with rain and absorb many, many times their own weight in water, which they release to plant roots as the soil dries out. Look for these "water blankets" in gardening catalogs.

๐ Water either early in the morning or after the sun has set. This saves loss from evaporation. About one-third of the water that's sprayed overhead during the heat of the day is lost to evaporation before it gets to the plants. Let the water run out of the hose end with a gentle stream that penetrates the mulch and soaks the area around each plant. Or use soaker hoses—but lay them out efficiently so that they do not soak a lot of unplanted space or wet the ground too deeply.

๐ Stop the drips. Check all connections and faucets to be sure your hose is not leaking. A slow drip all day long can waste from 15 to 40 gallons a day.

๐ Use "recycled" water. "Gray" water from dishwashing, baths, and laundry should never go to waste during dry spells or drought. Even if you take a shower, plug up the tub to capture the water, and use it for watering plants.

DRIP IRRIGATION

You can cut the amount of water you use in your garden 50 percent with drip irrigation. You'll also get more food and flowers for your H_2O—the lengthy, slow trickle provided by a drip system has increased yields by as much as 84 percent over other methods of watering.

How does drip irrigation work? If your sprinkler throws out more water than the ground can absorb, the soil will become waterlogged and less productive. When soil moisture is constant, soil organisms thrive and create more humus, which makes soil loose, fluffy, and able to hold moisture.

The great virtue of drip irrigation is that it delivers very small amounts of water directly to the plant roots over a long period of time, allowing your garden to produce more food with less water and losing no water to evaporation of windblown spray or puddles.

๕OURCE

For a complete explanation of how to install a drip irrigation system contact: Harmony Farm Supply, P.O. Box 451, Dept. HS, Graton, CA 95444 (Catalog $2), or the Urban Farmer Store, 2121 Taraval Street, Dept. HS, San Francisco, CA 94116 (Catalog $1).

LANDSCAPING

Lawn Care

Lawn care is the most popular "gardening" activity in the United States, even more so than growing vegetables, flowers, fruit, or houseplants. But the American obsession with the "perfect" lawn comes with an astounding price tag. It costs $6 billion a year to keep American lawns green and weed-free, and that doesn't include the toll in polluted groundwater such activity takes on the environment.

If you maintain a lawn, you could be applying anywhere from 3 to 10 pounds of pesticide each year. According to a 1980 National Academy of Sciences report, our gardens and lawns receive the heaviest pesticide applications of any land area in the United States.

If you're using a chemical care company that relies on any of the chemicals listed above, cancel your contract immediately. If you're not, don't start. Instead, practice chemical-free growing techniques that minimize growth of pesky insects, weeds, or diseases.

○ Grow grasses that do well in your locality and in the "micro-climate" around your house. Each grass type requires

---

WHAT LAWN CHEMICALS AFFECT BESIDES GRASS

○ 2,4-D, the most commonly used herbicide on home lawns, was formerly a component of the defoliant Agent Orange. It contains traces of highly toxic dioxins. Skin exposure has resulted in acute delayed nervous system damage in humans. Other possible effects: skin rashes; eye, throat, and respiratory tract irritation; lymphatic cancer. May be toxic to birds and fish.

○ Chlorpyrifos can affect the central nervous system. Overexposure can lead to profuse sweating, nausea, blurred vision, lack of muscle coordination. It can also cause kidney, liver, and bone marrow problems. Extremely toxic to birds, fish, bees, crustaceans, and aquatic insects.

○ Diazinon causes eye irritation and skin rashes. It inhibits proper function of nervous system and also causes headaches, dizziness, flulike symptoms, muscle twitches. It may contribute to birth defects. Highly toxic to birds, waterfowl, fish, bees, crustaceans, and aquatic insects.

○ Benomyl is classified by the EPA as a possible carcinogen. It causes birth defects and decreased sperm counts in laboratory animals. Highly toxic to birds.

○ Captan is both carcinogenic and mutagenic. Very highly toxic to fish.

○ Dicofol contains traces of DDT and causes skin rashes and disorders. Reproductive hazard to birds and fish.

○ Methoxychlor causes kidney, liver, and testicular damage. Very highly toxic to fish, amphibians, and insects and moderately toxic to birds and mammals.

different amounts and combinations of fertilizers, pesticides, water, and mowing. Before you embark on a new lawn-care program, identify what kind of grass you have and what kind of care it demands.

◐ Mow your lawn only as it needs it. And don't always mow it to the same height. Adjust your mowing to the time of the year, the amount of rainfall, and how high the grass has gotten. If the grass has gotten too tall, don't mow it down to 1 inch all at one time. Mow gradually, cutting no more than an inch off with the first mowing. Allow the grass to recover for a day or two, then cut off another inch. Continue cutting an inch at a time until you reach the desired height.

◐ Water wisely. Some grasses need more water than others, and all grasses are affected by the kind of soil they're growing in. So know what kind of grass you have before you set about watering it once a week. When you do water, soak the grass, not just the top of the blades. There are many varieties of water sprinklers on the market; short of having an underground sprinkling system, the best portable sprinkler to get is the "impulse" variety, which shoots water out in a jet as the sprinkler head turns. Impulse sprinklers have the greatest range and uniformity of watering, although, like most sprinklers, dripping can lead to a heavy accumulation of water at their base. So don't place the sprinkler in the same spot time after time.

◐ Establish "tolerance levels" for weeds. All lawns harbor some weed species, whether herbicides are used or not. The trick is to keep weed populations low enough so that the grass still looks good to the naked eye.

◐ Monitor your lawn to detect problems before they turn into epidemics. Regularly inspect your lawn for signs of bugs, weeds, or disease.

◐ Regularly maintain healthy, dense grass to discourage lawn pests that normally grow in your area.

◐ If pest populations appear likely to exceed tolerance levels, use cultural and biological controls. If weeds are the problem, check for soil compaction, too much or too little fertilizer, or the way you water. If insect numbers are growing or disease is threatening, check for excessive layers of thatch. (Thatch is the buildup of matted grass clippings and roots that sits on the surface of the soil. Thatch is beneficial for lawns if it is less than ½ inch thick. A thicker layer may keep out water, air, and fertilizer; harbor insects; and give rise to disease.)

Most pest problems can be solved by accurately detecting the underlying causes and changing them. For example, chinch bugs can be kept at low numbers in lawns by increasing moisture levels in the soil during the summer. Most lawn diseases, on the other hand, can be kept in check by reducing the availability of water on leaf surfaces—so water in the morning, instead of at night, when it takes longer for surface water to evaporate. And weeds

---

ORGANIC BUG CONTROLS FOR YOUR LAWN

- **Milky spore disease** *(Bacillus popillae)*—controls grubs of Japanese beetles.
- **Green lacewing larvae** *(Crysopa carnea)*—controls aphids.
- **Nematodes**—control sod webworms and army worms.
- **Big blue-eyed bugs** *(Geocoris* species)—prey on chinch bugs and other pests.

---

can be controlled by raising the height of your mower to encourage grasses to shade out weeds.

○ Use least-toxic chemical controls. Safer insecticidal soap can kill aphids, fleas, and other lawn pests. Margosan, an oil of low toxicity extracted from the neem tree, shows promise for use against a variety of lawn pests. Of the conventional synthetic pesticides, the synthetic pyrethroids should be selected over organophosphate- or carbamate-based products, because they can target pests and will remain in the environment for a shorter time. Make sure you read the labels for these toxic ingredients before you buy any chemical lawn treatment products.

How to Fertilize Your Lawn the Chemical-Free Way

According to the Lawn Institute, if you leave it alone, your grass will convert organic matter into nutrients to keep the lawn growing. In fact, grass clippings themselves are a good source of free fertilizer: They can provide up to one-half of the nitrogen needed by a lawn.

Grass clippings left on the chemical-free lawn will begin to decompose almost immediately. (Chemical fertilizers slow the activity of decomposers—earthworms, bacteria, fungi, and other microorganisms—and stall the breakdown of clippings, causing thatch.) The only times you should remove clippings

SOURCE

The Common Sense Pest Control Quarterly, Volume II, Number 2, Spring 1986. This is a publication of the Bio Integral Resource Center, a nonprofit corporation formed to provide practical information on the least toxic methods of managing pests. For more information, contact BIRC at P.O. Box 7414, Berkeley, CA 94707.

are when converting from a chemical system, after the first mowing in the spring to help the grass green up, and after the last fall mowing to reduce the chance of disease. Also, remove clippings whenever you cut off more than one-half of the top growth.

Overfertilizing makes nitrogen immediately available to the roots, so the roots don't have to work to seek out nourishment. They grow on top and don't loosen the soil, leading to soil compaction, insects, and diseases. Synthetic fertilizers can also slow down and even kill off biological processes. The dead roots don't break down, the lawn gets "soft," and there's excessive runoff—forcing you to water and fertilize more frequently.

⊙ **Feed the soil, not the plant,** to break this cycle. Slowly soluble natural fertilizers, like blood

meal or organic mixes, feed the roots and allow the plants to build up a good supply of the carbohydrates that enable grass to endure stress. These organic fertilizers are usually moderate in nitrogen content, not acidic to the soil, and water-insoluble—they won't run off into the sewer the next time it rains. Some varieties of organic fertilizer include alfalfa meal, blood meal, and cottonseed meal. You can also make your own by mixing 2 parts dried blood, 1 part rock phosphate, and 4 parts wood ashes, all of which should be available at your local garden supply store.

Nitrogen, among other things, makes the grass grow quickly and grow green. But in addition to nitrogen, grass needs other "nutrients": phosphorus, which aids in root growth; potassium, which makes grass more resistant to heat, cold,

BRIGHT IDEA

Arnold Palmer is not only a champion golfer but an avid proponent of natural lawn care as well. On the more than twenty golf courses he owns and manages, including the site of the annual Bay Hill Classic in Orlando, Florida, all-natural fertilizers are used to keep the greens green and healthy.

Each year, the typical golf course may need at least four or five applications of fertilizers to stay verdant and pounds of fungicides to suppress common diseases. But natural fertilizers, composed of bone meal, feather meal, wheat germ, soya, muriate of potash, enzymes, and soil microorganisms work even better—and can cut fertilizer applications in half. Part of their secret is the 100 million beneficial microorganisms they contain per gram of material. The microorganisms and enzymes decompose the other ingredients, slowly releasing nutrients to the soil, where they become available to the plant roots. The greens stay green longer and the soil's ability to hold water is increased.

Source

A complete line of organic lawn and garden fertilizers, insect traps, and bug sprays has been developed by Ringer Natural Lawn and Garden Products. For a product catalog, call toll-free 800-654-1047.

For a thorough description of organic lawn care, including types of grasses to grow in what part of the country, techniques for mixing fertilizers, and watering and identifying bugs and diseases, see *The Chemical Free Lawn* (Rodale Press, 1989) by Warren Schultz.

---

draught, disease, and traffic; calcium, to improve the way grass uses nitrogen; magnesium, to enhance the growing process called photosynthesis; and sulfur, which improves grass color and enhances growth. Bone meal, wood ashes, dolomitic limestone, and elemental sulfur all can be applied to your garden to give it these boosts.

© Fertilize only once or twice if you live in the North, and two or three times if you live in the South, rather than every week or month. Studies have shown that lawns fertilized every month during the summer require 13 percent more water than those fertilized only once.

"Global ReLeaf"

If you plant three trees on the southeast and southwest sides of your home, you can cut your air-conditioning bill by 10 to 50 percent. You'll also be helping to clean up the air and cool the globe.

Burning fossil fuels like coal and oil releases carbon dioxide (CO_2) into the atmosphere, where it traps the sun's rays before they can bounce back into outer space. In less than two centuries, fossil fuel combustion and forest destruction have increased the levels of carbon dioxide in the atmosphere by 25 percent, turning the earth into a planetary hothouse.

Because they use carbon dioxide as they grow, trees can offset and even reduce CO_2 emissions. According to the American Forestry Association, the nation's oldest citizens' conservation organization, there are at least 100 million spots around our homes and in our towns and cities suitable for trees. Planting those 100 million trees could offset America's CO_2 emissions by 18 million tons a year, saving American consumers $4 billion annually!

But trees do more than just absorb CO_2, especially in cities. Studies done in Sacramento, California, show that tree-filled neighborhoods can be up to 9 degrees cooler than unshaded streets. And Lawrence

Livermore scientist Art Rosenfeld says, "If you planted three trees for every unshaded air-conditioned house in America and gave those houses light exterior surfaces, you could save about a third of the 100 billion kilowatt hours consumed each year by residential air conditioners."

When they shade houses and buildings and pavement from the sun, they help cool down the "heat islands" that build up around pavement and other dark surfaces that reduce evaporation and absorb the sun's heat. "Nature's air conditioners" also help clean up the air, by filtering airborne particles with their leaves and branches.

While the vast expanses of tropical forests that serve as the earth's "lungs" are being lost at an alarming rate, even in the United States, only one tree is being planted for every four that die or are removed in our cities and towns. Planting trees is a positive step you can take right now—in your backyard, on your street, and in your city or town—to stop the CO_2 buildup and reduce global warming.

Landscape Design Tips

◗ **Enhance your landscape while maintaining lawns, trees, and plantings by using readily available, recyclable materials and some ingenuity.**

- Old tires become planters when filled with topsoil and planted with tomatoes or strawberries.
- Plastic jugs with the bottoms removed provide protection against late frosts for plants set out in spring.
- Old wooden windows can serve as parts for a greenhouse or cold frame.
- Railroad ties can be used to build raised beds for planting and terracing.
- Old tires and miscellaneous lumber can be transformed into a playground.

To care for your trees and bushes organically:

◗ **As in the vegetable garden, plant pest-resistant species.** For example, planting oak trees in an area already or soon to be infested with gypsy moths is an

SOURCE

The American Forestry Association has launched a nationwide campaign to get 100 million trees planted in American communities by 1992. For a Citizens' Action Guide, write: Global ReLeaf, P.O. Box 2000, Washington, DC 20013.

HOW TO PLANT A TREE FOR A COOLER, CLEANER WORLD

1. Locate a clear, open site for your tree, with generous rooting area and good drainage.

2. Loosen and blend the soil in the entire planting area 6 to 10 inches deep. In the center, dig a hole at least as wide, but only as deep as the root ball.

3. Remove tree from burlap or container and place on solidly packed soil so that the root collar (where the tree's main stem meets the roots) is slightly above the surrounding grade.

4. Backfill the hole and lightly pack the soil into place around the tree.

5. Spread a 2- to 3-inch layer of mulch in the entire area, keeping a 6- to 8-inch distance from the tree trunk.

6. Stake the tree so that it can flex in the wind. Attach stake to the tree by using discarded rubber innertubes. Remove them after six months.

7. Water thoroughly, but do not flood the hole. Water twice a week during dry periods.

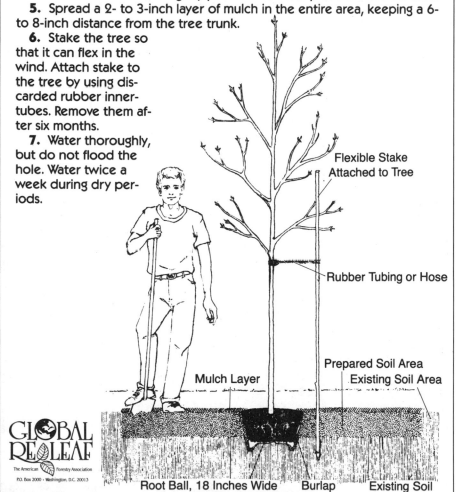

Flexible Stake Attached to Tree

Rubber Tubing or Hose

Prepared Soil Area

Existing Soil Area

Mulch Layer

Root Ball, 18 Inches Wide

Burlap

Existing Soil

GLOBAL RELEAF

The American Forestry Association

P.O. Box 2000 · Washington, D.C. 20013

invitation to disaster. Your county extension agent can provide you with lists of more suitable, resistant plant species and varieties for your area.

◑ Use low-toxicity pest controls. *Bacillus thuringiensis* (B.t.), a naturally occurring bacterium, is extremely effective against many caterpillars, including the gypsy moth and the cabbage worm. Other strains of B.t. are effective against mosquitoes, black flies, and wax moths. (Scientists have found seventy-two different varieties of B.t. in soil samples from such disparate places as caves in West Virginia, the Himalayas, a car bumper in Iceland, and the bottom of a cat's foot *(B.t. fluffiensis)*. Milky spore disease is an effective biological control for Japanese beetles. Other relatively safe pesticides include fatty-acid soaps, effective against insects, fungi, and weeds, and horticultural oils, which control scales and mites.

To Fight Gypsy Moths

Homeowners and scientists have been trying to stop the spread of gypsy moths for at least a century. Each voracious eater can devour up to 50 square inches of leaves from the time it hatches in the spring until it wraps itself in a cocoon two months later. According to the U.S. Forest Service, at their peak in 1981, gypsy moths defoliated more than 13 million acres of trees. Hundreds of communities in the United States are infested with gypsy moths.

The "gypsy" deserves its name:

It begins life as an egg, then turns into a caterpillar, before resting in its pupa and finally becoming a moth.

Eggs are deposited by the female moth in masses of between 100 and 1,000 eggs in late summer, usually in August. These masses may be deposited on branches or trunks of trees, under rocks, or on many other objects. The masses will hatch in late April or early May. Once the larvae hatch, they move to the tops of the trees and begin eating leaves. Caterpillars are not easily noticed on the ground during these early stages of feeding and growth. In fact, you may not notice them until June or July, after they are fully grown and much of the damage they do to the trees is already done.

◑ Don't overreact. Avoid knee-jerk reactions to any pest. Learn to tolerate some defoliation, and make organic protection of your trees a regular part of your landscaping upkeep.

◑ Keep trees in good health. Watering during dry periods will help trees recover from defoliation. Mulching will prevent excessive water loss. And keep construction activity at a distance so as not to compact soil and prevent moisture from penetrating to small feeder roots.

◑ Properly fertilize to keep your trees as healthy as possible.

◑ Diversify the plantings in your landscape. Gypsy moths like oaks, alder, aspen, birch, hemlock, and willow—so plant dogwood, ash, maple, tulip poplar, holly, walnut, sycamore, and mulberry instead.

❂ **Encourage the moth's natural enemies to stay in the area.** As many as thirty-eight bird species, including black-capped chickadees, blue jays, tanagers, orioles, catbirds, and robins feed on gypsy moths. To attract them, build bird houses or nesting platforms. Beetles, wasps, flies, mice, spiders, and ants will eat various stages of the moth, so fight your natural instinct to kill these creatures whenever you see them outdoors. And maintain the area beneath the trees as much like a forest as possible. Removing all leaves and litter eliminates the hiding places for the moth's natural enemies (and removes acid-rich nutrients as well).

❂ **Scrape egg clusters off trees, wood piles, stone walls, and other hiding places.** Dunk them in soapy water, creosote, or kerosene and then discard in garbage or by deep burial.

❂ **From May through July, apply "repel'm" or some other sticky tape completely around the trunk of your tree.** It will trap and kill larvae before they become caterpillars. And the double-band variety forms an impenetrable barrier that caterpillars cannot cross.

❂ **Place burlap collectors on trees from May through mid-July.** Cut a piece of burlap 8 to 12 inches wide and long enough to

BRIGHT IDEA

The U.S. Department of Agriculture has begun testing a virus that kills nothing but gypsy moths. Unlike chemical pesticides, the virus supposedly poses no threat to the environment and is transmitted from one generation of gypsy moths to the next. For several years, the U.S. Park Service has successfully used the virus, nicknamed "Abby," to combat gypsy moths in parts of Rock Creek Park, in Washington, DC.

SOURCE

For more information, contact the USDA's Insect Pathology Lab in Room 214, Building 011A, Beltsville, MD 20705; telephone: 301-344-3689, and ask about "Abby."

wrap completely around the tree. Using a piece of string or rope, tie the burlap piece around the tree at shoulder height. Fold the upper half of the burlap over the lower half and let it hang. Every day, collect and destroy the caterpillars that hide under the burlap.

Protecting Roses and Other Plants from Aphids*

Growing roses may demand more pesticide applications than any other flower in your garden. Their scourge: aphids, one of the most common garden pests, which relentlessly suck sap out of leaves. Although these minuscule bugs have plenty of natural predators (like ladybugs and lacewings), beneficial insects rarely appear on the scene until *after* aphid populations have begun attacking plants. Thus, there's usually some lag time between the moment you first spot aphids on the growing tips of roses, and the time their natural enemies move in. Any measures you take to control the aphids should not kill off their predators, too.

   ◑ Establish tolerance levels. All plants can withstand some degree of infestation. By carefully observing your roses (or other plants) in early spring, you can note when aphids first appear, see how long it takes for their natural enemies to show up, and decide whether or not the amount of plant damage that

*(Source: *Common Sense Pest Control Quarterly,* Volume II, Number 2, Spring, 1986)

occurred during the "lag time" was tolerable.

If aphids have started to damage your plants, try these least-toxic control options:

   ◑ "Shoot" them with a strong jet of water from the hose. You may have to hose off the plants several times, three or four days apart, to keep aphid numbers down until the natural enemies appear. Hose plants early in the day so the leaves dry before nightfall.

   ◑ Wipe small colonies of aphids off leaves and buds with your hands (wear gloves). Severely infested sections of plants can be pinched or pruned and disposed of in compost or a bucket of soapy water.

   ◑ Spray with an insecticidal soap. However, do not apply to plants in full sun in the heat of the day. Wait for cooler temperatures and or shadier times to spray. As with other pesticides, the more you use insecticidal soap, the sooner the bugs will become immune to it. Use only when and where the soap is truly needed.

   ◑ Take measures to control ants. In some areas of the country, certain ant species will protect aphids from their natural enemies to ensure that the aphids continue to excrete a honeydew on which the ants feed. If you see ants crawling on aphid-infested plants, you can assume the ants are playing this protective role. Apply a band of sticky material like Stickem or Tanglefoot around the trunk of roses or other woody plants to keep ants away. For annual vegetables and flowers, which cannot be painted with a sticky band, consider using a boric acid–based ant bait as a home-made insect control.

© **Avoid dosing your roses with highly soluble nitrogen fertilizer.** Aphids reproduce best when the plants they're eating contain high levels of nitrogen. So use less-soluble forms of fertilizer (ask your nursery for advice), and space the feedings out over the growing season. If you're growing plants primarily for their flowers or fruit, use fertilizers that are higher in phosphorus than nitrogen.

Those Damned Mosquitoes!

Mosquitoes are among the most widespread of all flying insects. One species or another, particularly the house mosquito *(Culex pipiens)* has been found on practically every spot of land on earth. Nevertheless, mosquito control agencies in the United States and Canada dole out more than $80 million every year in a futile attempt to destroy insects that, for the most part, cause little more discomfort than an itch. The public spends even more than that for aerosol insecticides, repellents, window screens, and other controls. That's a lot of money to waste on a bug we'll just never be able to wipe off the face of the earth.

The squandered money is compounded by the potentially dangerous side effects involved in spraying massive quantities of toxic chemicals into our air or over our water. Not only do we and our pets inhale these toxins, but the pesticides can kill off the natural enemies of other insects that otherwise would be under control, forcing us to contend with even more bothersome bugs.

Electric bug zappers are even less effective than pesticides in killing mosquitoes. An extensive study on bug zappers in Ontario, Canada, showed that of 20,000 insects killed, only 4 percent were mosquitoes. Ground fogging is not a choice alternative, either. Though fogging may kill many adult mosquitoes, most species regularly fly over a mile in the course of looking for food and breeding grounds; recruits from surrounding areas can move into a fogged area within twenty-four hours or less.

The problem is that most mosquito control efforts are still directed against the adult mosquito, instead of going to the source—water—where the mosquito's larval stages can be destroyed before they mature into biting pests.

There is generally no justification to treat for mosquitoes in wilderness areas, especially with toxic chemicals. Not only can these chemicals destroy animal life—as DDT did when it began to kill off the sea osprey twenty years ago—but they don't work. Though it may be possible to reduce mosquito populations somewhat, it is impossible to eradicate them altogether: They will show the same evolutionary ingenuity as other bugs and develop an immunity to the pesticides you apply.

At home, however, it is somewhat easier to control mosquito populations because the area you're concerned with is smaller and because the controls are more accessible. If mosquitoes are bothering your home, take the following steps:

◑ Since it is adult mosquitoes that do the biting, try to destroy mosquito populations before they "grow up." Destroying the habitats of their larvae— standing water—is particularly effective.

◑ Survey your premises for standing water in which mosquitoes could develop. Chances are that the pests are being produced within a few yards of where you were bitten.

◑ Gradually working outward from the house, check the periphery and nearby neglected areas and vacant lots in your neighborhood. Look for old tires and similar miscellany behind garages and gas stations.

◑ Simply empty the container, remove it, or turn it upside down so that it no longer collects water.

◑ Since you will not be able to kill mosquito populations completely, take other measures to reduce the likelihood that you will be bitten: Do your outdoor chores at times other than dawn and dusk, when mosquitoes are most active; wear light clothes in the woods, since mosquitoes appear to be attracted to dark surfaces; wear long-sleeved shirts,

MOSQUITO SOURCES AROUND THE HOME

Tin cans, jars, and other containers
Watering cans, buckets
Clogged roof gutters
Saucers under potted plants
Cisterns
Old tires
Leaf-filled drains
Rain barrels
Watering troughs
Sumps
Poorly constructed cesspools
Septic tanks
Ornamental ponds
Over-irrigated lawns and fields
Street gutters
Catch basins at road corners
Plastic wading pools
Boats that have not been drained
Standing water in tire ruts
Puddles from evaporative cooler drains
Dripping outdoor faucets
Leaky pipe joints
Tree holes
Drain outlets from air conditioners
Vaults in water-softening tanks
Vaults in utility meters
Bird baths
Wheelbarrows or tilt-up carts
Wells

long pants, and a hat if necessary. You can apply repellent to your clothes rather than to your skin because the major objective of mosquito repellents is to mask the initial stimulus that carbon dioxide from our breath provides the mosquito. For the same reason, you can burn citronella candles on your porch or patio to repel mosquitoes.

◑ To keep mosquitoes out of your house, repair holes in

For more information, write for a copy of *Those Damned Mosquitoes* (20 pages), Massachusetts Audubon Society, South Great Road, Lincoln, MA 01773 ($2.00); or "Mosquitoes—The Water Connection" in the *Common Sense Pest Control Quarterly*, Vol. 3, No. 2 (Spring 1987), P.O. Box 7414, Berkeley, CA 94707 ($1.00 plus legal-sized self-addressed, stamped envelope).

screens and fill cracks around doors, windows, and other spots where mosquitoes may be sneaking in.

Gardening Tools

As much as possible, stick to tools that only require one power source: you. You'll save money on fuel costs, pump less CO_2 and other pollutants into the air, and conserve water.

○ **Instead of using a gasoline-powered leaf blower, rake.**

○ **Don't wash off sidewalks and driveways with water;** sweep once or twice and let the rain do the rest.

○ **If you have only a small**

The Solar Solution to Night-time Lighting Problems

Several innovative manufacturing companies have developed outdoor night lights that are powered by the sun. By using photovoltaic cells that charge by day and release their energy at night, these lights will burn no fossil fuels and yet do the same job a normal light will do. Available products include:

○ Walk lights for paths and driveways
○ Patio lights
○ Security and area lights
○ Illuminated house numbers

Catalogs listing these and other solar products, such as calculators and car batteries, can be obtained from Sunergy, P.O. Box 177, Princeton, NJ 08542 (telephone: 800-247-6627); or The Solar Electric Catalog, 175 Cascade Court, Rohnert Park, CA 94928 (telephone: 707-586-1987).

lawn to maintain, consider using the most energy-efficient mower on the market today: one that's pushed by you . . . minus the gasoline.

© Unless your hedge resembles a stretch of tropical jungle, trim it with hand-powered shears, not electric ones.

© Share tools with neigh-bors. Not only will you save money in purchasing and maintenance costs, but you'll consume far fewer products that you eventually have to throw away.

3 IN THE GARAGE

Driving a fuel-efficient car may be the simplest and most immediate step you can take to help stop global warming and reduce acid rain. Why? Consider these facts:

○ Passenger cars consume one of every six barrels of oil;

○ Burning just one gallon of gasoline produces almost twenty pounds of carbon dioxide, the chief cause of global warming.

○ The average American car pumps its own weight in carbon into the atmosphere each year.

And things are getting worse instead of better. In 1988, oil use for transportation increased 10 percent; transportation now generates over 33 percent of all carbon emissions in the United States.

Our dependency on oil is attached to a stupendous price tag, and it's a lot more than what we pay for a gallon of gasoline at the pump. The Worldwatch Institute has calculated that the hidden cost of the automobile to the average American taxpayer is close to $2,400 per passenger car, once the expense of building and maintaining roads, regulating and policing traffic, caring for accident victims, and loss of land to paved roads is computed into the price. If these expenses were reflected in retail fuel prices, a gallon of gasoline might cost as much as $4.50.

Then there is the unexpected—and sometimes inestimable—expense incurred when pristine environments like Alaska's Prince William Sound are ravaged by oil spills or other disasters. Exploration and production of oil even threatens large areas of tropical rain forest. As you read these words, Conoco, Occidental, British Petroleum, Shell, and Exxon are all pushing their way deep into sensitive tropical forests in search of "black gold."

Researchers at the University of California estimate that the use of gasoline and diesel fuel in the United States alone may cause up to 30,000 deaths every year. The American Lung Association estimates that air pollution from motor vehicles, power plants, and industrial fuel combustion costs the United States $40 billion annually in health care and lost productivity.

ⓞ One significant step you can take is to **drive a more fuel-efficient car, and drive it more efficiently.** Improving auto fuel economy would extend oil supplies long enough to develop renewable energy sources safely and would make the use of renewable energy feasible. One change alone, the increase in the average fuel efficiency of American automobiles from 13.1 miles per gallon (mpg) in 1973 to 17.9 miles per gallon in 1985, cut U.S. gasoline consumption by 20 billion gallons per year, lowering oil imports by 1.3 million barrels of oil

per day. The U.S. average fuel economy of new cars and light-duty trucks combined increased 66 percent between 1975 and 1985.

HOW MUCH ENERGY CAN BE SAVED?

ⓞ Reducing auto weight can save 25 percent of the energy used in the typical car.

ⓞ Simply installing the most efficient tire available on the market today would improve the fuel economy of most cars by 1 to 3 miles per gallon.

ⓞ "Continuously variable transmissions" give a car an unlimited number of gears; they offer fuel savings of 20 to 24 percent, particularly in urban stop-and-go driving.

What You Can Do to Conserve Energy on the Road

More than one-third of the petroleum we use in this country is burned as fuel for private automobiles and light trucks. In addition to saving oil and reducing air pollution, energy-conscious driving and good car maintenance can save you $70 to $100 a year in gasoline and diesel costs.

Here are some ways you can practice energy conservation on the road:

ⓞ **Use public transportation, a motorcycle, a moped, a bicycle, or walk to your destination.**

THE FEDERAL GOVERNMENT'S IMPACT ON FUEL ECONOMY

According to Amory B. Lovins, director of research at the Rocky Mountain Institute in Colorado, the Reagan fuel-efficiency rollbacks led to an increase in U.S. crude oil use of 295,300 barrels a day—equal to the amount the Interior Department hopes can be extracted from the Arctic National Wildlife Refuge in one year. We should insist that the federal government play a positive, not a negative role in energy conservation efforts.

The federal government has the power to influence fuel economy positively in three very important ways:

○ **By increasing motor vehicle fuel-efficiency standards.** U.S. Senators Tim Wirth and John Heinz believe it is "reasonable to target a standard of at least 38 miles per gallon by the end of the century."

○ **By increasing the tax on gas guzzlers and using revenue from this tax to provide rebates to purchasers of very efficient "gas sippers."** Cars which get less than 22.5 mpg should be considered guzzlers. Revenue from taxes on these cars could be used to fund research on renewable energy sources, generate support for mass transit, and promote various methods of protecting and improving air quality.

○ **By supporting mass transit.** American cities were once serviced by a network of efficient and well-functioning urban and interurban rail systems, known as trolleys. But beginning in the 1930s, the General Motors Corporation, with counterparts in the oil, steel, and tire industries, began acquiring and dismantling the systems that made trolley travel possible. By the late 1950s, about 90 percent of the trolley network had been eliminated.

The federal government should mount an aggressive campaign to promote transportation alternatives to the car in every urban center in America.

○ **Share your ride.** Join a car pool or a van pool. If you and other commuters added just one person to your pool, the nationwide gasoline savings would amount to more than 33 million gallons of gasoline each day, enough to drive all the way around the world 34,000 times.

○ **Eliminate unnecessary trips.** Can you cut out one driving trip per week by using the telephone or combining errands?

○ **Drive at a steady pace.**

○ **Minimize braking.** Anticipate speed changes. Take your foot off the accelerator as soon as you see a red light or slowed traffic ahead. Energy losses due to braking and idling can amount to as much as one-third of a vehicle's original kinetic energy.

○ **Don't let the motor idle for more than a minute.** Turn off the engine. It takes less gasoline to restart the car than it takes to let it idle. Generally, there is no need to press the accelerator down to restart the engine.

ⓞ **Don't overfill or "top off" your tank.** Remove the nozzle or ask the gas station attendant to remove it when the automatic valve closes, to eliminate any chance of spillage.

Another Alternative to Gasoline?

Wood alcohol (methanol) has been on hand for more than fifty years. It's abundant, packs more power than gasoline, and creates only half as many noxious emissions. In March 1988, the South Coast Air Quality Management District in California adopted a sweeping new antipollution program for the Los Angeles area. Though more than 100 specific measures are included in the 5,000-page plan, the centerpiece would do away with gas-burning vehicles over the next two decades. City buses would have to drive on "clean fuels" by 1991, and by 1993 so would taxis and rental cars. And by 2009, strict new emissions standards would lock new gas guzzlers out of the market. Every filling station in the region would be required to devote at least one pump to clean energy. (Only seven methanol pumps are in operation in California currently, but both ARCO and Chevron have pledged to set up dozens more by 1990.)

Car owners anxious to make the switch to methanol-burning cars may be able to look to Ford and General Motors for vehicles. The two automotive giants are hand-building models that can run on gasoline, methanol, and several other fuels, singly or in combination. Engines in both feature an optical scanner that analyzes what's in the fuel line and regulates fuel injection accordingly. Both Ford's "flexible fuel" Crown Victoria and GM's "variable fuel" Chevy Corsica

BRIGHT IDEA

Thousands of residents in Burnaby, British Columbia (a suburb of Vancouver), are powering their cars with cooking fuel in the largest experiment of its kind in North America.

In an effort to find ecologically cleaner alternatives to gasoline, car owners have turned to compressed natural gas, an abundant fuel source that minimizes air pollution, can help reduce the greenhouse effect, and decreases dependence on foreign oil. Natural gas costs half as much as gasoline, and cars using it for fuel get twice as much mileage from gas as they get from gasoline. The move is completely sanctioned and supported by the Canadian government, at both the local and federal level.

should be available commercially by 1993.

Still, methanol is not the perfect solution. Though it produces little of the smog-forming soot, hydrocarbons, or nitrogen oxides associated with gasoline, methanol emits even higher levels of formaldehyde. Like gasoline, methanol also releases carbon dioxide, which causes the greenhouse effect. And it is considerably more expensive than gasoline in terms of energy delivered: a gallon of gas produces 1.7 times as much energy as a gallon of methanol for approximately the same price.

Where Are You Going to Park?

Parking a car at home, at the office, and at the shopping mall requires an average of 4,000 square feet of asphalt. To accommodate America's millions of cars, over 60,000 square miles of land have been paved over—about 2 percent of the total surface area in the United States, an area as large as the entire state of Georgia. World-

---

FIVE WAYS TO CURB TRAFFIC

Here's how six cities around the world are discouraging traffic in already congested areas:

Hong Kong
Electronic sensors on cars record highway travel and time of day. Drivers are issued a monthly bill (commuter hours are the most expensive).

Singapore
Automobiles entering downtown Singapore during rush hour are required to display a $30-a-month sticker, but cars carrying four or more passengers may pass without charge.

Gothenburg, Sweden
To encourage pedestrian traffic, the central business district has been divided into pie-shaped zones, with cars prohibited from moving directly from one zone to another. Autos move in and out only by way of a peripheral ring road.

Rome and Florence
All traffic except buses, taxis, delivery vehicles, and cars belonging to area residents have been banned between 7:30 A.M. and 7:30 P.M.

Tokyo
The buyer of a standard-size vehicle must show evidence that a permanent parking space is available for the car before he can close the sale. To comply with the law, some drivers have constructed home garages with lifts to permit double-deck parking!

(Source: *Sierra* magazine, May/June 1989)

wide, reports the Worldwatch Institute, at least a third of an average city's land is devoted to roads, parking lots, and other elements of infrastructure for cars. In American cities, close to half of all urban space serves as a parking pad or thoroughfare for the automobile; in Los Angeles, the figure reaches two-thirds.

If devoting so much space to concrete doesn't immediately strike you as preposterous, there are other environmental consequences that will. Wherever concrete is laid, natural areas are destroyed, fewer trees that could halt global warming and minimize air pollution remain standing, and fewer of the insects, birds, and wildlife that maintain the natural web of life survive.

Because manufacturing cement and asphalt are such energy-intensive processes, it rarely makes sense to break up pavement once it's laid down. But it does make sense to minimize the need for new roads and parking lots by driving less, car pooling, and supporting community plans to control traffic.

Why Not Bike?

You could save 407 gallons of gasoline each year—half the amount burned by a typical American car annually—if you biked to work instead of driving.

Bicycles outnumber cars worldwide by two to one, with most of the 800-million bicycle fleet concentrated in the Third World, particularly China and India. Bicycles transport more people in Asia alone than do automobiles in all other countries combined.

Here in the United States, 80 million recreational cyclists and 2.5 million bicycle commuters have discovered the joy of biking:

◉ Bicycling reduces dependence on scarce, polluting oil supplies almost completely. You can travel hundreds of miles by bicycle on no more than a thimbleful of oil.

◉ Bicycling creates no air pollution. Because you do not burn any kind of fuel but your own when you bicycle, you can ride through the environment without leaving a trace (noxious or otherwise).

◉ Bicycling is great exercise and helps keep your weight under control.

◉ Apart from walking (and distance permitting), there is no more energy-efficient way to get to work than by bike. More than half of all commuting trips are 5 miles or less in length, a distance that could easily be covered by bicycle.

The impact of bicycling on air pollution is immediate, since the shorter the car trip, the dirtier air emissions become. Research in Dallas, Texas, indicates that if you reduced the distance you travel by car by just .6 percent and bicycled instead, you could actually reduce your auto's emissions by 1.8 percent. And the EPA has estimated that a 2.4 percent shift from car to bike could reduce vehicle carbon monoxide emissions by 5 percent or more.

RIGHT IDEAS

○ In Boulder, Colorado, the Downtown Management Corporation is purchasing 100 "roadster" bikes for people to use freely to do their shopping or run errands. Users simply leave a credit card as a deposit, which is returned when they return the bike.

○ In Los Angeles, "Trip Reduction Ordinances" urge employers of more than 500 people to attempt to reduce the number of cars bringing employees to work each day. This will gradually be extended to include smaller firms employing as few as 100 workers.

○ In Gainesville, Florida, 10 percent of parking spaces are reserved for bicycles, removing one of the biggest obstacles bicyclists face: lack of a secure place to leave a bike.

"BIKE TO WORK" DAYS

Several U.S. cities have helped increase the number of bicycle commuters by organizing Bike to Work days. You can do the same in your community by taking these steps:

○ **Join your local bike club.** A bike club will instantly identify others you can bike to work with, and it will be easier to generate a widespread community event if you have an organization behind you.

○ **Pick a date for the event, based on the likelihood of good weather and the opportunity to work with or around other events such as street fairs and local or national holidays.** If possible, give yourself six months to organize the logistics.

○ **Recruit sponsors who will financially support your organizing efforts or will work with you to provide incentives to encourage as many people as possible to participate in the event.** Restaurants play a key role because they can offer riders free breakfast snacks upon arriving at the workplace or at designated food stations along the way.

○ **Get as many employers in your community to support the event as possible.** One firm that participated in a Bike to Work day in California raffled off everything from records to dinner passes—but only employees who bicycled could participate. The city of Westerville, Ohio, provides fifteen minutes additional vacation time every time a person bikes or walks to work. And several firms have passed along lower health insurance premiums to bicycle commuters.

○ **Publicize the event to your community.** Put up notices on bulletin boards and in company newsletters. Let employees know bicycling is endorsed by their company.

(Some employers attach a letter or notice to their employees' paychecks a couple of weeks before the event.)

◑ Recruit volunteers to hand out the food and register bicyclists at each food station. These locations need to be well publicized before the date, and banners should be placed at the establishments. The locations should be spread out around the city to provide close proximity to all major workplaces.

◑ Hand out stamps, stickers, pins, or t-shirts proclaiming "I biked to work" to all participants.

◑ Invite the media to cover the event. You may even be able to get your local newspaper or television or radio station to become a sponsor. Maybe the city's most popular weather forecaster can broadcast the morning weather report from one of the cycling "pit stops."

BUYING A CAR

Buying a car, whether used or new, gives you the perfect oppor-

tunity to trade in your gas guzzler for a gas sipper.

◑ Study the market before you buy. Review mileage test results publicized by *Consumer Reports* and motor industry magazines. Generally, the best fuel economy is associated with low vehicle weight, small engines, manual transmissions, low axle ratio, and low frontal area (the width of the car times its height).

◑ Buy the most energy-efficient car of the size and style you want. Don't let the car price alone determine your choice. Make your decision on the basis of the combination of purchase price and your estimated fuel costs. Remember that the lighter the car, the less fuel it burns. Each addition of 100 pounds decreases fuel economy by 1 percent.

◑ Choose accessories wisely and use them sparingly. Purchase only the optional equipment and accessories you really need. Air conditioning, automatic transmission, and power steering require considerable energy, all of which is derived from burning gasoline. Other optional equipment, such as power brakes and electric motor-

RIGHT IDEA

To encourage more commuters to leave their cars behind, the city of Boulder, Colorado, began organizing Bike to Work days four years ago. Today the program is a major success. At least thirty Boulder businesses participate in the Corporate Challenge—a contest among employers to have the greatest number of employees riding to work that day.

driven windows, seats, and radio antennas, consume less energy for their operation. But all accessories add to the vehicle weight, reducing fuel economy.

o Don't buy an air conditioner unless you really need it. Even when you're not using it, an air conditioner adds to the weight of the car. Besides, air conditioners are the biggest source of CFCs in the United States. According to *U.S. News and World Report,* an estimated 90 to 95 million auto air conditioners are in use in the United States. Each installed auto air con-

THE TEN MOST FUEL-EFFICIENT CARS AVAILABLE IN AMERICA TODAY

American cars average only 19 miles per gallon of gasoline. But even achieving just 30 mpg is not very ambitious when you consider the kind of gas mileage the cars below are already attaining:

Car	City/Highway mpg
1. Geo Metro, 5 gears	53/58
2. Honda Civic CRXHF, 5 gears	50/56
3. Geo Metro LSI, 5 gears	46/50
4. Honda Civic CRX HF, 5 gears	45/52
5. Ford Festiva, 5 gears	39/43
6. Geo Metro LSI, automatic 3-speed	38/40
7. Ford Festiva, 4 gears	38/40
8. Isuzu I-Mark, 5 gears	37/41
9. Geo Spectrum, 5 gears	37/41
10. Toyota Tercel, 4 gears	35/41

(Source: U.S. Environmental Protection Agency, 1989)

ditioner contains at least 2.5 pounds of chlorofluorocarbons (CFCs); and the annual recharge of the air conditioner can require an additional pound of CFCs.

○ **Buy a light-colored car with tinted glass.** It will require less air conditioning.

CAR MAINTENANCE

○ **Have your car tuned as needed.** For most cars, that means every 5,000 to 10,000 miles. Regular tune-ups extend engine life, improve performance, and reduce air pollution. A poorly tuned car could use as much as 3 to 9 percent more gasoline than a well-tuned one. Over time, the tune-up will pay for itself in gasoline savings and car reliability.

○ **Keep the engine filters clean.** Clogged filters waste gasoline.

○ **Use the gasoline octane and oil grade recommended for your car.** If you change the oil yourself, do so carefully so as not to spill any on the ground; afterward, take the used oil to your service station for recycling.

BRIGHT IDEA

Over 200 million gallons of used oil are generated each year by people who change their own motor oil. Less than 10 percent of this oil is recovered through recycling, even though used oil is still a valuable resource. Most of the time, the oil is dumped into the street or down a sewer, where it can contaminate our drinking water supplies.

In 1977, a chemical engineering professor at the University of Alabama organized Project ROSE (Recycled Oil Saves Energy) to help Alabama citizens recycle used motor oil. The program has two goals: to increase public awareness of the hazards of dumping used oil; and to organize a convenient used oil recycling network for individual communities. In 1988, 6.2 million gallons of used oil were recycled in Alabama, about 35 percent of the total used oil generated by vehicles in that state.

Project ROSE communicates its message through the media, schools, special events, and civic and volunteer organizations. Twice a year, Project ROSE airs public service announcements on radio and television, publishes press releases in local papers and magazines, and distributes brochures. In addition, the state telephone service and power company include information about Project ROSE with their bills at least once a year. Posters are distributed to service stations that collect used oil from consumers, while several larger cities pick up the used oil with curbside collection. In Tuscaloosa, the garbage trucks are fitted with racks to carry the used oil, increasing the convenience of this form of recycling for citizens.

⭐️ SOURCE

For more information, contact Project ROSE, P.O. Box 6373, Tuscaloosa, AL 35487-6373; telephone: 205-348-4878.

The EPA has compiled a directory of state used-oil recycling contacts. For your copy, contact U.S. Environmental Protection Agency, OS-323, 401 M Street, SW, Washington, DC 20460.

◐ **Check tire pressures regularly.** Underinflated tires increase gas use. You can lose about 2 percent in fuel economy for every pound of pressure below the recommended pounds per square inch.

◐ **Consider radial tires.** You can boost your gas mileage 3 to 5 percent in the city, 7 percent on the highway, and 10 percent at 55 miles per hour after the tires are warmed up for twenty minutes. Radial tires last longer, too (but for safety's sake, never mix them with conventional tires).

◐ **Remove unnecessary weight from the car.** The lighter the car, the less gas it uses. An extra 100 pounds in weight decreases fuel economy about 1 percent for the average car, 1¼ percent for small cars.

◐ **Use unleaded gas and a high quality multi-grade oil.** The Greenhouse Crisis Foundation reports that approximately 14 percent of the drivers in this country use leaded gas in vehicles that require unleaded gas. Such fuel switching adds significantly to automotive emissions, including hydrocarbons, nitrogen oxide, and lead, all of which contribute to the greenhouse crisis and acid rain, as well as to serious health problems.

◐ **Wash your car at home.** The average automatic car wash probably uses ten times too much water and a big charge of electricity to do a job you could easily do in your driveway with a bucket, hose, and sponge.

Warning! Do not have your car's air conditioner "serviced." This usually does nothing more than release CFCs (48% of the coolant!) into the atmosphere. Lost coolant from automobile air conditioners contributes 16 percent of ozone destruction, according to *Consumer Reports.* Leave the air conditioner alone unless you're sure it's broken. If you must have it replaced, take it to a dealer who can trap ozone-destroying CFCs that remain inside the unit before a service technician attempts to repair it.

SOURCE

For more information, get a copy of "Can We Repair the Sky?" care of Consumers Union/Reprints, P.O. Box CS 2010-A, Mount Vernon, NY 10553; or *Protecting the Ozone Layer: What You Can Do* (33 pages), Environmental Defense Fund, 257 Park Avenue South, New York, NY 10010 ($2.00).

◦ Use a repair shop that uses CFC recycling equipment. Most repair shops will just vent the CFCs remaining in the auto air conditioner into the air and refill the unit with new CFCs. But inexpensive machines, called "vampires," can now capture, clean, and recycle the used CFCs.

◦ If possible, buy a smaller air-conditioning unit for your car. Present car air conditioners are often capable of cooling a small apartment.

4 AT THE SUPERMARKET

When you go grocery shopping, for the most part you intend to buy food. But when you come home and unpack your bags, you'll find a lot more there than milk, bread, and eggs. First are all the grocery bags themselves; then there are the various containers the food is packed in: cardboard boxes that hold plastic margarine tubs, microwave popcorn, or just one cup of soup; styrene plastic egg cartons; cellophane wrappings; plastic bags or plastic cartons for the fresh fruit or vegetables. By the time the end of the week rolls around, you've got the nonfood leftovers to contend with: empty cans and boxes, used and discarded paper towels, throwaway bottles and empty plastic milk jugs, the aluminum trays from TV dinners, and other assorted types of trash that add up to at least 4 pounds of garbage per person per day—160 million tons a year.

You throw out your own weight in packaging alone every thirty to forty days! In fact, nearly $1 of every $10 Americans spend for food and beverages today goes to pay for packaging. According to the U.S. Department of Agriculture, Americans spent more for food packaging in 1986— $28 billion—than the nation's farmers received in net income. That's a lot of money to spend on products whose manufacture and disposal are linked to almost every environmental problem plaguing us today:

‪○‬ Shrinking landfill space: Packaging accounts for one-third of all municipal waste by weight and as much as 50 percent by volume.

‪○‬ Acid rain and global warming: Production of plastics and synthetic materials uses more energy than any other sector of the chemical industry. In fact, producing plastics consumes 3.5 percent of all oil used in the United States. Not only does this dependence on oil considerably deplete an already declining fuel source, but burning oil during the manufacturing process itself contributes directly to global warming and acid rain.

‪○‬ Toxic contamination: The Food and Drug Administration is considering whether to allow the use of polyvinylchloride (PVC) plastic as a food packaging material for milk, salad dressing, oil, frozen vegetables, cereals, and more. A known human carcinogen, PVC is currently used in construction materials and for some nonfood containers. Because recent technological advances have decreased its potential to contaminate food, industry is interested in using PVC for food packaging. But to do so will triple the amount of PVC in trash within five years, increasing the toxic air pollutants emitted when incinerators burn the stuff. If it's landfilled instead, the PVC could take as many as four centuries to decompose, possibly contaminating groundwater in the process.

Plastic is the most rapidly growing component of trash. In fact, it's designed to become garbage—and stay garbage. For example, a squeezable ketchup bottle is made of six layers of plastic, each of which does a different job (one gives the bottle shape, another strength, a third flexibility, and so forth). But few recycling processes can handle more than one type of plastic.

Less than 1 percent of all plastics are currently recycled (even though recycling the 20 billion plastic bottles and 1 billion pounds of plastic trash bags currently used by Americans could reduce our need for landfills by 30 percent). More than forty-six different types of plastic are in common use, and the number will probably grow by the turn of the century.

Carbonated beverage containers contribute significantly to garbage overload. Aluminum soda cans and glass and plastic bottles account for more than 5 percent of household wastes in many areas, but you could easily eliminate them from your trash altogether if legislation putting a refundable deposit on beverage containers existed in every state. A study by the Beer Wholesalers Association found that, within two years of its implementation, the New York deposit law had saved $50 million on cleanup expenditures, $19 million on solid waste disposal costs, and $50 to $100 million on energy, while increasing net employment by at least 3,800 jobs— and all this in New York alone.

In environmental terms, the reward is no less impressive. Every

BRIGHT IDEA

Innovative American entrepreneurs are getting their hands on some of the 200 million pounds of plastics that are being recycled each year and turning them into a wide variety of useful, durable products:

○ Aqua Glass, a manufacturer of fiberglass bathroom units, incorporates recycled PET bottles—the kind used for soft drinks—into its line of residential and commercial bathtubs, shower stalls, sinks, and spas.

○ Wellman, Inc., a recycler in Clark, New Jersey, converts PET soda bottles into carpets, filling for pillows and mattresses, and liners for landfills. Wellman is also transforming the glut of green plastic from soda bottles into a nonwoven "geotextile," that can be used to prevent soil at landfill sites and railroad track beds from shifting.

○ Plastics Recycling, Inc. of Iowa Falls, Iowa, is turning containers made of more than one form of plastic (like ketchup bottles) into car stops in parking lots, fence posts, two-by-fours for park benches and boat docks. This "plastic wood" is not slippery, and it doesn't rot or corrode.

Meanwhile, the city of Minneapolis has banned most plastic food packaging from grocery stores and fast food restaurants until the city can work out an acceptable way to recycle plastics.

---

ton of crushed waste glass (or "cullet") used to make new glass saves the equivalent of 30 gallons of oil and replaces 1.2 tons of raw materials. Recycling an aluminum can saves 95 percent of the energy used to make aluminum from scratch—and cuts air pollution by a corresponding 95 percent. In fact, the energy needed to make 1 ton of virgin aluminum could be used to recycle 20 tons of aluminum from scrap.

Even recycling plastics saves twice as much energy as burning them in an incinerator creates (while avoiding toxic air pollution). And producing a fabricated plastic product from scrap instead of virgin resin saves some 85 to 90 percent of the energy otherwise used.

Beyond a doubt, one of the simplest and least expensive steps the federal government can take to reduce garbage overload immediately in the United States is to pass nationwide deposit legislation.

RIGHT IDEA

"Reverse vending machines" accept returned beverage containers and disburse deposit refunds, either in the form of cash or vouchers. In the machines, cans are flattened, glass bottles are crushed, and plastic bottles are granulated to confetti-size pieces, compacting volume for efficient collection. As an incentive to their customers to use the machines, supermarkets in San Diego, Huntington Beach, and other California cities award instant cash prizes to recyclers and make them eligible for even bigger payoffs—like a brand-new Alfa Romeo Spider Graduate convertible car. For more information about the reverse vending machines, contact their manufacturer: Environmental Products Corporation, 11240 Waples Mill Road, Fairfax, VA 22030-6032; telephone: 703-591-1001.

WHAT CAN YOU DO TO CUT "PACKAGING POLLUTION"?

◐ If you can't recycle something, reuse it. Buy products that will last. If you must buy plastic and glass bottles, don't throw them away. Use them to hold leftovers in the kitchen, to store bobby pins in the bathroom, to hold paper clips in the office . . . you get the idea.

◐ Whenever possible, buy returnable bottles and cans. In addition to soft drink and alcoholic beverages, returnable milk bottles are still available in many places, including states without a bottle bill. Each bottle may be reused as many as forty or fifty times.

◐ Buy products that can be recycled—and recycle them. Newspapers, aluminum and steel (not tin) cans, glass of all shapes and colors, and a growing number of plastic milk jugs and soda bottles can be recycled at home. Call the department of public works in your city for more information. Also, the Yellow Pages list many scrap-metal companies that will pay for aluminum, copper, brass, lead, batteries, radiators, and insulated wire.

◐ Buy biodegradable products. Avoid most plastics, especially polystyrene plastics (such as Styrofoam), which cannot be recycled at all. Buy waxed paper instead of plastic wrap; for microwaving, buy glass casseroles with lids instead of microwave wrap.

◐ Avoid excessive packaging. Buy soap that comes wrapped in paper instead of liquid soap that comes in a plastic bottle. Slice your own cheese instead of buying the individual, plastic-wrapped slices. Buy fresh produce and bag it yourself, instead of buying food that's prepackaged in steel or tin cans, cardboard, or plastic containers.

○ **Buy fewer things.** The best way to keep packaging out of the trash is not to buy it in the first place. If you don't really need it—or can borrow it from someone else—don't buy it.

○ **Reuse what you do buy.** Buy products that will last.

○ **Buy in bulk.** Select the largest size possible of household products like shampoo and detergent, and transfer to smaller containers for easier use if necessary. Or buy products in concentrated form and add the water to them when you get home. Instead of buying a six-pack of soda, buy one large bottle. And if your store has a bulk foods department, use it. You'll end up using—and throwing away—fewer containers.

○ **Choose paper instead of plastic.** If you must buy throwaway products, opt for paper, which is biodegradable.

○ **Reuse plastic bags.** If you end up with some plastic sacks anyway, use them several times before you throw them away. They can be used to store leftovers or for wrapping up sandwiches to take to school, the office, or on a picnic. And you can avoid buying plastic garbage bags by using plastic grocery bags in your garbage pail instead.

In any event, bring your bags, whether plastic or paper, back to the grocery store with you for a refill the next time you shop.

○ **Leave the bag ties at the store.** In the produce section, the bulk foods department, or anywhere else you bag your own food, forego using the plastic or metal ties the store provides for closing

BRIGHT IDEA

When the first Body Shop opened in Berkeley, California, in 1970, people passing by would frequently stop outside the tiny emporium to watch employees cut and wrap soaps by hand. Five stores and almost twenty years later, the Body Shop still offers the high-quality items that attracted customers to it in the first place: biodegradable soaps, perfumes, and lotions simply wrapped in paper, for sale at prices everyone can afford. The company also offers an all-purpose biodegradable cleanser called "Bio-Clean" that's concentrated so a few drops go a long way—and a bottle lasts a long time.

The Body Shop offers its products via mail order, but there's a particular benefit to dropping by one of the five locations the next time you happen to be in the San Francisco Bay area: If you bring along your own empty bottles, the Body Shop will fill them for you with lotions, oils, or hair care products—at a reduced price.

For a copy of the company's catalog, contact The Body Shop at 1341 Seventh Street, Berkeley, CA 94710; telephone: 415-524-0216.

the bags. You can knot the corners of the bags together to keep the bag closed just as effectively.

€ **Object to new throwaway products before they get established in the marketplace.**

There wouldn't be a market for disposable contact lenses, one-use-only razors, or plastic diapers if people wouldn't buy them in the first place. If a new, objectionable product hits the shelves of your

NOT SUCH A BRIGHT IDEA

€ **The plastic can.** In 1985, Coca-Cola launched a product destined for the environmental graveyard: a plastic can.

Made of clear plastic with an aluminum top and a polyvinylchloride label, the can sparked nationwide protests from professional recyclers, environmentalists, and local officials opposed to adding yet another unrecyclable product to the solid waste stream. Because the can could be mistaken for an all-aluminum container, it could gum up the works of aluminum recycling equipment. And if it became popular with consumers, it could pull the financial rug right out from under aluminum recycling, the backbone of the recycling industry.

Almost as soon as the plastic can hit grocery store shelves, a citizens' group rose up to mobilize grassroots opposition. The Coalition for Recyclable Waste mounted a formidable national letter-writing campaign to make it clear to Coke, and eventually to another manufacturer, the Original New York Seltzer company, that consumers, recyclers, and environmentalists were unalterably opposed to the use of this can. The result: Both Coca-Cola and Original New York Seltzer abandoned the plastic can, and the entire manufacturing facility, Petainer, shut down its United States operation. Just to make sure Coke, Original New York Seltzer, or any other company doesn't try to resurrect the idea, legislation banning the plastic can has been passed in Connecticut and Minnesota.

€ **The throwaway camera.** Now Kodak is manufacturing a throwaway plastic camera.

The company's target market is tourists who accidentally leave their cameras at home. All the consumer needs to do is buy a camera, take the pictures, and ship the whole thing off to a photo finisher. The finisher will remove and develop the film, send you the pictures, and toss the camera itself into the garbage.

Such convenience isn't cheap, and the high retail price doesn't include the hidden costs to you and others of disposing of yet another throwaway item at the dump.

To urge Kodak to pull its disposable cameras off the market, call 800-242-2424 (the Kodak hotline). Your complaint will be reported to a consumer representative and included in a report to senior company executives. Or write to the Kodak Information Center, Department 841 K, 343 State Street, Rochester, NY 14650.

®RIGHT IDEA

Eat candy to save the rain forests? You can if the candy is Rainforest Crunch, a sweet brittle made of cashew and Brazil nuts harvested in the Amazon rain forest. Rainforest Crunch is the premiere product of Community Products, Inc., which was founded by Ben Cohen of Ben & Jerry's Homemade Ice Cream. The goal is to provide the people who live in tropical rain forests with an economic incentive to keep the forests intact. The company will buy 150,000 pounds of nuts a year, to be made into both candy and ice cream. Forty percent of the profits will be donated to organizations working to protect the rain forest.

grocery store, complain to the store manager and write the manufacturer a letter.

○ **Buy eggs in cardboard cartons, not plastic.**

○ **Buy concentrated, multipurpose products, like laundry soap that is also a bleach or a fabric softener—to cut down on packaging.**

○ **Buy products in cardboard.** Fifty percent of cardboard supermarket packages are made from recycled paper. Recycled packaging can be identified by the recycling symbol on the package or by a gray interior, found in paperboard boxes containing cereals, detergents, and cake mixes.

○ **If possible, buy unbleached paper versions of products such as coffee filters, milk cartons, toilet paper, and paper towels.** The chlorine that is used to bleach paper pulp to make it "ultra white" has been linked to the highly carcinogenic substance dioxin. Not only has dioxin been found in the soil and water around paper mills, but traces of dioxin have been found in the paper products themselves. Though the United States as a whole has been slow to act on controlling the use of chlorine bleach in paper manufacturing, throughout Europe, the need for highly bleached paper products is being re-evaluated.

®OURCE

The Pennsylvania Resources Council has prepared a kit that includes a 20-page booklet, *Become an Environmental Shopper: Vote for the Environment,* and a product list of 400 items in recyclable or recycled packaging. Copies can be obtained for $5.00 by contacting PRC at P.O. Box 88, Media, PA 19063.

Sweden, for example, has stopped the sale of chlorine-bleached disposable diapers. And in Austria, consumers are using unbleached brown coffee filters and milk cartons.

○ **Stock up on cloth napkins and towels** so you don't need to use the throwaway kind.

○ **Buy non-aerosol sprays.** Though all aerosols sold in the United States now meet legal requirements for levels of CFCs, the chlorofluorocarbons still permitted can destroy the ozone that filters the sun's rays.

○ **Buy rechargeable batteries for flashlights and other household gear.** Many batteries contain hazardous materials, including cadmium and mercury. If possible, use electricity instead of batteries; the slight amount of energy you'll consume from the electrical outlet will be more than offset by the fact that manufacturing batteries can take fifty times more energy than they produce. If you use a lot of batteries, buy the rechargeable kind, and recharge them regularly.

○ **Borrow or rent items you don't use that often, and maintain and repair the items you own to ensure longer product life.** In other words, buy less. You'll have less to throw away.

○ **Shop at farmers' markets or co-ops.** Local markets will have fresher produce that consequently may be contaminated with fewer pesticides than the supermarket equivalent. Foods will not be so

---

IDENTIFYING AND AVOIDING CFCs

Chlorofluorocarbons (CFCs), halons, and other man-made chemicals are putting a hole in the earth's protective ozone layer and contributing to the greenhouse effect. Unfortunately, products that contain these chemicals are not required to be labeled, so you could accidentally buy—and use—a product containing halons or CFCs without even knowing it. Several products still contain dangerous CFCs and halons. The Natural Resources Defense Council suggests that you check the labels of products like aerosols, foam plastic materials, fire extinguishers, and aerosol dust removers for photographic equipment, and avoid items that contain any of the following chemicals:

CFC-11	Trichlorofluoromethane
CFC-12	Dichlorodifluoromethane
CFC-113	Trichlorotrifluoroethane
CFC-114	Dichlorotetrafluoroethane
CFC-115	(Mono)chloropentafluoroethane
Halon-1211	Bromochlorodifluoroethane
Halon-1301	Bromotrifluoroethane
Halon-2402	Dibromotetrafluoroethane

☾ 🅑RIGHT IDEA

One way you can pressure companies to be environmentally responsible is by exerting your buying power. The New York–based Council on Economic Priorities has produced a pocket-size handbook to help you purchase products from nonpolluting companies. You can use the handbook before you go shopping to identify items to buy or avoid, based on how they're manufactured and on the company's environmental practices in general. For a copy of the guide, write to *Shopping for a Better World,* Council on Economic Priorities, 30 Irving Place, New York, NY 10003 ($5.00).

heavily wrapped in plastic or paper, either.

○ **Support deposit legislation.** Urge your state representatives to pass a statewide bottle bill, and tell your Member of Congress you support deposit legislation nationwide.

Pesticides in the Grocery Store

With each passing day, it seems as if another cancer-causing chemical is showing up on our food . . . and staying there. After ranking twenty-nine environmental problems under its jurisdiction, the Environmental Protection Agency concluded that only indoor radon pollution and worker exposure to chemicals pose a greater risk of cancer than pesticide residues on food. EPA also noted that more than 70 of the roughly 360 pesticide ingredients used by farmers are "probably carcinogens." Yet the agency has completely banned only three pesticides since it was established in 1970 and has seriously restricted only a handful of others.

CAN YOU BELIEVE IT?

○ We throw away enough glass bottles and jars to fill the 1,350-foot twin towers of New York's World Trade Center every two weeks.

○ Consumers and industry in the United States throw away enough aluminum to rebuild our entire commercial air fleet every three months.

○ Americans go through 2.5 million plastic bottles every hour: one for every resident of the state of Iowa.

○ We throw away enough iron and steel every day to supply all the nation's automakers every day.

(Source: Environmental Defense Fund)

PICK THE BEST PACKAGE

When you go shopping, if all other considerations are equal, pick a product wrapped in the least amount of packaging. The following list provides some guidelines that will help you make your decision. In the ratings column, a check (✔) means the item can be reused or recycled; a zero (0) means it can be incinerated or landfilled; a minus (−) means it cannot be disposed of easily and should be avoided if at all possible.

Kind of Package	Grocery Store Item	Rating
No packaging or natural package	Melons, pineapples, other fruits	✔ +
Returnable glass bottles	Milk bottles	✔
	Soda and beer bottles in states with deposit laws	✔
Reusable containers	Cookie and cracker tins, heavy-duty plastic plates on which some microwave dinners are packaged, sturdy glass vegetable or juice jars	✔
Uncoated paper	Bags of candy, cookies, chips, and other snacks	0
Uncoated cardboard	Cereal boxes, detergent boxes, dessert mix boxes and boxes of dry food that don't have a cellophane window	0
All-steel cans	Many canned fruits and veggies	0
All-aluminum cans	Beverage containers	✔
Steel cans with aluminum tops	Pull-top cans	0
Glass bottles with twist-off tops	Soft drinks	✔
Wax paper	Liners in cake boxes and other foods	0
Cellophane, plastics	Windows in paper boxes	0
	Plastic bags	−
Coated paper	Paper milk and juice cartons	0
PVC	Clear plastic bottles and plastic wraps	−
Aluminum-foil–based containers	Foil-lined boxes and bags	−
Collapsible metal tubes	Toothpaste, hand cream	−
Metal and plastic pumps	Toothpaste pumps	−
Aerosol cans	Toiletries, deodorants, hairsprays, insecticides	−

☼ **B**RIGHT IDEAS

○ *Seventh Generation.* If you can't find the biodegradable items you're looking for in your local grocery or department store, you may be able to order them by mail. Seventh Generation, a company based in Vermont, stocks biodegradable toilet paper and sanitary napkins, nontoxic cleaners and bug sprays, solar calculators, and water-saving shower heads, among many other environmentally sound items. For a complete product catalog, send $2 to Seventh Generation, 10 Farrell Street, South Burlington, VT 05403.

○ *Cheaper & Better.* The ultimate way to avoid excessive packaging is by making your own products at home (at a fraction of the price) and storing them in the bottles and cans you haven't been able to bring yourself to throw away. Recipes and formulas for over 300 high-quality foods, cleansers, creams, and even sun tan lotion are included in *Cheaper & Better: Home-made Alternatives to Storebought Goods* (423 pages), by Nancy Birnes, Harper & Row, 1987.

Just because a pesticide is registered by the U.S. Environmental Protection Agency and your state does not make it safe.

A 1982 U.S. Congressional staff report indicated that between 79 and 84 percent of pesticides on the market have not been adequately tested for their capacity to cause cancer; between 90 and 93 percent of pesticides have not been adequately tested for their ability to cause genetic damage; and between 60 and 70 percent have not been fully tested for their ability to cause birth defects.

Hundreds of chemicals have been registered with false, misleading, or inadequate health and environmental test data. Some chemical companies have not updated or "re-registered" their products to keep pace with modern safety standards. "Backdoor" registrations, such as "emergency exemptions" and "special local need permits" allow untested or unsafe products to be marketed and their uses expanded. And the risk/benefit formula used for regulating pesticides may result in unacceptable risks not only for such vulnerable segments of the population as children and pregnant women, but for all people exposed.

A tolerance level for a chemical residue on a particular fruit or vegetable is based on the EPA's estimate of how much of that commodity is consumed yearly by the average American. As Americans for Safe Food, a national coalition dedicated to creating a healthier food supply, notes, someone who is fond of, say, eggplant only has to eat more than 7.5 ounces—less than half a pound—per year to be exposed to what the EPA has determined could be an unsafe level of pesticide residue. Children and the elderly may not be as able as the "average American" to detoxify or eliminate pesticides. And infants are particularly vulnerable, both because they eat higher levels of foods that contain cancerous residues, and because some pesticide residues are concentrated in breast milk.

How Can You Play It Safe?

❍ **Buy pesticide-free produce.** Wherever possible, buy organically grown fruits and vegetables.

❍ **Get to know your grocery store manager.** Urge him or her to stock more contaminant-free fruits and vegetables.

❍ **Don't buy "perfect" food.** If it's not good enough for the worms, should you eat it?

❍ **Wash all fruits and vegetables before eating them, preferably in a diluted solution of a mild dishwashing liquid like Ivory Soap and water.** Peel everything, especially citrus fruits. And don't use those new pesticide- and wax-removing washes. They cost eight times more than dishwashing liquid, but private tests have shown that they may not do a better job.

❍ **Buy foods in season, and encourage your market to stock locally grown produce.** To produce and transport out-of-season products usually requires excessive energy consumption, as well as preservatives and pesticides to keep produce looking "just picked." Local products are usually treated with fewer chemicals be-

SOURCE

Two groups can help you get more pesticide-free food into your grocery store:

❍ Americans for Safe Food, a coalition spearheaded by the Center for Science in the Public Interest, is organizing a national campaign to let grocery stores know that consumers want food free of potentially dangerous pesticides, fumigants, growth promotants, antibiotics, hormones, and additives. For more information and a copy of *Guess What's Coming to Dinner: Contaminants in Our Food* ($3.50), write to them at 1501 16th Street, NW, Washington, DC 20036.

❍ National Coalition Against the Misuse of Pesticides is a national network committed to pesticide safety and the adoption of alternative pest management strategies that reduce or eliminate a dependency on toxic chemicals. Their address is 530 7th Street, SE, Washington, DC 20003.

☀️ **B**RIGHT IDEA

Mothers and Others for Pesticide Limits

For years, the Environmental Protection Agency has allowed food growers to apply chemicals to hundreds of fruits and vegetables even though many of those chemicals are known or "probable" carcinogens. The problem is especially acute for children. According to the Natural Resources Defense Council (NRDC), a highly respected environmental research group, as many as 6,000 American preschoolers could eventually get cancer from ingesting chemical residues on U.S. produce—particularly apples treated with the ripening agent Alar.

On February 27, 1989, NRDC released its data in a report titled "Intolerable Risk: Pesticides in Our Children's Food" and announced the formation of Mothers and Others Against Pesticides, headed by actress Meryl Streep, to educate the public about pesticide hazards. The ensuing national uproar brought about what no level of EPA or Congressional activity had been able to achieve: enough public concern—accompanied by a significant drop in apple sales—to prompt many apple growers voluntarily to stop using Alar in their orchards. NRDC is still pressuring EPA to issue a total ban on Alar so that those apple growers who don't support the voluntary ban will be unable to use the chemical.

WHAT DOES "ORGANIC" MEAN?

According to the Organic Foods Production Association (OFPANA), "organic foods are foods produced under a system of ecological soil management that relies on building humus levels through crop rotation, recycling organic wastes, applying balanced mineral amendments, and using varieties resistant to disease and pests.

"When necessary, botanical or biological controls with minimum impact on health and the environment may be used. Organic foods are processed, packaged, transported, and stored to retain maximum nutritional value without the use of artificial preservatives, coloring or additives, irradiation or synthetic pesticides."

For information on how to certify that food is truly organically grown, write OFPANA, 125 West 7th Street, Wind Gap, PA 18091; or call 215-863-6700.

SOURCE

For a copy of the executive summary of "Intolerable Risk: Pesticides in Our Children's Food" ($5.00), contact the Natural Resources Defense Council, 740 West 20th Street, New York, NY 10011.

For an analysis of the levels of Alar found in apple juice, see the article "Bad Apples" in the May 1989 issue of *Consumer Reports*.

cause they're consumed sooner and don't have to survive cross-country transport.

When the Package Itself Is a Problem . . .

The Food and Drug Administration has found that lead levels in tomatoes packaged in lead-soldered cans can be twenty times higher than in tomatoes from cans with welded seams. Because lead intake can be particularly dangerous for children under the age of six and for fetuses, *Consumer Reports* recommends that wherever possible, you buy cans that have not been sol-

dered with lead. Here's how to tell the can types apart:

Peel back a bit of the label on the can. A soldered seam has a crimped joint, which means the edges are folded over, and a smear of silver-gray metal on the outside of the seam. A welded seam is flat, with a thin, dark, sharply defined line along the joint.

The next time you go grocery shopping, make sure that you check cans of tomatoes and other canned foods for lead-soldered seams. Or play it safe—buy fresh produce and make your own sauces and servings.

SOURCE

If your grocery store does not stock organically grown food, you can order your own from one of the 300 growers, wholesalers, and distributors of organic food in the United States and Canada. Names and addresses are provided in the *Organic Wholesalers Directory and Yearbook,* published by the California Action Network. The directory can be ordered for $19.00, plus $1.75 for shipping and handling from CAN, P.O. Box 464, Davis, CA 95617; telephone: 916-756-8518. An abbreviated list of organic food mail order suppliers is also available from Americans for Safe Food.

BRIGHT IDEA

Cornell University's Integrated Pest Management program has reported that New York farmers raising twenty-seven different crops have saved money by cutting back on pesticide use—with no loss in crop production. The farmers use pesticides only when they're needed. Instead of spraying automatically at certain times of the year, they use data on temperature and humidity to predict past outbreaks. When an attack looks likely, they consult specialists who help devise appropriate spraying plans. *Newsweek* reports that last year, apple growers participating in the Cornell experiment used 38 percent less pesticide than in 1975. Of the 3,200 acres of alfalfa monitored under the program, only 57 ended up needing any pesticide at all.

BUY AND EAT LESS MEAT—AND SUPPORT WISE USE OF AGRICULTURAL LAND

It is widely recognized that adopting a healthy diet would significantly reduce the 1.4 million deaths that occur annually from heart disease, stroke, cancer, and other chronic illnesses, as well as reduce the associated pain and suffering, medical bills, and loss in productivity. Such a diet would favor whole grains, vegetables, and fruit over animal and other fatty foods, sugar, and salt.

But this "low impact" diet helps restore health to the environment, too. Consider these facts:

○ The intensive exploitation of marginal agricultural land for production of foods for people and animals has been largely responsible for the massive erosion and irretrievable loss of billions of tons of topsoil annually.

○ Animal agriculture consumes one-third of the raw materials used for all purposes in the United States.

○ Over 90 percent of all agricultural land in the United States, more than half the total land area, is used to produce animal "crops." Over two-thirds of all cropland is used for livestock agriculture.

○ Producing meat consumes at least ten times more water than producing grain. Just one chicken slaughtering plant uses 100 million gallons of water each day—the equivalent of the amount of water used by a community of 25,000 people.

So eating less meat helps conserve resources. It helps save energy, too. It takes 5 to 20 calories of fossil fuel to produce 1 calorie of food energy in the form of meat. But it takes only ¼ or ½ calorie of fossil fuel to produce 1 calorie of plant food energy. Even under energy-intensive Western agriculture, production of plant foods

SOURCE

Several excellent vegetarian cookbooks are available from your bookstore or library to help you prepare delicious, meat-free meals. They include:

  Ⓣ *The New Laurel's Kitchen,* by Laurel Robertson, Carol Flinders, and Brian Ruppenthal, Ten Speed Press, P.O. Box 7123, Berkeley, CA 94707

  Ⓣ *Vegetarian Times Cookbook,* P.O. Box 570, Oak Park, IL 60303

  Ⓣ *World of the East Vegetarian Cooking,* by Madhur Jaffrey, Alfred A. Knopf, New York, 1988

is ten to a hundred times more efficient in terms of energy than meat production.

Already, many more people, while not cutting meat out of their diets completely, have reduced the amount of meat they eat each week. Here's what you can do:

Ⓣ **Eat less meat.** According to the Greenhouse Crisis Foundation, if Americans were to reduce their meat intake by even 10 percent, the 12 million tons of grain saved annually would be enough to feed all people on the earth who starve to death annually. Reducing beef intake would also reduce deforestation caused by tree cutting for grazing land.

Ⓣ **Prepare meals from fruits, grains, and vegetables.**

Ⓣ **Support measures for controlling agricultural use of marginal land.**

HELP YOUR SUPERMARKET BECOME MORE ENVIRONMENTALLY AWARE

In addition to buying products that have a low impact on the planet, encourage your grocery store to operate more responsibly, too.

Ⓣ If you are part of a local environmental group or civic association, **request a meeting with the store manager to discuss the options available to the store to conserve energy, purchase organic produce, stock items that come in recyclable packaging, etc.**

Ⓣ **Meet with the consumer affairs representative.** Larger supermarket chains will have a consumer affairs representative responsible for implementing changes at all of their stores. In addition to in-store practices like those described above, urge the chain to print environmental messages on their grocery bags or to prepare an

![lightbulb] **B**RIGHT **IDEA**

Since 1989, Canadians have been able to choose environmentally sound products such as re-refined motor oil, insulation material made from recycled paper, and selected items made from recycled plastic. How do they know these products are environmentally "okay"? Because they're marked with the environmental choice logo, three birds entwined to form a stylized maple leaf. The logo was cooperatively developed by representatives of consumer groups, manufacturers, and the government to help consumers make "green" purchasing decisions in order to reduce waste and pollution as well as to encourage the development of environmentally safe products. For further information, contact the Canadian Standards Association, 178 Rexdale Boulevard, Rexdale, Ontario M9W 1R3; telephone: 416-747-4017.

inexpensive educational pamphlet or "bag stuffer" about the environment. Stores could also give shoppers discount coupons for "low impact" products (those that come in recyclable glass or aluminum or come wrapped in paper instead of plastic) or for the store's own "bio brands" (see below).

◑ Encourage grocery store chains to stock their own brands of recyclable/biodegradable products. Many stores could break new ground and create a profitable new niche for themselves by stocking a "bio brand" of many items.

◑ Set up a newspaper recycling operation outside the grocery store. Many stores already allow their customers to recycle their newspapers in bins set up outside the grocery store.

◑ Urge each grocery store to work with the local utility to conduct an energy audit. The utility can help the store identify many opportunities to conserve energy; at the same time, the grocery store can serve as an example to other businesses in the community.

5 AT SCHOOL

*S*chools can suffer from the same pollution problems as homes. But fixing those problems may be more challenging than tackling your own leaky windows or tightening your water faucets. A school administrator has many needs to attend to. Despite the best of intentions, the school's budget and other extenuating circumstances may require the administrator to make tough choices that may or may not favor the environment. You can help educate your school district and influence school policy by playing an active role in the Parent-Teacher Association, by voicing your concerns to the school board at meetings and through letters and petitions, and by educating the media about important environmental problems and opportunities your school faces.

Most of this chapter contains suggestions for what an administrator can do to "green up" his or her school. But, as a parent or student, you can play an important role too, beginning with the following actions:

◐ **Start an Ecology Club.** Beginning with students in your biology or science classes, form a club to promote energy conservation and other environmental projects. A science teacher can act as an adviser. The club can set up a recycling center, build a display on energy-efficient driving, conduct an environmental audit of the school, or sponsor an ecology fair on the anniversary of Earth Day (April 22).

The club can also become a force for change in the school. As an official school entity, you can pressure school administrators to enact more environmental regulations, urge the Parent-Teacher Association to get involved, and lobby the school board. You can also write a regular environmental column for the school newspaper and perhaps give an award to the "environmental teacher of the year."

○ Set up an Environment Committee of the PTA. As a concerned parent you can work closely with your local PTA to ensure that the school your children attend is as environmentally responsible as possible. Attend PTA meetings to raise environmental issues important to your school, like solid waste, energy conservation, and indoor air pollution.

○ Urge the PTA to endorse an environmental curriculum for your school, beginning with the resources listed later in this chapter.

○ Supplement what your children are learning about the environment at school with lessons you can teach them at home. Again, refer to some of the materials listed as resources at the end of this chapter.

○ Encourage students and teachers to use buses or other **mass-transit rather than their own cars.**

○ Support special parking privileges to students and teachers who drive fuel-efficient cars or who car pool.

○ If a new school is being built in your community, attend planning meetings to ensure that it is as efficient as possible.

○ Encourage publications like *Weekly Reader* and *Scholastic* to run regular features on the environment.

○ Urge high school shop classes to offer courses in tuning up car engines to maximum efficiency. Then, during an "Ecology Week" or on Earth Day, offer tune-ups to students and teachers driving to school.

○ Make use of school resources available in your community. Find out if universities and colleges in your area conduct research on tropical forests, new grains and plants, agriculture, or medicines. If they depend on tropical plants for their research, warn them about the impending destruction of tropical rain forests and enlist their help in presenting community programs, talking to reporters, and learning about further sources of information.

THE THREE R's

When it comes to the "three R's"—reduce, reuse, and recycle—schools, colleges, and universities have as much to learn about garbage overload as do the rest of us.

A school can spend as much money disposing of its trash as it does on buying textbooks. The amount of trash created in schools has grown steadily over the last ten years, as cafeterias and dining rooms have switched to serving more and more meals and snacks on paper and throwaway plastic instead of conventional tableware, glass, or reusable plastic. In schools all over America, napkins, plates, cups, forks, knives, and spoons are tossed into the garbage can thousands of times a day, five days a week, along with the bags from potato chips, candy bars, and Popsicles, all standard school lunch fare. In some schools, even if hamburgers are cooked on the spot, they are wrapped in colorful (and throwaway) aluminum foil to resemble a Big Mac or a Whopper.

Thus our schools are teaching students a set of values about our throwaway society that they'll keep with them all their lives. After all, if the school doesn't think it's important to minimize waste and recycle, why should the student?

Here are just a few ways to reduce garbage overload at schools:

◐ **Take lunch to school in reusable containers.** Lunch boxes and heavy-duty plastic containers are better than throwaway bags, plastic wrap, and waxed paper.

◐ **Work with your Parent-Teacher Association and student council to identify ways your school could reduce the amount of garbage it produces.** Encourage your school to:

* Stop using throwaway dishes, cups, and utensils for regular school meals. For carry-out items, use only paper products, not plastic.
* Replace the "fast food" approach with fresh-cooked foods and meals that minimize waste and taste better, too! One old-fashioned sectioned plate could hold a burger, french fries, fruit, and drink and create no waste other than a napkin.
* Put separate garbage cans in the cafeteria for organic (uneaten food), paper, and other kinds of trash. The organic waste can be composted on the school grounds and used as fertilizer on lawns, fields, and flower beds.
* Set up a paper recycling operation. In addition to paper trash created in the cafeteria, students throw away a lot of paper during the course of a day. Any recycling program that's set up for the cafeteria should include a plan to collect paper from classrooms and, for colleges and boarding schools, dormitories as well. Every classroom could have a special box or bin just for paper, while dormitories could put recycling boxes in the laundry rooms. Contact the city's public works department, or check the telephone book for listings of paper recyclers.

● Offer broken desks, chairs, and other equipment to salvagers or charities to repair and resell. The minimum amount of remaining trash can be hauled to a landfill.

● **Turn class projects into demonstrations about the amount of garbage your school produces.** As a science or civics project, you could build a "Mount Trashmore" just out of the foam plastic cups students use for a month. Accompany it with a display about shrinking landfill space in your community, and suggest alternatives for the school to adopt.

Schools can take many other steps to insure a healthier environment for their students and to minimize the impact they as institutions have on the environment. You can help get them started.

● **Attend school board meetings to make your views known.**

● **Involve the PTA in lobbying school board members to support sound environmental management.**

● **Urge your local newspaper to editorialize in favor of a greater school board commitment to the environment.**

● **Network with other parents, students, and teachers concerned about environmental issues.**

● **Prepare a checklist for your local school board of concerns relating to the school environment itself.**

ENVIRONMENTAL ALERTS IN AND AROUND THE CLASSROOM

Radon

On April 20, 1989, the Environmental Protection Agency urged all school buildings to be tested for radon contamination. EPA expects that at least 10 percent of schools have a radon problem, the same percentage of residences that exceed safe radon levels around the United States.

Basements and rooms at ground level stand the greatest risk of radon contamination. Because ventilation systems work poorly in many schools, contaminated air that enters rooms from the foundation of the building concentrates instead of dispersing.

SOURCE

The EPA has issued a guide to help schools measure radon and reduce high levels. For more information, write for a free copy of *Radon Measurements in Schools*, Office of Radiation Programs, Environmental Protection Agency, Washington, DC 20460.

EPA recommends that all schools take the following actions:

◐ **Test frequently used rooms on the basement and ground-level floors, as well as gymnasiums, cafeterias, libraries, and offices.**

◐ **Conduct tests in the cooler months of the year** when doors and windows are likely to be closed and concentrations of the gas are probably high.

◐ **Take immediate corrective action if the school has a radon problem.** Seal cracks in the foundation of buildings to prevent gas from seeping in, improve ventilation, and increase air pressure within a building to keep out the gas.

Asbestos

Asbestos is a naturally occurring mineral that was used widely in schools and commercial buildings because its fibers are fireproof, strong, and don't corrode easily. However, when disturbed during renovation, reconstruction, or demolition, asbestos fibers may become suspended in the air for many hours, making it possible to breathe asbestos into the lungs. According to the EPA, there is no safe level of exposure to asbestos.

Asbestos fibers have been used in floor tile, sealants, plastics, cement pipe and sheet, paper and textile products, and insulation. They've been sprayed around pipes and boilers and used in fireproofing and soundproofing or for decorative purposes. They've also been manu-

factured into yarn, cloth, and other textiles that were later made into fire-resistant curtains or blankets, protective clothing, electrical insulation, thermal insulation, and packing seals. Though the raw textile products may contain as much as 85 percent asbestos, they are typically coated with plastics before assembly into a final product. Because such products are not required to be labeled as containing asbestos, most of them are not. These products may release asbestos dust if cut or torn, and some products emit asbestos during normal use. A significant quantity of uncoated fabrics remains in use, especially in schools and fire departments.

The Environmental Protection Agency, under the Toxic Substances Control Act, requires that all schools be inspected to determine the presence and quantity of asbestos; the local community must be notified of the results and signs posted in the building. Corrective actions, such as asbestos removal or encapsulation of the asbestos material on site, are left to the discretion of the school administrators. If a school administrator suspects that asbestos poses a problem in his or her school, specially trained experts, not the school's maintenance staff, should be asked to clean it up.

The Asbestos School Hazard Abatement Act of 1984 (ASHAA) established a $600-million grant and loan program to assist financially needy schools with asbestos abatement projects. The program also compiles and distributes information concerning asbestos and establishes standards for cleanup programs. For more information call the toll-free ASHAA hotline (800-835-6700).

Other Environmental Concerns

Schools can take many other steps to ensure a healthier environment for their students and to minimize the impact they as institutions have on the environment. Here are some things to be alert to:

○ Ask school officials to check for lead in drinking water. The solder that connects pipes in most plumbing systems is about 50 percent lead (since 1986, solder is required to contain no more than .2 percent lead, though enforcement of this requirement has been spotty at best). In addition, many drinking fountains contain lead-lined cooling tanks or pipes. The longer water sits unused in the lead fountains or pipes, the more lead may dissolve into it. In older buildings, the calcium carbonate found in hard water will eventually build up a protective shield around the pipes and solder. But in schools less than five years old (and in those with soft water), that shield has not had time to develop completely. Thus, buildings that have been constructed in the last five years or which have softer water warrant special scrutiny.

In your home, you can let your water run for one or two minutes to flush the lead out of the pipes and down the drain. But in elementary and secondary schools, it would be impossible to monitor every child who drinks water from a school fountain to make sure they let the water run before drinking it. EPA recommends several steps school officials can take if lead is detected in your school's drinking water: Change the piping that carries the water to the fountains, replace the drinking fountains themselves, or chemically change the water as it enters the school building. Usually lead contamination within a building is restricted to just one solder or a cluster of pipes. Encourage your school officials to take these steps if necessary.

○ To conserve water and reduce water bills, ask school officials to install toilet dams in school toilets. If they are replacing toilets, pressure them to buy those that use less, rather than more, water to flush.

SOURCE

For more information and a complete set of recommendations, see *Lead in School Drinking Water,* available through the Government Printing Office, Department 36ES, Superintendent of Documents, Washington, DC, 20402-9325 (telephone: 202-783-3238), $3.25, stock number 055-000-00281-9.

SOURCE

Planning for Non-Chemical School Ground Maintenance is the title of a 77-page information packet available from the Northwest Coalition for Alternatives to Pesticides (NCAP). The booklet documents the evolution of an integrated pest management program for school grounds maintained by the 4-J School District in Eugene, Oregon, and is an invaluable resource for other school districts wishing to reduce their reliance on landscape pesticides. The booklet costs $7.00 post-paid, and can be ordered from NCAP, P.O. Box 1393, Eugene, OR 97440; telephone: 503-344-5044.

○ **Also to conserve water, ask the school to install low-flow shower heads on showers in school gymnasiums.** They should also install faucet aerators, tighten all sink faucets, and check exterior faucets and watering faucets for leaks. A company that manufactures these devices might be willing to donate some to the school in exchange for positive publicity. If school maintenance personnel don't have time to install them, a group of parents and students could.

○ **Insist that bugs and weeds on school grounds be controlled organically.** The same principles that apply to organic gardening around your home can be put to work on school grounds as well: Using slow-release, organic fertilizers, composting yard wastes for additional fertilizer, and attracting friendly insects and birds to prey on pests should all be part of school grounds maintenance.

SAVE ENERGY

The United States uses more energy per pupil than most countries in the world use per capita. According to Educational Facilities Laboratory, a nonprofit organization that researches and provides information on the building and operation of facilities for public institutions, fifteen children in a classroom use as much energy during the school year as the average house with a gas furnace uses in a full year. U.S. schools spend at least $2 billion on energy: $42 for every child and about $1,000 for every classroom in public schools.

But schools don't have to rack up such high energy bills. An efficiently managed building could save as much as 30 percent in energy— about $15 per pupil, $375 per classroom, and $665 million nationally. Maintenance staffs can tune up the school building to improve its performance the same way you tune up your car.

☀ 𝓑RIGHT IDEAS

◐ The Aurora, Colorado, public schools used less energy in 1979 than in each of the three previous years, even though they added 242,000 square feet of classroom and warehouse space. This reduction was accomplished by improving the energy efficiency of existing buildings and by using solar energy in new construction.

The district tuned heating, ventilating, and boiler units and replaced caulking and weather stripping in its buildings. It sponsored a contest, awarding cash prizes to the top three schools that reduced energy consumption the most. And it put active solar energy systems into five new elementary schools, which use half as many BTUs per square foot as other elementary schools. By combining the solar systems with energy efficiency, the schools are expected to get 85 percent of their heat from the sun. For more information, contact the Aurora Public Schools, 1085 Peoria Street, Aurora, CO 80011.

◐ Harnessing the earth as well as the sun, a few districts are experimenting with "underground" schools as a way to cut energy costs. The Norman Rockwell School in suburban Omaha, Nebraska, opens to street level, facing the southeast. But all other levels, attended by all students except kindergarteners, are below ground, and there are no other exterior windows. The outside is visible from all parts of the school—classrooms look into the library, which faces the open front. The main hallway is flooded with sunlight from skylights.

Above ground, the media center serves as a passive solar collector. Heat passes through its large windows, and the school's twenty heat pumps distribute it to the rest of the building. An awning shields the windowed area from the summer sun, but because most of the building is underground, it is naturally cooled. A backup boiler adds more heating or cooling when necessary, which doesn't occur until the outside temperature drops below 40 degrees. For more information contact the Millard Public Schools, 5606 South 147 Street, Omaha, NE 68137; telephone: 402-895-8200.

Here are areas in which you can ask school officials to take further appropriate steps:

◐ **To reduce acid rain and global warming, all school vehicles should be as energy-efficient as possible.**

◐ **Ask your local utility to conduct an energy audit of the school or buildings on campus to identify spots where energy is leaking out of the building.** Caulk, weather-strip, and insulate as needed.

◐ **Use fluorescent lights.** New lighting technologies use 75 percent less electricity than conventional systems by converting more of the electricity to light rather than heat. Your school will not only pay less for lighting, it will reduce its air-conditioning costs at the same time, as fluorescent lights generate less heat.

○ **Turn off the lights in rooms not being used.** An energy study in a Las Vegas high school discovered a fantastic amount of electric energy was being used during the evening cleanup period. The school consumed 30 percent of its total energy between 4 P.M. and midnight, when the school's normal daily population of 1,100 shrank to three custodians. Merely by switching off the lights and air conditioning in areas where they had finished their work, the custodians could cut the school's daily electric power consumption by 15 to 20 percent.

○ **Regularly inspect building facilities.** Inspections can pinpoint energy waste from poor thermal insulation on steam and hot-water lines, in air-conditioned spaces, and on chilled water pipes or cold-air ducts.

○ **Keep condensers for air conditioning, refrigeration, and drinking water fountains free of paper and other foreign material that might interfere with air flow or heat transfer.**

○ **Keep heat transfer coils free of dust, which can reduce efficiency by 25 percent or more.**

○ **Maintain the building's furnace so that it operates as efficiently as possible.** Inefficient combustion increases fuel bills in two ways: Extra fuel to produce the required heat adds 5 to 15 percent to the fuel bill, and soot buildup on heat-transfer surfaces can add 8 percent to a furnace's fuel consumption. Maintenance staff should maintain the fuel/air ratio specified by the manufacturer, check burner alignment and condition, and maintain the recommended fuel oil temperature at the burner tip.

○ **Choose the most energy-efficient heating, ventilating, and air-conditioning (HVAC) system for your school.** According to the National Bureau of Stan-

SOURCE

A comprehensive picture of the many steps schools and colleges can take to conserve energy is presented in *The Economy of Energy Conservation in Educational Facilities,* available from the Academy for Educational Development, 1255 23rd Street, NW, Washington, DC 20037 (91 pages, $4.00 plus $2.00 shipping and handling).

For more information, contact your state energy office and your state education department, which may have an office responsible for energy conservation in school buildings; also contact your local utility.

dards and the General Services Administration, energy consumed by most HVAC systems could be cut 30 percent by selecting and maintaining the right size model.

○ **Plant trees.** Planting trees along a south wall provides shade in summer, when the trees are in leaf, and admits sun in winter, when solar heat gain may help.

○ **If you are building a new school, install windows made of shaded or double- or triple-glazed glass.** Shaded glass admits only one-quarter of the heat trapped by unshaded glass exposed to sunlight. Double-glazing (two layers of glass with an insulating air space between) prevents winter heat loss as well as summer heat gain. Double-glazed, shaded, heat-absorbing glass reduces heat gain by about 85 percent. Reflective glass cuts heat gain by one-third or so.

ON COLLEGE CAMPUSES

The modern environmental movement was born on hundreds of college campuses twenty years ago, when millions of students organized the widely publicized events on April 22, 1970, which became known as Earth Day.

Campuses are still crucibles for important environmental activity. You can get involved in the following ways:

○ **Conduct a campus-wide environmental audit.** Campuses consume huge quantities of energy and resources and generate substantial amounts of waste, often unknowingly. A campus audit can pinpoint opportunities to minimize waste generation, reduce water and air pollution, and conserve energy and water. It can also reveal whether a university is investing its financial resources in companies that pollute and suggest alternative investment options. And an audit may help university officials find ways to change their procurement practices, so that they buy less plastic and more recycled paper, glass, and aluminum. As with a study performed at UCLA in spring of 1989, an audit can become the basis for a campus environmental blueprint.

○ **Urge your student government to pass resolutions supporting environmentalism.** The resolutions should reflect concern for the health of the planet and call for bold changes in individual behavior and institutional practices. Earth Day 1990 can provide guidelines for

SOURCE

To help conduct an audit on your campus, a step-by-step guidebook has been prepared by Earth Day 1990, P.O. Box A.A., Stanford, CA 94309; telephone: 415-321-1990. Check for price.

BRIGHT IDEAS

○ The State University of New York at Stony Brook replanned the use of its entire heating and air-conditioning system in order to meet federal temperature level guidelines. First the physical plant staff determined how and what could be changed; then they sought cooperation throughout the campus for changes that included shutting down one of the two main refrigeration units in the air-conditioning system; lowering thermostats and hot-water temperatures in the boilers; recirculating warm return air; closing down heating motors and fans at night; monitoring boiler operations; and recovering heat wasted by boilers. (Special arrangements were made for laboratories that needed humidity control.) This campus conservation program involved no initial costs beyond the regular budget. During the first year alone, the school saved 1.53 million gallons of fuel oil, valued at over $1 million.

○ Benedict College of Columbia, South Carolina, studied the heat-retention qualities and needs of each building on campus and then installed storm windows and insulation where needed. Thermostats were set at levels required by the government. Boilers were run on schedules to match individual building occupancy needs and were started only when outside temperatures dropped below 40 degrees F and the relative humidity level rose to above 70 percent. Boilers were never run for more than six hours at a time, and boilermen were placed on flex-time to eliminate overtime. The initial cost of the project: $28,900. Savings amounted to $91,400 during the first year alone.

○ The University of California at San Francisco uses cogeneration, the simultaneous production of useful electrical power and heat, in its medical center to recover and use steam heat that would otherwise be vented. The hospital had been firing three steam-run generators to produce electricity twenty-four hours per day as a source of emergency power. Although essential for emergency standby purposes, the power system was wasting both the electricity it produced and the steam heat released from the generators. The cogeneration process recovers wasted steam and uses it to provide most of the heat required for a number of buildings near the hospital, turning a necessary but energy-wasting electric power source into an effective heating conservation project. The project cost $247,000, but annual savings in heating costs are $87,000, paying back the entire cost of the project in less than three years.

(Source: *Energy Conservation Idea Handbook,* Academy for Educational Development)

ℱOURCE

The National Wildlife Federation is urging college campuses to participate in community projects that will help reduce global warming. For more information about NWF's "Cool It!" campaign, contact the National Wildlife Federation, 1400 16th Street, NW, Washington, DC 20036; 202-797-5435.

the text of resolutions you may be considering.

○ **Create a coalition of campus groups to promote environmental issues.**

○ **Organize a teach-in on Earth Day.** On Earth Day (April 22), you and other groups can co-sponsor teach-ins and seminars open to both the campus and the public at large.

○ **Hold a film festival.** Myriad feature and documentary films have been produced that address important environmental issues. Check the Appendix at the end of this book for organizations that offer film and videotapes.

ENVIRONMENTAL EDUCATION

There's no better place for students to learn how to protect the environment than at school. Unfortunately, teachers are often forced to stretch their tight budgets by relying on the very industries that pollute for educational materials that frequently do little more than justify polluting practices.

The following nonprofit organizations have developed excellent environmental education materials that are available to teachers, parents, and students at reasonable prices. Some also offer special "hands on" environmental education programs for teachers and students. If you are a teacher, you can use these materials to supplement your textbooks; if you're a parent, they will provide you with lessons you can teach at home. And if you're a student, you can show them to your teacher as an example of the material your class should be studying.

○ **Washington State Department of Ecology,** 4350 150th Avenue, NE, Redmond, WA 98052. *A-Way with Waste,* a 297-page curriculum guide, covers recycling for grades K–12. It includes a comprehensive bibliography and resource list that can be used to augment studies in the classroom.

○ **Center for Marine Conservation,** 1725 DeSales Street, NW, Washington, DC 20036. The Center for Marine Conservation has prepared a series of books, reports, slide shows, and posters on the protection of whales, seals, and sea turtles. It also offers a kit on cleaning up beaches and preventing "marine debris." And its book *The Ocean: Consider the Connections* . . . offers many educational activities for children of all ages.

◐ **Earthwatch Teacher Fellowships,** 680 Mt. Auburn Street, Box 403, Watertown, MA 02172. One of the primary goals of Earthwatch, a scientific research organization, is to train teachers and students in biological research skills. Each year Earthwatch awards fellowships to outstanding teachers who accompany Earthwatch expeditions and help document fascinating environmental problems around the world. At least 1,000 teachers have participated in Earthwatch expeditions, 500 of whom have been supported with full or partial fellowships.

◐ **Environmental Protection Agency,** Office of Community and Inter-governmental Relations (A-108 EA), 401 M Street, SW, Washington, DC 20460. EPA provides *Education Materials for Teachers and Young People* (grades K–12), an annotated list of educational materials on environmental issues. Materials range from workbooks and lesson plans to newsletters, films, and computer software intended for young people. Educational materials available from sources other than EPA are listed alphabetically following the name of the sponsoring organization or group. A separate listing of selected EPA publications and other material available from EPA's Public Information Center is also included.

◐ **Greenhouse Crisis Foundation,** 1130 17th Street, NW, Suite 630, Washington, DC 20036. The Greenhouse Crisis Foundation is working with the National Science Teachers Association and the National Council of Churches to distribute its 24-page citizens' guide to global warming. *The Greenhouse Crisis: 101 Ways to Save the Earth* ($5.00). A poster entitled "10 Ways to Save the Earth . . . and How You Fit into the Puzzle" accompanies the guide.

◐ **National Audubon Society**—*Audubon Adventures,* 613 Riversville Road, Greenwich, CT 06831. *Audubon Adventures* offers a bimonthly newspaper and leader's guide for elementary school classes and other groups of children in grades 3–6 covering a wide range of topics.

◐ **National Wildlife Federation,** 1400 16th Street, NW, Washington, DC 20036. Educational materials include a series of film strips on wildlife, forests, water, soil, clean air, and public land; the NatureScope Library, a fifteen-issue magazine series for grades K–7; and the Discover Insects kit. Subscriptions to *Ranger Rick* magazine and *Your Big Backyard* (aimed at ages three to five) are also available. NWF's complete *Nature Education Materials* catalog can be ordered by calling toll-free 800-432-6564.

◐ **National Geographic Society,** Dept. 89, Washington, DC 20036; telephone: 800-368-2728. The National Geographic Society has produced hundreds of films, books, videos, puzzles, maps, charts, and other educational tools that touch on every aspect of the natural history of the earth. Two catalogs are available: a comprehensive *Educational Services Catalog* and a *Film and Video Catalog.*

◐ **Sierra Club,** 730 Polk Street, San Francisco, CA 94109. For the last four years, Sierra Club has been offering a week-long environmental education workshop for teachers at the Club's Claire Tappan Lodge in the Sierra Nevada Mountains.

◐ **World Wildlife Fund,** 1250 24th Street, NW, Washington, DC 20037. World Wildlife Fund has produced a special environmental education package to accompany the Smithsonian Institution Traveling Exhibit, "The Tropical Rain Forest: A Disappearing Treasure." The education kit is designed for grades 2–6 and includes a 28-page booklet describing the threats to endangered rain forests, an illustrated teacher's manual, a full-color poster, and a lively six-minute video called "Rain Forest Rap." The Vanishing Rain Forests kit is $20; the "Rain Forest Rap" video is $15.

6 AT THE OFFICE

If you work in an office, you can save at least seventeen trees and keep 60 pounds of air pollution out of the skies for each ton of paper you recycle. Recycling office paper even helps reduce acid rain: Nationwide, office waste paper recycling programs have the potential to conserve the energy equivalent of 384 gallons of oil per recovered ton of paper. Given that as much as 85 percent of all office waste is discarded paper—and that over 4 million tons of office waste paper are disposed of each year—it is hard to imagine how your office could do more sooner to improve the quality of the environment than by setting up an office-wide paper recycling program.

Office paper is prized by recyclers because the long fibers found in high-quality bond and computer paper allow it to be reprocessed into other quality products, like stationery. But short-fibered waste paper is valuable, too, because it can be processed into lower-grade products like toilet paper and paper towels. Bergstrom Papers of Neenah, Wisconsin, which converts more than 160 tons of waste paper a day into paper for all kinds of uses, has never owned a forest. In fact, as many as 200 paper mills in the United States rely exclusively on waste paper to produce their products. And the market for waste paper is growing. According to the American Paper Institute, at least 19 million tons of waste paper are now being reprocessed annually into cardboard boxes, newspapers, and assorted office paper, with another 5 million tons of waste paper being exported overseas.

Recycling paper can save a city as much as $50 a ton in landfill costs for every ton that is not thrown away. But recycling makes economic sense for corporations, too, especially if they have to pay to cart their own trash away. The city of Palo Alto helped the Syntex Company develop a comprehensive recycling program that initially saved the company $60,000. Now, with the addition of a glass recycling component, recycling is reducing Syntex's disposal costs by $2,300 per month.

WHAT CAN YOU DO?

To get the most out of the paper you do use while recycling the rest:

○ **Use less paper.** Avoid making copies of everything, and use both sides of the page when you're making rough drafts of documents or letters.

○ **Use your computer or word processor more.** Most computers can be set up so that one terminal can "talk" to another electronically. Instead of using paper pads to leave messages for other employees, use electronic mail.

○ **Recycle your own waste paper internally into message pads and internal memos, and take waste office paper home to use as scratch pads.**

○ **Encourage your company to buy recycled paper for use as stationery and envelopes.** In addition to saving resources and reducing pollution, using recycled paper will help boost demand for re-

---

WHY RECYCLE?

○ To save forests: Recycling one ton of office paper saves seventeen trees.

○ To save energy: It takes 60 percent less energy to manufacture paper from recycled stock than from virgin materials; every ton of recycled paper saves 4,200 kilowatts of energy, enough to meet the energy needs of at least 4,000 people.

○ To save water: Making paper from recycled paper stock uses 15 percent less water than making paper "from scratch"; recycling one ton of paper saves 7,000 gallons of water, enough to supply the daily water needs of almost thirty households.

○ To reduce garbage overload: Every ton of paper not landfilled saves 3 cubic yards of landfill space.

BRIGHT IDEA

AT&T has set up a model in-house office paper recycling program in its New Jersey offices that is efficient, cost-effective, and popular with its employees.

Two clearly marked bins sit at every desk: one for trash—coffee cups, dry ink pens, leftovers from lunch—and one for paper. The employee separates recyclable paper from the rest of his or her trash merely by tossing it in the right bin. Because processing waste paper is getting more sophisticated, more materials can be recycled, including envelopes with cellophane windows, file folders, and glossy magazines. The paper clips and staples don't have to be removed before recycling, either.

AT&T earned more than $372,000 in 1987 alone from selling its recyclable waste paper, while avoiding disposal costs. So far, the effort has saved about 62,395 trees (the capacity of a nice-size park) and the energy equivalent of 9,176 barrels of oil, enough to fuel 1,250 cars for a year.

cycled products and help lower the cost of recycled paper, which is currently higher than that of paper made from virgin fibers.

◐ Set up an easy system to encourage in-office recycling. Separate your office paper from other trash as you're throwing it away by putting a separate trash can next to your desk for any kind of office paper. (When Hewlett-Packard installed desktop recycling containers for all of its employees at its corporate headquarters in Palo Alto, the company's monthly recycling tonnage almost doubled!) Arrange with a paper recycler in your community to pick up the waste paper on a regular basis.

◐ Recycle newspapers. Newspapers received in offices stack up even more quickly than they do at home because usually more than one newspaper is received. Newspapers can be bundled and delivered to your local recycling center weekly or monthly. If others in your office building recycle their papers as well, the recycling center may be willing to visit your office on a regular basis and pick up all the papers at the same time.

◐ Avoid throwaway lunch containers. Steer away from restaurants that serve their food on hard or styrene foam plastic. Since plastics are so difficult to recycle, stick to packaging made out of recyclable paper, aluminum, or glass. If possible, bring your lunch to work in recyclable containers. And stock up on glass plates, cups, and glasses and regular silverware for use—and reuse—in the office.

*B*RIGHT IDEA

New York City's Office Paper Recycling Service (OPRS) recovers almost 1,300 tons of paper per year from over forty companies operating in and around Manhattan, including Consolidated Edison, Columbia University, the New York Power Authority, Metropolitan Transportation Authority, Chemical Bank, and The New York Times.

OPRS helps an office start and maintain its own recycling program by pinpointing the easiest and most effective ways for that particular office to recycle. OPRS provides desktop folders, central collection boxes, containers, signs, posters, and brochures and other materials to get employees involved in recycling.

At the same time, the New York City Department of Sanitation collects office paper from city agencies. In 1987 alone, a thousand tons of paper were collected from thirty-four different city agencies, the sale of the paper more than paying for the cost of the program. By 1991, the program is projected to serve approximately 83,000 city employees.

○ If your city is instituting a residential recycling program, urge legislators to extend the program to offices and other commercial buildings. Work with other companies to lobby officials, educate the media, write letters to editors, and gain support from local environmental groups and recycling companies.

THE AIR YOU BREATHE

If your job is giving you a headache, it may not be just because you don't like your boss or you've got too much work to do. Significant air pollution problems, primarily created by poor ventilation, plague many offices, especially those in which the windows are sealed

*S*OURCE

Many paper manufacturers, including Garden State Paper Company, Neenah, and Smurfit, make recycled paper. But if for some reason, your printer cannot obtain recycled paper stock from these companies, you can order it from Earth Care Paper Company, P.O. Box 3335, Madison, WI 53704. The company's catalog offers stationery, gift wrap, and greeting cards, as well samples of high-quality office paper, window envelopes, and copy paper.

HOW TO SET UP AN OFFICE RECYCLING PROGRAM

1. **Establish a contact with a reputable waste paper dealer.** Look in the phone book under waste paper dealers or find out who recycles paper in your locality from the Paper Stock Institute of America, 330 Madison Avenue, New York, NY 10017; telephone: 212-867-7330.

2. **Get the support of your boss.** Once you've located a market for your paper, enlist the support of the chief executive of your organization to ensure maximum participation in the program.

3. **Appoint a recycling coordinator.** The coordinator will work with the waste paper dealer and employees to set up and implement the program.

4. **Determine the number of people who will be asked to participate and the types and amounts of waste paper that will be generated.** A good rule of thumb for determining how much waste paper your company will generate is to estimate that each participant will produce about one-half pound of paper per day.

5. **Ask employees to separate their recyclable paper from other office wastes.** The most common methods are the desktop container, a second trash can, or a central collection area. Each collection receptacle should have a recycling logo or other identifying graphic on it and should list what items are and are not acceptable for recycling. In some offices, white and colored paper are put in different boxes for recycling.

6. **Decide how the paper will be collected and stored.** Most systems use central boxes where employees place separated paper; these boxes are collected by janitorial or mail-room personnel and placed in a central area for pickup by the waste paper dealer.

7. **Coordinate your collection program with your purchases of new paper.** For example, if your program is designed to collect only white paper due to its high value, then purchase only white paper wherever feasible. And eliminate purchases of contaminants such as plastic window envelopes and labels that are not water-soluble.

8. **Involve all employees.** In a brief fifteen- to twenty-minute session, you can discuss the program's goals, methods of sorting and collection, and acceptable and unacceptable items.

9. **Publicize the success of the project and encourage maximum participation.** Once the program is successful in one area, you can expand it to additional buildings in your firm or to other offices in your building.

10. **Develop a cost-benefit analysis of the program,** based on whether you or the waste paper dealer will pay for such items as desktop units or other storage devices, boxes and pallets, and the cost of training. Determine the approximate value of the waste paper, and whether you can save on waste collection and disposal costs.

(Source: *Resource Recycling* magazine, May/June, 1984)

closed. If you're experiencing headaches, burning eyes, sneezing, dizziness, nausea, or other similar symptoms, you may have "sick building syndrome." Poor lighting, noise, vibration, being too hot or cold, and psychological stress may also cause or contribute to these symptoms.

There is no single manner in which these health problems appear. You might feel ill as soon as you enter your office, then feel better as soon as you leave; in other cases, the symptoms may continue until you treat the illness itself. Sometimes many workers in a single building come down with the same disease; in other cases, health symptoms show up in just one especially sensitive individual.

The Source of the Problem

Three factors make for poor indoor air quality in office buildings: the presence of indoor air pollution sources; poorly designed, maintained, or operated ventilation systems; and uses of the building that were unanticipated or poorly planned for when the building was designed or renovated.

These specific factors could be fouling your office air:

Tobacco smoke
Asbestos from insulating and fire-retardant building supplies
Formaldehyde from pressed wood products
Carpeting and office furnishings
Cleaning activities and the use of cleaning materials
Restroom air fresheners
Paints
Adhesives
Copying machines
Photography and print shops in the same building as your office
Dirty ventilation systems
Water-damaged walls, ceilings, and carpets
Pesticides from pest management practices

Mechanical ventilation systems are designed and operated not only to heat and cool the air, but also to draw in and circulate outdoor air. When they are poorly designed, operated, or maintained, however, ventilation systems can themselves contribute to indoor air problems by not bringing in enough air or bringing in polluted air.

In addition, buildings originally designed for one purpose may end up being converted to use as office space. If not properly modified during building renovations, the ventilation system can contribute to indoor air quality problems by restricting air recirculation or by providing an inadequate supply of outside air.

What to Do

○ Wherever possible, select offices whose windows open—and keep them open, even if it's just a crack.

○ Speak up if you or others at your office are experiencing health or comfort problems that you suspect may be

caused by indoor air pollution. Talk with your own physician and report your problems to the company physician, nurse, or health officer so that they can be added to the record of health complaints.

○ **Talk with your supervisor, other workers, and union representatives;** urge that a record of reported health complaints be kept by management, if one has not already been established.

○ **Ask the building manager to consider hiring a commercial company that conducts building investigations to diagnose the problem or problems and to suggest solutions.** Carefully select such companies on the basis of their experience in identifying and solving indoor air quality problems in nonindustrial buildings.

○ **Call the National Institute for Occupational Health and Safety (800-35NIOSH) for information on obtaining a health hazard evaluation of your office.**

○ **Call your state or local health department or air pollution control agency to talk over the symptoms and possi-** ble causes of the problems you are experiencing.

○ **Work with others to establish a smoking policy that minimizes nonsmoker exposure to environmental tobacco smoke.**

The Environmental Protection Agency estimates that 467,000 tons of tobacco are burned indoors each year, creating smoke that contains forty-three known carcinogens. Because smoke diffuses rapidly through buildings and persists long after smoking ends, the only practical way to eliminate exposure is to remove the source.

ENERGY

Many of the energy-saving steps you take in your own home can just as easily be applied to your office: turning off lights when you're not in a room, turning off electrical equipment when no one is using it, particularly at the end of the day, or using blinds, curtains, or shutters to keep sunlight from heating up your office and forcing you to use your air conditioner. Commercial buildings account for 27 percent of all electricity used in the United

SOURCE

Many offices have already created smoke-free zones. If you would like to add yours to the list, this booklet will help guide you through the process: *A Decision-Maker's Guide to Reducing Smoking at the Worksite,* available free from the Office on Smoking and Health, 5600 Fishers Lane, Park Building, Room 1–10, Rockville, MD 20857.

BRIGHT IDEA

Though you can control smoking in your own home, reducing smoking in the workplace can be more difficult. Many businesses have developed creative programs to help their employees stop smoking:

◐ The 4,000 employees of the Hartford Insurance Group in Hartford, Connecticut, are offered a stop-smoking program on company time for just $50; if the participant stops smoking for three months, he or she not only gets back the $50 but also, as an added inducement, receives an extra $10, paid for from fees paid by those who do not complete the program successfully. Hartford also holds its own no-smoking day and no-smoking "fair" each January to take advantage of New Year's resolutions to stop smoking. And the company offers a "quit smoking" motivation and education program two or three times a year.

◐ Employees of MSI Insurance in Arden Hills, Minnesota, were given fourteen months to prepare for a policy that banned smoking everywhere except in one area of the cafeteria on January 1, 1985. In an effort to assist and encourage smokers to stop, a series of incentives and events were staged throughout the year, and an interim policy limiting smoking to designated areas was established. The "countdown" began November 17, 1983:

- On MSI Cold Turkey Day, smokers were encouraged to stop smoking for at least twenty-four hours; those who did were eligible for a drawing for a frozen turkey.
- In December, three more pairs of turkeys were awarded to quitters who were still off cigarettes and to their non-smoking support buddies.
- In May, those who were smoke-free for six months were eligible for a drawing for a free YMCA membership.
- Those who remained smoke-free for one year were eligible for a weekend vacation.
- On July 4, those still smoking were invited to "Declare Your Independence from Smoking." If successful, one month later they became eligible for a set of barbecue tools.

The company now has a near total smoking ban in place.

SOURCE

Representative Claudine Schneider (R–RI) has calculated that for a company in the top tax bracket with a 10 percent gross profit margin, each dollar of electricity savings is equivalent to $15 in new sales revenues. But any company, no matter how big or profitable, can take advantage of energy-efficient lighting technologies to save energy and money. Representative Schneider's office has prepared a "High Efficiency Lighting Fact Sheet" that describes ways businesses can cut their electricity bills by 50 percent. For a free copy, write to Representative Claudine Schneider, 1512 Longworth Office Building, Washington, DC 20515.

States. One of the most effective ways to reduce global warming is by increasing the energy efficiency of heating, cooling, and lighting in buildings.

What Can You Do?

○ **Use less energy to light the same amount of office space.** Lighting and the air conditioning it requires consume roughly 60 percent of a commercial building's electricity. Over the lifetime of a building, lighting expenditures can amount to nearly half the original cost of constructing the building!

A package of measures already on the market, including better controls, reflectors and spacing, improved bulbs, and fluorescent tubes can reduce lighting energy required in commercial buildings by over half. Microelectronic sensors that measure sunlight and sense people entering and leaving rooms can cut energy use for lights in half yet

again. You can use less light in your own office by using desk lamps instead of overhead lights. Furthermore, every improvement in lighting efficiency lowers the generation of waste heat and saves on air conditioning. The California Energy Commission calculated that in a typical Fresno office, every 100-watt savings on lighting means an additional 38-watt savings on air conditioning.

○ **Have your office windows glazed with low emulsive film.** Because low emulsive film is transparent, it won't interfere with your view. But it does reduce the amount of ultraviolet rays that can get into your office from regular sunlight, so office spaces will stay 30 to 50 percent cooler.

○ **Install an "energy management and control system" (EMCS).** An EMCS automatically regulates the operation of the heating, ventilating, and air-conditioning system, the lighting, and possibly

SOURCE

The Department of Energy has identified twenty-nine ways for industry to recover waste heat and fifty-one ways to make its processes more efficient. If fully implemented, such measures would cut the energy use of existing industries by nearly 50 percent. For a copy of DOE's *1990–1994 Multi-Year Conservation Plan,* write U.S. Department of Energy, Office of Conservation, Washington, DC 20585. Also request copies of *Buildings and Community Systems* and the "Program Overview" fact sheets on lighting research, advanced window technologies, roofing, indoor air quality, and building efficiency.

other systems in buildings. EMCS ranges from simple point-of-use timers to sophisticated microprocessor-based systems. According to the American Council for an Energy Efficient Economy, computerized EMCS equipment typically provides a 10 to 20 percent energy savings by eliminating unnecessary equipment operation and varying air and water temperatures depending on climatic conditions.

○ Use a laptop computer. Growth in the use of microcomputers has boosted energy use in many offices. But for offices where word processing is the primary computer need, laptop computers can do the job just as well—and use 10 to 30 percent less energy in the process.

○ Car pool or "telecommute" to work. And urge your employer to increase ride sharing by raising parking fees, giving subsidies to car pools, and letting more employees "telecommute" by working at home or in small neighborhood offices through telephones and computers.

7 IN YOUR COMMUNITY

While it's true that you can change the world, you'll probably get a lot more done if you have some help. In fact, progress usually happens a whole lot faster when an entire community bands together to protect the planet. The pace picks up even more when local government gets into the act, bolstering citizen ingenuity with money, resources, and in some cases, credibility. Here are just a few examples of the many creative ways communities are solving their environmental problems.

152

Cutting Back the Trash

Over 400,000 tons of municipal solid waste are generated daily in the United States, and rising disposal costs are draining municipal treasuries like never before. The *Christian Science Monitor* reported that in 1980, a city of 100,000 paid approximately $1 million a year to dump its garbage, about what it spent on libraries. Today, the same city may spend $10 million, more than for police or firefighters. Closing a city's landfill, which could increase that city's disposal costs by almost 500 percent, will only make matters worse—and EPA expects nearly half of all existing landfills to close by 1991.

Incineration is not the answer, either. Not only are incinerators the most expensive solid waste management technology a community can choose, but for every 100 tons of garbage burned, 30 tons of toxic ash are produced, and disposing of ash can cost four times as much as garbage disposal. The health implications of garbage incineration are just as astounding. Incinerator emissions of chromium alone will increase cancer deaths by 1,000 for every million people exposed. Dioxins, perhaps the most toxic synthetic chemicals ever produced, could also be released, leading to birth defects, spontaneous abortions, neurological disorders, liver disease, skin disease, and immune dysfunction.

Fortunately, communities are left with the alternative they should have chosen in the first place: recycling. According to Neil Seldman of the Institute for Local Self-Reliance, of all the waste disposal options, "recycling requires the least amount of capital, provides the most flexibility and costs the least." A ton of waste can be recycled for only $30, compared to the $50 a ton it costs to landfill waste and from $64 to $75 to incinerate it. In addition, every ton of material that is reused saves from one and a half to three tons of virgin materials. The Sierra Club once determined that each year the United States throws away enough steel to reconstruct the entire borough of Manhattan! According to the EPA, if the United States recycled all of the recyclable glass, aluminum, paper, and plastic it would otherwise trash in a landfill, we'd save the equivalent of 10.1 billion gallons of gasoline, enough to fill the tanks of 15.4 million cars for a year.

Although the great majority of the solid waste we generate is recyclable, currently an average of only 10 percent of the entire waste stream is recycled (as opposed to 50 percent in Japan).

To get at the glass bottles and aluminum cans that make up 5 to 10 percent of household waste, ten states have passed mandatory "bottle bills": California, Connecticut, Delaware, Iowa, Maine, Massachusetts, Michigan, New York, Oregon, and Vermont. And at least eight states (Oregon, Rhode Island, Connecticut, New Jersey, Maryland, Florida, Pennsylvania, and

RIGHT IDEA

Recycling is making the biggest dent in our trash on the local level as communities pass new packaging laws and institute procedures that make it easy for residents and businesses to recycle.

○ In Seattle, containers of recyclable cans, bottles, newspapers, and junk mail are collected separately at no charge. But citizens have to pay $13.35 a month to have one can a week of ordinary garbage picked up and $5 for each additional can. Now 55 percent of Seattle's households separate recyclable trash to reduce charges. And rather than dumping its sewage sludge in Puget Sound, as it used to, Seattle processes it and sells it as a rich commercial fertilizer. Reportedly, trees fertilized with Seattle sludge grow twice as fast.

○ In Rhode Island, citizens use a separate 20-gallon trash container to throw out their aluminum and tin cans, glass containers, and plastic soda and milk bottles.The penalty for not cooperating is simple: If the recycling bin isn't put out on the day the trash is collected, the household's regular garbage doesn't get picked up either.

○ Rockford, Illinois, offers its residents the most blatant incentive to recycle: Each week, if a trash bag chosen at random is free of aluminum and newspapers, the household that discarded it wins $1,000.

○ And in Minnesota, state and local economic development funds helped Rubber Research Elastomerics, Inc., open a free disposal center for used tires (240 million are produced annually in the United States—enough to stretch from New York City to the outer islands of Japan). From the 4 million tires it recycles each year, the firm produces "tirecycle," which is used as a substitute for raw rubber in doormats, garbage cans, and other products. Meanwhile, the state stands to save more than $100,000 a year in waste-tire-related costs.

New York) and the District of Columbia have adopted variations of mandatory recycling.

In addition to promoting recycling and reuse, deposit legislation is more effective at reducing litter than any other measure on the books. Except in California, where the state's one-cent refund doesn't generate many returns, bottle bills have led to the recycling of 80 to 95 percent of the beverage containers sold.

The environmental payoff is just as great: Each recycled aluminum can saves the energy equivalent of half a can of gasoline; producing aluminum from scrap instead of bauxite ore decreases air pollution by 95 percent. As for glass, the Congressional Research Service says that every 10 percent of

SOURCE

Hundreds of communities and industries are making recycling work for them. Their stories are told in three highly informative handbooks:

○ *Coming Full Circle: Successful Recycling Today,* 162 pages ($20.00), Environmental Defense Fund, 1988, 257 Park Avenue South, New York, NY 10010. An excellent primer on recycling that highlights successful local and state recycling programs, identifies potential markets for recyclable materials, and includes lists of state recycling hotlines, recycling industry associations, and ordinances dealing with solid waste.

○ *Proven Profits from Pollution Prevention: Case Studies in Resource Conservation and Waste Reduction,* 316 pages ($25.00), Institute for Local Self-Reliance, 1986, 2425 18th Street, NW, Washington, DC 20009. An easy-to-read compendium of case studies illustrating how various industries reduce waste by meeting environmental regulations through pollution prevention, rather than pollution control.

○ *Beyond 25 Percent: Materials Recovery Comes of Age* ($40.00), also from the Institute for Local Self Reliance. An excellent primer on recycling, composting, and the potential of "total materials recovery," with in-depth information on fifteen American communities that recover high levels of materials from their trash.

crushed used glass added to a glass plant's furnace reduces the plant's energy needs by 5 percent.

Some cities are taking more preemptive steps. Minneapolis and St. Paul have passed ordinances banning from store shelves and fast-food restaurants any plastic carry-out food packaging that cannot be recycled. Bills banning disposable diapers have been introduced in the Washington and Oregon state legislatures. And in 1988, local governments in Berkeley, California, and Suffolk County, New York, banned the use of polystyrene plastics such as Styrofoam for fast foods or other foods packaged by local retailers.

How Cities Can Promote Recycling

Here is a five-point plan for getting recycling off the ground in your city:

1. Organize neighborhood associations into a strong coalition of recycling advocates, and take your concerns to city council meetings.
2. Ask the city council to appoint a task force to determine how much money the city will save in garbage disposal costs by recycling instead of dumping.
3. Publicize the results of the task force findings in local

BRIGHT IDEA

The McToxics Campaign

Polystyrene plastic cups and food containers from one day's sales at McDonald's take up 50,000 cubic feet of landfill space.

Styrene plastic is nonrecyclable and nonbiodegradable. Hazardous wastes are produced during its manufacture, and when it is incinerated, it releases the pollutant carbon monoxide and could release carcinogenic styrene oxide. In almost all cases, paper packages are sufficient substitutes for styrene plastic.

Getting McDonald's 10,000 restaurants to stop using plastic burger boxes could have a stunning domino effect on the rest of the fast food industry. With this thought in mind, the Citizens Clearinghouse for Hazardous Wastes (CCHW) launched a national campaign to get McDonald's to "Hold the Toxics!" Waving signs, posters, and fliers, CCHW supporters picketed various McDonald's outlets to emphasize their demand for all-paper packaging. In California, Concerned Neighbors in Action placed orders for McNuggets and burgers wrapped in paper. When the servers wouldn't oblige, the bulky plastic boxes were left on the counter and people carried away their food in napkins.

Based on the public uproar, McDonald's decided to recycle something— its corrugated cardboard. The company also announced plans to begin a trial recycling program for styrene plastic (which CCHW says can't be done) and launched an educational campaign on waste reduction. But it's still serving coffee, burgers, and other meals in plastic. For more information, get the "McFact Pack" ($5.00) from the Citizens Clearinghouse for Hazardous Wastes, Inc., P.O. Box 926, Arlington, VA 22216. And the next time McDonald's (or any other fast food restaurant) serves your order in plastic, leave the packaging on the counter.

---

newspapers and on radio and television. You may want to hold a news conference on the steps of City Hall or at the local garbage dump.

4. Urge your city to take the steps listed below for creating a recycling program.

5. Identify a specific date on which the city will begin implementation of its recycling program.

The steps that follow are things your city administration can do to follow through on the initiatives of citizens who have raised vital environmental issues:

◐ **Hire a full-time recycling coordinator.** Recycling programs are most effective when they are part of a city's overall solid waste management plan, not when they're an afterthought or implemented outside the regular garbage collection program. A recycling coordinator will develop a comprehensive plan to incorporate recycling into everyday solid waste management.

© Help create a market for recycled products. No matter how much paper, glass, and aluminum is recycled, it will ultimately get trashed if there is no demand for the materials collected. To encourage the use of recycled products, governments can require their purchasing agents to buy competitively priced goods that contain a certain percentage of recycled material. Reports, laws, and tax forms can be printed on recycled paper; government buildings can be heated with waste oil; and public roads can be paved in part by recovered rubber.

© Make recycling mandatory. This is the single most effective way to make recycling work. And several national public opinion polls indicate that Americans over-

whelmingly support mandatory recycling laws.

© Ban the disposal of specific recyclable materials and adjust disposal fees. Give a discount to those who recycle, or charge according to the amount of trash they throw out.

© Keep it simple by providing separate containers for different recyclables and clear instructions on how to recycle.

© Have recycled materials picked up the same day as regular garbage. Curbside collection programs are much more successful than any other in getting people to recycle.

© Educate the community about the importance of recycling. Simple fliers can be distributed door-to-door, posters can be displayed in store windows, and articles can be run in the local daily or weekly newspaper.

© Recycle the city's own gar-

BRIGHT IDEA

© The state of Maryland has been buying recycled paper since 1977. Over 1 million reams of recycled bond and $17 million in recycled paper products have been purchased thus far. The Maryland state government now buys half its bond paper from recycled paper manufacturers and almost all of its tissue and towel products from reclaimed fiber mills, saving enough energy to heat nearly 9,000 homes for a year.

© FSC Paper of Chicago promises to buy all of a community's waste newspapers if the local newspaper publisher agrees to buy FSC's newsprint, which is made with 100 percent recycled fiber. One of FSC's customers, the *Chicago Sun Times,* uses about 45 percent recycled newsprint. According to Cynthia Pollock Shea of the Worldwatch Institute, if the United States recycled just half the newsprint consumed annually, it would divert enough trash from landfills to fill 3,200 garbage trucks every day.

RECYCLE YOUR NEWSPAPERS

Many localities have begun city-wide newspaper recycling operations. If yours is not one of them, you can still recycle your own papers:

1. One day each week, bundle together the week's newspapers or stack them inside a paper grocery bag. Do not include the glossy magazine section of the paper, which pollutes the rest of the newsprint.

2. Contact the office of solid waste management in your city or county for a list of locations that accept recycled paper or the name of your state recycling coordinator. You can also contact your state recycling coordinator (see Resources chapter).

3. When you have accumulated enough paper to fill the trunk of your car, load it up and drop it off at the recycling center.

4. If you do not have a car, ask friends who do to join your recycling effort and you can recycle your papers together. If you live in an apartment building, talk to your tenants association about setting up a building-wide recycling program, similar to the ones managed by the Environmental Action Coalition of New York City (see Bright Idea on page 174).

5. Organize neighborhood support for a city-wide, mandatory curbside recycling program, which is proven to be the most effective way of getting people to recycle.

ORGANIZING CHECKLIST

1. Work with others in your neighborhood who support mandatory recycling.

2. Circulate a citizens' petition to urge your city council to adopt recycling provisions. You can collect signatures by going door-to-door or by posting petition sheets at the check-out counters of local businesses that support recycling.

3. Identify members of your city council who support curbside recycling, and ask them to introduce ordinances that will make it mandatory.

4. With or without the support of council members, hold a public hearing on recycling and encourage everyone who goes to bring a week's worth of newspapers with them. Present the petitions to your city council during the public hearings.

5. Alert the media to the "recycling controversy," and urge them to do feature stories on garbage overload in your neighborhood.

6. If the city council appoints a committee to study recycling and make recommendations, serve on it.

7. Meet with neighborhood associations in other cities and counties, and work together to enact state-wide recycling legislation.

bage. Your city can set a great example for the rest of the community by setting up in-office paper recycling programs, using returnable bottles, installing "reverse vending machines" to redeem bottles and cans on the spot, and composting the debris accumulated from maintaining city lawns, trees, and parks.

Hunt the Dump

Your community may be one of thousands that is unknowingly being exposed to hazardous waste. How?

American industry generates about 250 million tons of hazardous materials each year, and as much as 90 percent of it may be disposed of improperly. In many instances, you can both see and smell the substances: Dark smoke rising from a stack at the local factory, oil floating on the surface of your river or creek, or black "goop" bubbling or seeping up from the ground near your home are all pretty hard to miss.

But just because you don't see or smell anything, doesn't mean you don't have a problem. According to the Environmental Protection Agency, there are over 30,000 hazardous waste sites in the United States. If you have any reason to suspect that your community is being contaminated by hazardous materials, the Citizens Clearinghouse for Hazardous Waste of Arlington, Virginia, recommends you ask the following questions:

1. **Where is the dump?** Is it close enough to your home, neigh-borhood, or community to contaminate your drinking water or create other health problems associated with decomposing solid or hazardous waste?

2. **What is the history of the dump itself?** Who dumps (or dumped) there? What is or was disposed of? Is the site lined to prevent the waste from leaking into the groundwater? (Most impoundments are unlined.) Have any citizens' complaints been filed?

3. **Has any environmental testing been conducted?** By whom, the industry dumping its waste there, the EPA, or local or state agencies? Were any carcinogenic or hazardous substances found to be leaking out of the site?

4. **Who owns the site now?** Does the site have a permit to legally accept hazardous wastes? Is it still operating, or is it abandoned?

For information, look to your local planning board, city hall, county health department, and local newspaper library. The planning board may have the original design plans and future plans for the site on file. You can find out who owns the property at city hall. Your city's department of public works should have records on permits, the site's operating history, and whether the site's operators have been cited with any violations, though it may be impossible to find out what's been dumped there without scientific testing. And the health department can tell you whether the materials leaking at the site are hazardous. If they are, take immediate measures:

SOURCE

For more help, contact the Citizens Clearinghouse for Hazardous Wastes. CCHW was founded in 1981 by Lois Gibbs, a housewife from Love Canal, New York, who captured national attention by organizing her neighborhood to protect itself from life-threatening chemical hazards. The organization collects information on chemicals and their effects, various disposal methods, and technology for cleanup, and helps people fight for their rights by providing direct assistance. CCHW has produced over three dozen citizens' guidebooks. For more information, contact CCHW, P.O. Box 926, Arlington, VA 22216; telephone: 703-276-7070.

○ **Hold a meeting with your neighbors to determine a course of action.** Ask someone from the health department to attend, as well as your city council representative and state legislator.

○ **Working with your member of Congress, ask the U.S. Environmental Protection Agency for help in cleaning up the site.** Getting EPA's cooperation will not be easy, since the agency doesn't have nearly enough resources to clean up all of the hazardous waste sites it knows about. Involving your member of Congress

THE EMERGENCY PLANNING AND COMMUNITY RIGHT-TO-KNOW ACT

In November 1986, Congress passed a law designed to help America's communities deal safely and effectively with the many hazardous substances in use today. Called the Emergency Planning and Community Right-to-Know Act, it has two main purposes: to encourage and support emergency planning for responding to chemical accidents; and to provide local governments and the public with information about possible chemical hazards in their communities.

For the law to work, industry, interested citizens, environmental and other public interest organizations, and government at all levels must work together to prevent chemical accidents and to reduce the risk to the public from releases of toxics into the environment. The act establishes a Local Emergency Planning Committee, an ongoing forum at the local level for discussion and a focus for action. For more information, see "Chemicals in Your Community: A Guide to the Emergency Planning and Community Right-to-Know Act"; available free from the U.S. Environmental Protection Agency, Washington, DC 20460.

BRIGHT IDEA

O In 1975, the Minnesota Mining and Manufacturing Company (3M), established the 3P Program—Pollution Prevention Pays—to stress pollution prevention, beginning with product development and manufacturing. The program had three goals: to "re-invent" products so that they could be made from materials that don't pollute, to redesign products so that they could be manufactured without creating pollution, and to retool the manufacturing equipment itself. As of March 1988, the 3P Program's 2,261 projects had saved the company $420 million. The planet was better off, too: An anticipated 120,000 tons of air pollutants, 14,000 tons of water pollutants, 1.6 billion gallons of waste water, and 313,000 tons of sludge and solid waste were not discharged into the surrounding environment, thanks to the program.

O The Hill Air Force Base in Ogden, Utah, has also dramatically reduced waste and costs by replacing chemicals with machines. To strip paint from aircraft and ground support equipment, the base uses a conventional sandblasting process that relies on recoverable plastic beads instead of sand. The process has reduced hazardous waste by 94 percent while eliminating 200,000 gallons of waste water. Raw material costs immediately fell by more than 90 percent, and energy costs have been nearly halved. The savings on operating costs during the first month covered the entire cost of the new blasting equipment.

and other local officials will help focus EPA's attention on your problem.

O If hazardous materials continue to be dumped at the site, work with others in your community to get the dumping stopped. Lawyers in your community may be willing to provide legal advice "pro bono" (for free).

O Contact the news media. Negative publicity about the site may help persuade the responsible company to stop dumping and begin cleaning up. It will also help convince elected officials to take the problem seriously.

PROTECTING YOUR LOCAL WATER SUPPLY

Local impacts on water quality can be severe, and everything from building construction to lawn maintenance plays a role.

Because they generate so much sediment, construction sites are a major source of water pollution: Erosion rates from construction sites can be ten to fifteen times those of agricultural lands, even though much smaller areas are involved. Other pollutants include chemical fertilizers, pesticides, petroleum products, miscellaneous wastes dumped on the site, construction chemicals, and debris.

Each time it rains, asphalt, tar, oil, gasoline, fertilizers, litter, road salt and sand, and pet waste may be washed off residential and urban streets, roofs, lawns, and other areas into lakes, rivers, or aquifers. Then there are the toxic chemicals homeowners themselves use indiscriminately around the house, frequently throwing a container that still holds some toxics into the trash (usually to end up in a landfill) instead of taking them to a local hazardous waste facility.

What You Can Do

◐ Do not dump "leftover" toxic chemicals onto the ground or into the street, where they can run into the sewer. But don't throw them out with the weekly trash, either. When you've finished with a container, close the cap or lid tightly and store it in a box on a shelf in your basement or garage (out of the reach of children) until you've filled the box. Then call your community's public works department to get the location of the nearest hazardous waste facility. Hopefully, you'll be using so few toxics that you won't have to make this trip more than once or twice a year.

◐ Organize a "Clean Sweep" project in your neighborhood or community. If enough of your neighbors want to join you in safely disposing of their toxic containers, organize a "clean sweep" of the entire neighborhood: Pick a convenient Saturday or Sunday in the spring or fall, when most people are involved in yard and household cleanup projects anyway. Through fliers, local newspaper articles, and word of mouth, urge people to put all of their toxic containers in a cardboard box or heavy-duty paper bag and place them on their curb. (Discourage people from putting the containers themselves right on the street just in case they are leaking.) Then recruit someone in the neighborhood who has a station wagon or pickup truck to make the rounds from street to street; you may even be able to get your city's public works department to donate a truck and driver for the day of the pickup. When the "sweep" is finished, take all of the materials you've collected to the nearest hazardous waste facility. Make sure the media are on hand to report how many containers were kept out of the landfill—and how many toxics won't be leaking into the groundwater—to make everyone who participated feel good about doing it again next year.

◐ Encourage your local government and community businesses to use sand instead of salt to de-ice streets and walkways, and to avoid excessive use of chemical fertilizers on public or commercial lawns and parks. Attend city council meetings to make your opinions known, write letters to the editor, or ask your neighbors to sign a petition calling for chemical-free management of community property.

◐ Work with your city government to protect any wet-

lands that may remain in your area. Acre for acre, wetlands match the most productive ecosystems in the world. They help maintain and improve water quality by removing and retaining nutrients, processing chemical and organic wastes, and reducing sediment from floods. Every citizen can help protect wetlands by supporting wetland conservation initiatives, by donating wetlands or funds for purchasing wetlands to private or public conservation groups or agencies, and by pressuring communities to maintain wetlands as open space.

◐ Support ordinances to control litter and make pet owners clean up after their pets on the street.

◐ Plant trees. Because they absorb carbon dioxide in the process of growing, trees help clean up the air and reduce global warming. (One acre of trees can absorb 2.6 tons of carbon dioxide—enough to offset the CO_2 produced by driving a car 26,000 miles.) But trees also protect water supplies by preventing soil erosion, holding land in place with their roots. Slopes leading down to streams that feed into rivers and lakes, as well as the

BRIGHT IDEA

Martha's Vineyard is just a small island off the southern coast of Cape Cod, Massachusetts. But on one day in the fall of 1985, a hazardous household waste collection from among the island's 15,000 year-round residents yielded 670 gallons and 2,900 pounds of toxic materials, mostly in the form of leftover cleansers, polishes, paints, and pesticides. To prevent these materials from accumulating in landfills and eventually seeping into the aquifer that supplies drinking water for the entire island, the Martha's Vineyard Refuse Disposal and Resource Recovery District has opened New England's first permanent facility for collecting, sorting, and storing household hazardous waste. The collection center is little more than a modified truck trailer where technicians and chemists, provided by a private waste-disposal company, sort materials as they are brought in. Containers of liquid waste are packed in an absorbent material inside steel or plastic drums until the facility's forty-eight-drum capacity is reached. Then the waste is shipped off for permanent disposal in a licensed hazardous waste dump. In addition to keeping hazardous waste out of the town landfills, the regularly scheduled collections provide an opportunity to educate island residents about dangerous substances that are commonly used in the home. For more information, contact the Martha's Vineyard Refuse Disposal and Resource Recovery District, P.O. Box 2248, Oak Bluffs, MA 02557; telephone: 508-693-3479.

BRIGHT IDEA

Green Shores in Baltimore

The Chesapeake Bay is one of the most important sources of seafood in the world. It's also one of the most endangered, due to the tremendous overflow of fertilizers and pesticides that run into its waters via nearby streams and rivers. In 1988, in an effort to help keep these pollutants out of the bay, the city of Baltimore, in conjunction with Maryland's state government, initiated a program to plant trees along the city's three main streams. In addition to enhancing the streams' beauty, the trees minimize pollution and sedimentation by filtering soil and reducing run-off of harmful phosphorus and nitrogen. So far, 6,000 trees have been planted. For more information, contact Baltimore's City Forester at 301-396-6108.

shores of the rivers and lakes themselves, should be planted with trees to reduce runoff pollution and erosion.

FOR THE BIRDS

Nearly half of all species of birds that live in North America are songbirds, and most of them survive each year because they can migrate to warmer habitats south of our borders before winter strikes.

Birds don't live long enough to survive more than a few seasons of hardship, so the deforestation that's going on in the tropics as well as in our own backyards can slice a bird population to shreds in just a few years. Communities can help protect migrant songbirds in several ways:

◑ **Protect your local woods and parks.** Every new trail or cleared area in a forest—even if that forest is nothing more than the woods surrounding a new subdivision—creates more edges and exposes nesting birds to dangers. Though cowbirds, starlings, grackles, and blue jays will survive such clearings, migrant birds needing cover to protect their nests and young from predators will suffer. Wherever possible and practical, support efforts to maintain woods and parks intact.

◑ **Reforest vacant lots.** It won't take long for migratory birds to discover these new "woods," which will soon become a regular stopping-off point on their migratory routes.

◑ **Share your knowledge of the importance of tropical forests with others.** Schedule programs, workshops, and meetings on tropical forest conservation at your school, church, club, and office. Show newspaper and TV reporters that your community is interested in saving tropical forests by helping them get in touch with local people—teachers, researchers, bird-watchers, or conservationists who are working on the issue and whose projects might make interesting news stories.

◑ **Encourage local fast food restaurants not to buy beef from Central America.** Yes, there is a connection between birds and burgers. It takes 55 square feet of tropical forest to produce enough hamburger to make a quarter

pounder. (In Brazil alone, an area the size of Maine has been converted to cattle ranches.) In the process of clearing the forest, more than the birds suffer: 500 pounds of globe-warming carbon dioxide are emitted for every 55 square feet of cleared forest land. Some 138 million pounds of beef were imported from Central America last year, with the primary benefit being that the cheaper meat lowers hamburger prices about a nickel.

◑ **Don't bank at an institution that funds deforestation.** Hundreds of American banks con-

BRIGHT IDEA

The rosy periwinkle of Madagascar is a tiny tropical forest plant that is successfully used to treat leukemia and Hodgkins' disease. Now it's being used to "treat" ignorance as well. The Rainforest Alliance's Periwinkle Project is educating doctors, pharmacists, and the public about the enormous medicinal value of tropical plants. It's goal: to advocate greater use of forests for medicinal research by pharmaceutical firms and medical research agencies (and less use as grazing land for exported beef).

Even though 25 percent of all drugs prescribed in the United States contain an active plant substance, only 1 percent of rain forest plants have been thoroughly researched for their medicinal value. The Rainforest Alliance is hoping that encouraging pharmaceutical giants to conduct more rain forest research will lead to greater protection of these endangered ecosystems.

The Rainforest Alliance provides posters and brochures to local volunteers to distribute to doctors' offices, pharmacies, and hospital waiting rooms. The volunteers then tell the Alliance where they've distributed the materials so the Alliance can follow up by contacting the medical staff with more information about "jungle pharmacy."

If you'd like to hang a poster in your doctor's office during your next appointment, contact the Rainforest Alliance, 270 Lafayette Street, Suite 512, New York, NY 10012; 212-941-1900.

tribute directly and indirectly to rain forest destruction by funding ill-conceived dams, road building, mining, and other damaging projects. Because of the enormous sums of money involved, these development loans are usually undertaken by the larger national banks like Bank of America or Citicorp. Instead of giving these banks your dollars to work with, bank with a small, local, socially responsible institution.

CLEAR THE AIR

Community governments can take several steps to clean up their air. The first begins with transportation.

Transportation is the single largest source of nitrogen oxides and carbon monoxide, compounds that pollute the air and cause acid rain. Pollution from individual vehicles can be cut significantly over the next ten to twenty years by setting more stringent emissions standards for cars, buses, and trucks, strengthening requirements to have vehicles inspected and maintained, and enacting stronger measures to prevent tampering with pollution-control equipment. Cities can begin by buying and maintaining fleets of energy-efficient cars and trucks.

Cutting the total number of vehicle miles residents travel would also reduce the amount of gasoline burned. To do so, cities could improve traffic flow, encourage drivers to use more public transit, provide preferred parking spaces for car and van pools, and include high-occupancy and bicycle lanes in all plans for new road construction. Fees for parking and automobile registration could also be increased, as a disincentive for people to own more than one car or to use the car

Working Assets, an innovative company that offers a variety of banking and money management services, invests its funds only in companies with a responsible environmental operating track record. They offer a money market fund, credit cards, long-distance telephone services, even a travel service. For more information, contact Working Assets Funding Service, 230 California Street, San Francisco, CA 94111; telephone: 800-52-APPLY.

Other investment firms that scrutinize a company's environmental behavior include the Calvert Social Investment Fund and the Dreyfus Third Century Fund. And recently, Fidelity Investments opened a fund that will invest in companies that deal with solid waste management, treatment for water and air, waste engineer consulting, asbestos work, and recycling.

LOS ANGELES CRACKS DOWN

The air over southern California is more polluted than anywhere else in the country. In 1988, the area violated the federal health standard for smog on 176 days, far more than any other city, and carbon monoxide pollution is worse than anywhere but New York. Fearing that the U.S. Environmental Protection Agency would take matters into its own hands, the South Coast Air Quality Management District voted to enact a far-reaching air pollution control plan that could become a model for the rest of the country.

Here is a sample of the provisions contained in the proposed law:

 Governmental bodies or businesses (including car rental agencies) with at least fifteen vehicles must switch to cleaner-burning fuels, such as methanol, by 1992, or whenever suitable engines become available.

 New barbecue grills that require starter fluid, which contributes to the formation of smog, will be banned, as will gasoline-powered lawn mowers and fast-wearing bias-ply tires that throw off small particulates as they wear.

 About 1,760 dry cleaners in the South Coast basin use perchloroethylene, which contributes to smog. Dry cleaners would have to use equipment that eliminates transfer of clothes from washer to dryer, during which "perc" leaks into the air. New equipment to capture emissions would be installed, and small dry cleaners would not be exempted from complying with the regulations.

 By 2010, the basin is expected to have at least 7 million cars and light-duty trucks. Regulations would limit the number of cars each household could register, with reduced registration fees for owners of vehicles that burn clean fuels.

they do own for commuting when they could just as easily take a bus, train, or subway.

A ROLE FOR COMMUNITIES IN PROTECTING THE OZONE LAYER

Local government can make a significant contribution to protecting the ozone layer by making it easy—and mandatory—for ozone-damaging chlorofluorocarbons to be recovered and recycled.

 Require recovery of CFCs when refrigerators and autos are junked. Any auto air conditioner or home refrigerator that is being discarded can easily be picked up by a permitted salvager or the local sanitation department and taken to a recycling center for reclamation.

A SMALL TOWN AND BIG SAVINGS

The town of Osage, Iowa, population 3,600, has committed to energy efficiency and conservation while other communities continue to drink up oil like water. The new insulated roof on the local hospital shaves utility bills by 20 percent. Since 1974, the community has cut its natural gas consumption some 45 percent and reduced annual growth in electricity demand by more than half, to less than 3 percent a year. When Osage Municipal Utilities offered to give every building in town a free thermogram, a test that pinpoints places where the most heat is escaping, more than half the town's property owners accepted the offer. Then the utility gave customers $15 fluorescent light bulbs . . . for free. The model conservation program saved the community an estimated $1.2 million in energy costs in 1988.

○ **Establish recycling centers for CFC reclamation.** State and local governments, working with industry, could establish centralized recycling centers to receive and reclaim CFCs so that they're not vented into the atmosphere. Existing recycling centers could also be required or encouraged to receive captured CFCs for reclamation.

○ **Educate auto repair shops about the proper maintenance of automobile air conditioners.** Given that almost half of the CFCs emitted in the United States come from automobile air-conditioning units—and that much of that is vented unnecessarily during routine maintenance checks of the equipment—communities could do the ozone layer a great service by educating vehicle repair shops about proper care of air conditioners. An explanatory flier could be prepared and distributed to all shops in the city, accompanied by local newspaper articles and radio and TV reports. The city could also publicize the fact that it is maintaining all of its own auto air conditioners properly . . . by leaving them alone.

HEAT ISLANDS AND GLOBAL WARMING

Heat islands. We've all been trapped on them, dark-colored, heat-absorbing surfaces like asphalt and concrete in the middle of a city where temperatures are 5 to 10 degrees higher than the surrounding neighborhood.

According to scientists at the Lawrence Livermore Laboratory in California, increasing the number and size of trees is the most cost-effective way to reduce the heat island effect in most cities. In fact, the *Journal of Arboriculture* reported as long ago as 1971 that one

◯ ℬRIGHT IDEA

In Orange County, California, the city of Irvine has approved what may be the nation's most comprehensive ordinance restricting the use of chlorofluorocarbons and other substances known to deplete the earth's ozone layer. The ordinance, which will take effect July 1, 1990, will prohibit the use of nearly all CFCs and related compounds in any industrial process, except in the manufacture of drugs and medical devices and when military specifications call for them. Though the ordinance will not bar the use of CFCs in automobile air conditioners and refrigerators, it will require service stations and repair shops to capture and recycle the coolant. And it will ban the sale and use of plastic foam food packaging containing CFCs, as well as the use of building insulation that contains the compounds.

In taking the action, Irvine joined a growing list of American cities and towns that are exploring ways they can help protect the ozone layer. Plastic foam packaging containing CFCs has been banned in Suffolk County, New York; Newark, New Jersey; Tempe, Arizona; Portland, Oregon; the State of Florida; and several other California cities (including Los Angeles, San Francisco, Berkeley, and Palo Alto). Vermont requires CFCs in car air conditioners to be recycled; as of 1993, CFCs will no longer be allowed in cars sold in Vermont.

---

large tree can produce a cooling effect similar to five average room air conditioners running for twenty hours a day.

Other studies have shown that the location of one or two trees to shade outdoor air-conditioning units could increase their efficiency by as much as 10 percent. Around homes and small commercial buildings, well-placed trees can cut home air-conditioning bills by as much as 50 percent, and because less energy is being used, air pollution and carbon dioxide production are reduced at the same time.

James Kielbaso, a professor at Michigan State University, has estimated that an 80-foot beech tree can remove as much carbon dioxide from the air as two single-family dwellings produce. Says Neil Sampson of the American Forestry Association, "Each healthy tree is a free-standing air conditioner and purifier that is doing its part toward making the world habitable for all life."

But as we've already noted, about four trees die or are removed for each new one planted in the average city. Not only do cities run out of space for trees or the money to pay for them, but disease and insects (most notably Dutch elm disease and the gypsy moth) are decimating acres of trees. Construction and development don't do much to protect trees either. In 1975, a major construction project installed new paths, curbing, and sewers in the Boston Common. The construction killed more trees in one year than Dutch elm disease had killed in three years, and the excessive drainage caused by the new sewers required that the trees be artificially irrigated the following year.

It's estimated that one acre of trees can absorb four tons of carbon annually, the amount released by burning 1,000 gallons of gasoline. According to the American Forestry Association, planting 100 million trees by 1992 could save ratepayers an estimated $3 to $4 billion each year while offsetting 18 million tons of carbon emissions.

FURTHER STEPS YOUR COMMUNITY CAN TAKE

◐ **Reduce pesticide use.** As a matter of course, communities should follow the lead of homeowners and use a minimum of pesticides on lawns and shrubbery, around schools, and on other public grounds.

◐ **Promote water conservation.** With water supplies becoming more and more scarce and expensive, utilities and communities have begun investing in water efficiency as a way to conserve their water resources.

In Arizona, the city of Glendale has implemented a cost-sharing program to help homeowners improve water efficiency in their homes. The city offers a $100 rebate to anyone who replaces a conventional toilet (3.5 to 6.0 gallons per flush) with a new, more efficient

BRIGHT IDEA

The heart of downtown Washington, D.C., has been revitalized, and that's in large part due to the variety of trees, landscaped parks, and plazas that have been erected in the middle of Pennsylvania Avenue. The trees, in particular, are thriving, because tree spaces were created both above and below ground. "Floating" sidewalks and plazas are covered with blocks and bricks that allow water and air to enter the soil below. An underground irrigation system provides water when needed, and monitors indicate when the water should be turned on. Because tree roots are allowed to grow rather than being compacted, fewer trees are dying on Pennsylvania Avenue than anywhere else in the city.

SOURCE

For guidance in chemical-free landscaping, see the 24-page booklet *Least Toxic Lawn Care*. Safe, effective methods for managing common insects, weeds, and rodents are described, as are new biological controls, mechanical techniques, and the least toxic pesticides. The booklet costs $5.75 postpaid and is available from the Bio Integral Resources Center, P.O. Box 7414, Berkeley, CA 94707.

model (1.6 or fewer gallons per flush), and $100 to anyone who converts a conventional landscape to one that requires less water.

As a prerequisite to constructing a new home, any builder in Morro Bay, California, must first save more water than the new home will use. Builders have the option of paying to replace a specified length of the city's leaky water mains, or finding twelve single-bathroom or ten multi-bathroom homes and performing a full replacement of toilets, shower heads, and kitchen and bathroom faucet aerators. Builders' efficiency improvements have retrofitted more than 4,000 Morro Bay homes, a third of the city's total, in the first two years of the program.

To reduce the water loss that usually accompanies lawn watering, California's North Marin Water District offers hookup-fee rebates to builders who follow the district's landscaping guidelines. Rebates for efficient landscapes average about $150 per dwelling unit, a 15 percent discount off the standard fee. In the second and third year of the program, 95 percent of new townhouses and apartments met the landscaping guidelines and now use 40 percent less outdoor water than their neighbors.

● **Promote least-cost utility services.** Utilities should be required to promote energy efficiency and to provide energy at the least possible cost to customers. More utilities should follow the lead of the Pacific Northwest Power Planning Council in Portland, Oregon. The council thoroughly analyzes supply and demand in looking at electrical resources. Thereafter, utilities in the region implement efficiency measures to avoid the need to construct numerous costly power plants. According to the council, if population and economic activity in the region grow moderately, the most recent plan still calls for cutting electricity use by 13 percent by 2006.

In Austin, Texas, the Northern States Power Company, a municipal utility, has been able to lessen electricity use and peak demand by of-

SOURCE

For more information on water-efficient devices, contact the Rocky Mountain Institute, 1739 Snowmass Creek Road, Snowmass, CO 81654-9199; telephone: 303-927-3128 or 303-927-3851. Or write for a copy of *Citizens Guide to Community Water Conservation,* National Wildlife Federation, 1400 16th Street, NW, Washington, DC 20036.

fering rebates to people who purchase efficient appliances and other equipment. The rebate program has helped reduce the need for new electricity sources by 20 to 40 percent. At least sixteen states have adopted least-cost planning policies and requirements.

◑ Make buildings more efficient. Energy audits should be done for every community building, so that caulking, insulation, and other energy conservation meas-

ures can be taken. At the same time, incandescent light bulbs should be replaced with fluorescent ones to reduce energy use.

8 IN YOUR APARTMENT

Ecologist Peter Harnik notes, "While a house and its parcel of surrounding land imply self-reliance and self-production, an apartment building implies cooperation, sharing, interdependence, and conservation. What apartment buildings lack in productive capacity—land to grow enough food or roofs to capture enough sunlight for their residents—they compensate for through impressive economies of scale: energy conserved by shared walls, a "critical mass" of participants for recycling, huge savings in transportation energy, and much more." Harnik offers these suggestions for turning your apartment building into an "ecological highrise."*

○ **Weatherize your apartment.** (See suggestions on pages 23–24 in chapter 1.)

○ **Use an exhaust fan** (one about 18 inches in diameter) in the top part of a south-facing window or in your kitchen (whichever gets hotter), to blow warm air out and suck cooler air through all the other windows. To cool just the room you're in, close the windows in every other room. Running the fan all night uses only as much electricity as two hours' worth of air

*Source: "The Ecological Highrise," by Peter Harnik. *Environmental Action,* September 1982.

conditioning . . . and is a lot quieter.

◐ **Turn off the pilot light if you've got a gas stove.** Buy yourself a flint flame starter. Each time you need heat, strike the flint as you turn on the burner.

◐ **Conserve water in the kitchen and bathroom.**

◐ **Cut back on garbage.** Buy beer and soda in returnable bottles and avoid excess packaging, especially throwaway diapers. Buy longer-lasting fluorescent light bulbs and rechargeable batteries.

◐ **Control bugs by preventing them.** Caulk all cracks, minimize uncovered trash and unwashed dishes, and try to locate specific areas of infestation. Spread a thin film of boric acid powder along baseboards or inside cupboards— well out of the reach of children. You can try sticky roach traps, but forget those "no pest strips" for flying insects—they emit a constant stream of nerve poison. Flypaper works better.

◐ **Use the roof.** The rooftops in dense urban areas represent a staggering waste of usable space that can be converted into a garden or a platform for hot-water-heating solar collectors.

◐ **Turn your building's basement into an "ecology center."** It can serve simultaneously as a recycling station, bicycle storage room, information distribution center, tool room, appliance center, and meeting room.

◐ **Set up a building-wide recycling project, collecting newspapers, aluminum, and glass.** Everyone bundles their own papers together and accumulates their own containers and takes them down to the basement. If the volume is large enough, you may be able to get a recycler to come and pick them up with other recyclables in your neighborhood. If not, perhaps people in your tenants association can alternate loading the materials into their cars and dropping

RIGHT IDEA

The Environmental Action Coalition runs an apartment building newspaper recycling program for the city of New York. EAC explains why recycling is important to the building's management, tenant organization, or co-op board of directors and distributes literature explaining why recycling newspapers helps protect the building's garbage incinerators and saves money at the same time. Then EAC helps the building staff set up a way to manage on-site recycling. The coalition also coordinates an agreement between the building and a private paper hauler who collects the paper and takes it to a recycling facility. For more information contact the Environmental Action Coalition at 625 Broadway, 2nd floor, New York, NY 10012; telephone: 212-677-1601.

them off at a community recycling center.

○ **Share appliances.** Harnik calls this the "ultimate test of your tenants' group, sort of a black belt for urban ecology." He advises you to think of all the items you own that you rarely use—slide projector, sun lamp, rollaway bed, ice cream maker, and who knows what else. If those items were contributed to a walk-in closet on each floor, you might only have to pay one-tenth or one-twentieth the cost of each to be able to use it more or less whenever you wanted. It might be worth setting up a "sharing room" just to get all that clutter out of your own apartment!

INDOOR AIR QUALITY

Apartments can have many of the same indoor air problems as single-family homes because many of the pollution sources—building materials, furnishings, and household products—are similar. Indoor air problems much like those caused in offices by such sources as contaminated ventilation systems, improperly placed outdoor air intakes, or maintenance activities also can occur in apartments.

Solutions to air quality problems in apartments, as in homes and offices, involve one or more of the following actions:

○ **Eliminate or control the sources of pollution.**

○ **Keep windows slightly open to increase ventilation.**

○ **Have the building install air filters and purifiers and other air cleaning devices.**

Work through your tenants' association to discuss air quality problems with your landlord. If you believe your building is "sick" and the landlord refuses to take action, contact your city's landlord/tenant commission or housing violations bureau and ask how you can get your landlord to cooperate. If you live in federally subsidized housing, contact the local office of the Housing and Urban Development Department.

ENERGY

Making your apartment more energy-efficient is a no-lose situation for both tenant and landlord. If you are the owner and pay all the heating bills, the fuel savings you realize from weatherizing your building will reduce your operating costs and increase the value of your building. If you are the tenant and pay your own heating bills, you'll save money and live more comfortably in the bargain. And you may be able to tolerate a small rent increase to help pay for weatherization if it saves you as much or more money in average monthly fuel bills.

The potential for improving the energy efficiency of U.S. buildings

is great. If all cost-effective conservation measures were employed, energy consumed in buildings could be reduced by 30 to 50 percent.

The Massachusetts Audubon Society estimates a typical apartment owner can save between $150 and $300 by taking the following steps to weatherize:

Step	Cost	Savings per Year*
1. Pull down window shades at night	$0	$5 per window
2. Weather-strip windows with rope caulk	$.50 per window	$5 per window
3. Weather-strip door and install doorsweep	$8/door	$10 per door
4. Turn down temperature setting on hot-water heater	$0	$30 to $60
5. Install low-flow shower head	$10	$15 to $50
6. Put aluminum foil reflectors behind radiators	$.50 per radiator	$3 to $5 per radiator

*Based on heating oil prices of $1.00 per gallon

○ **Keep your fireplace damper tightly closed except when it is in use.** When you do use the fireplace, turn your thermostat down to around 55 degrees F.

○ **Install temporary "shrink-to-fit" storm windows.** Using a double-stick tape, apply a very thin plastic film onto the window frame and heat it with a blow-dryer. The heat shrinks the plastic, taking out all the wrinkles and making the plastic all but invisible. With ready-made kits, you can insulate a large window for about $5.00. Buying the plastic and tape in larger packages brings down the cost considerably.

○ **Use drapes or thermal curtains to keep heat from escaping through windows.**

○ **Keep radiators clean and free of furniture.**

○ **Turn down your thermostat.** You can cut your heating bill by 2 to 3 percent for every degree

BRIGHT IDEA

A leaky wall outlet can cost $1 per year in wasted heat. If you have ten outlets on exterior walls, that's $10 in lost heat every winter. You can seal up these leaks by installing outlet and switchplate insulators, small foam pads that fit behind the cover plate. The insulators only cost about a dime each and take one or two minutes to install.

SOURCE

For a complete list of energy- and money-saving tips, write for a copy of *How to Weatherize Your Home or Apartment,* Environmental Science Department, Massachusetts Audubon Society, South Great Road, Lincoln MA 01773 ($3.50). The Society's "Energy Saver's Series" also includes the booklets *Saving Energy and Money with Home Appliances, Solar Ideas for Your Home or Apartment,* and *Financing Home Energy Improvements.*

BRIGHT IDEA

If any landscaping is going on around your apartment building, urge the owners to plant more trees to help reduce global warming.

you set back your thermostat. (For example, if you now pay $1,000 per year for heat with the thermostat set at 68 degrees, turning it down to 65 degrees will save you $50 to $90, depending on local energy costs.) And setting back the thermostat 10 degrees when you go to sleep at night can cut your daily fuel use by 10 percent.

○ **Turn off lights you don't need.** Wherever possible, replace your incandescent bulbs with fluorescent lights.

9 VACATIONS

With tourism becoming the number three industry in the world, vacationing has started to take its toll on the environment. Tour operators often pick the choicest—and most fragile—places to invade, without giving much thought to the impact hordes of tourists might have on the area's flora and fauna. And instead of managing their ecological tourist attractions like a renewable resource, they exploit them as if they were in the middle of a gold rush: They move in, take as much out of the region as they can, and then move on to the next motherlode.

There are hundreds of wonderful ways to give yourself—and the planet—a break, from saving endangered species to exploring the great outdoors to staying home and getting reacquainted with your own community. When you start planning your next vacation, consider these options:

WHERE TO VACATION

○ **Vacation at home this year.** Rediscover nearby attractions, and visit new museums, zoos, parks, botanic gardens, or historic buildings that you haven't had time to explore yet. Go to plays and movies, and spend the money you've budgeted for hotel bills on long, relaxing dinners with friends at expensive restaurants you'd otherwise think you can't afford. You'll save energy by not driving or flying long distances, and minimize the tension that frequently accompanies planning and executing a more ambitious travel plan.

○ **Save energy if you do go away.** Remember to turn off lights, lower heating temperatures in winter, and turn off air conditioning in summer.

○ **Choose a hotel or campground close to where you live.** A nearby hotel or campground often can provide as complete and happy a change from routine as one that is hundreds of miles away. You'll just get there sooner and have more time to relax!

○ **Plan to stay in one place if you do vacation away from home.** Unless you are traveling by train, "hopping around" by car eats up gasoline and adds to the tension.

○ **Take a train or a bus instead of a plane or even the family car.** Save gasoline and relax.

○ **Rediscover the pleasures of walking, hiking, and bicycling during your vacation.** They're the most energy-conserv-

ing means of transportation and the healthiest for most people.

○ **Observe the posted speed limits.** The average automobile will save 17 percent of its fuel driving at 55 miles per hour rather than at 65 miles per hour.

○ **Plan your trips carefully.** Record your gasoline use, and try to get more miles per gallon out of your car.

○ **Minimize your impact at tourist attractions.** Places like amusement parks, zoos, and even Disney World are notorious for the amount of trash they generate, primarily in the form of food wrappers and containers. Yet because each of these places is essentially a self-contained community, it should be easy to set up on-the-spot recycling and to get food and drink concessions to use recyclable containers. If you're feeling really ambitious, write a letter to the company that manages the attraction, urging it to adopt more environmentally sensitive operating practices. For a lower-key approach, refuse to take a beverage if it is served in a foam plastic cup. Or you can pack your own refreshments (in recyclable containers, of course) and reduce your contribution to solid waste altogether.

IF YOU GO HIKING OR CAMPING . . .

○ **Put nature first.** Wilderness areas will only help us escape the pressures of modern living as long as they keep their wilderness qualities. When you enjoy the out-of-doors, leave it as clean as (or cleaner than) you found it.

○ **Choose the right equipment.** Heavy, lug-soled boots can rip up fragile terrain; consider wearing a pair of light boots or well-cushioned running shoes whenever it is safe and conditions permit. Use light footwear in camp.

○ **Use established trails when possible.** Cutting switchbacks tramples vegetation and leads to soil erosion. Get good trail maps from the park ranger before you embark on your trip.

○ **Minimize your impact on your campsite.** Select a level campsite with adequate water run-off, and use plastic under your tent to stay dry without ditching. Locate your site at least 100 feet away from natural water sources. If possible, select a site that has already been used, to eliminate further expansion of the camp. And leave the campsite in as natural a state as possible.

○ **Don't be a litter bug!** Pick up litter as you encounter it on your hike. And carry out or burn all of your own garbage, especially plastic and metal packaging. Depending on local fire hazards, you may be able to burn paper trash. If not, carry it out as well.

○ **Use established latrines if they are provided.** If not, dig a "cat-hole" with a trowel in an area at least 100 feet away from water sources, trails, and camp. After carefully removing the surface dirt, dig a hole several inches deep, deposit all your human wastes and toilet paper, and recover with dirt and other debris.

○ **Wash yourself and your clothes at least 100 feet away from water.** Even biodegradable soap stresses the environment, so do as much of your cleanup as possible with soapless hot water. When using any soap to wash yourself or your dishes, use it well away from natural water sources and pour it into highly absorbent ground. That goes for tooth brushing, too.

○ **Protect water sources from contamination.** And boil, chemically treat, or filter your drinking water any time you are not sure of water purity.

○ **Seek the park ranger's advice before building a fire.** Where dead wood has accumulated on the forest floor and could fuel more hazardous fire situations, campfires may be encouraged. Other conditions may warrant only the use of self-contained canisters for cooking food. If you must build a fire, keep it small, and use only dead wood you find already on the ground. At the end of the evening, make sure your ashes are cool.

○ **Don't smoke in dry woods where you could spark a fire.** Scatter your ashes only when they are cool, and carry out all your cigarette filters.

○ **Minimize your use of mountain bikes.** Use bicycles on roads or designated bicycle trails, not on hiking-only trails. Riding off trails and taking shortcuts can lead to erosion.

(Source: Recreational Equipment, Inc.)

The Sierra Club has been organizing outings to explore and enjoy the wilderness since 1902. Literally hundreds of exciting, rewarding trips all over the world are offered every year to Sierra Club members or those applying for membership. For more information, contact Sierra Club Outing Department, 730 Polk Street, San Francisco, CA 94109.

FISHING

Monofilament fishing line and plastic debris have made fishing a dangerous sport for many creatures in the environment—and not just the ones we eat.

Monofilament fishing line that's lost or thrown overboard is lethal for sea turtles and birds. Plastic trash, particularly six-pack rings, bags, and nets can trap fish and birds and strangle them as they try to break free. Or they mistake the debris for food, and die from internal injuries, intestinal blockage, or starvation. Some birds unknowingly feed plastic debris to their young. Sea turtles often mistake bags and sheeting for jellyfish. Even the great whales are victims—several have been found dead with plastic bags and sheeting in their stomachs.

Plastics can also be a floating menace to navigation. Plastic rope and line fouls propellers, and plastic bags and sheeting clog seawater intakes and evaporators, causing engine failure, costly repairs, and annoying delays. This type of vessel disablement can be life-threatening.

According to the National Academy of Sciences, oceangoing vessels discard 14 billion pounds of cargo and crew wastes, including plastics, every year. While some litter sinks or rapidly decays, plastics have an estimated life-span of hundreds of years. In fact, plastics are now the most common man-made objects sighted at sea.

Effective December 31, 1988, it became illegal for any vessel to dump plastic trash in the ocean or navigable waters in the United States. Anyone who uses these waters must comply with the law, including all ships, from small boats to tankers, platforms and crew boats, commercial and recreational fishermen, marinas and private docks, and fish processing facilities. Violators caught dumping may be fined up to $25,000.

Here are ten steps you can take to keep plastic out of the water:

O On your boat, stow plastic trash and old fishing gear for proper disposal on land.

O Use reusable items such as washable dinnerware to minimize the amount of plastic

waste you generate. Secure trash bags and cans to a fixture on the boat (so that they're not accidentally washed overboard), and then make sure that all trash finds its way into this receptacle. Dispose of it at the dock.

◐ **If dockside facilities are inadequate, express your concerns to the marina owner, dock master, or port authorities.**

◐ **Contact the Coast Guard if you see other boat crews dumping trash overboard.** Get the vessel's name, number, location, and type of trash.

◐ **Properly dispose of lengths of old fishing line, since lost line can be lethal.**

◐ **For larger vessels, install a trash compactor.**

◐ **Where possible, retrieve trash found in the water or on shore.**

◐ **Clean up after picnics and beach outings.** In particular, dispose of plastic wastes in trash facilities to prevent plastic debris from blowing into the water from the beach. In particular, dispose of plastic wastes in trash facilities.

◐ **Break or cut the loops of plastic six-pack holders before disposing of them** to ensure that if the ring escapes into the water it will not entangle an animal.

◐ **Participate in local beach cleanup efforts.**

WHEN YOU FLY

Every airplane flight that serves even so much as a beverage and snack generates a mountain of trash by the time the plane lands. Here are a few things you can do to keep garbage overload to a minimum when flying:

◐ **Bring your own snack.** The truly dedicated traveler may find it just as palatable to bring along an apple or a sandwich as to eat one offered on the plane. (Yours will probably taste better than theirs, anyway!)

◐ **Write the airlines, suggesting they use heavy-duty (and reusable) plastic plates and real silverware.** This is especially appropriate for airlines that serve up their meals in cute (and wasteful) little bags and boxes that are also wrapped in plastic and then collected in another plastic bag.

SOURCE

For information on how to organize a beach cleanup, get a copy of *Get the Drift and Bang It: A Nuts and Bolts Guide to Organizing a Beach Cleanup Campaign the Easy Way* from the Oregon Department of Fish and Wildlife, P.O. Box 59, Portland, OR 97207.

**B**RIGHT IDEA

To date, twelve states have enacted legislation requiring that all plastic six-pack rings sold in their state be made of degradable plastic. If the ring is discarded improperly, the ultraviolet rays from the sun will cause it to break apart. As it breaks down, wind and rain cause it to become brittle and to disintegrate into smaller and smaller pieces. Generally, the process takes less than three months.

Anheuser Busch, Inc., the world's largest brewer, voluntarily changed all of its six-pack rings to degradable plastic in 1987. And the Outboard Marine Corporation has begun packaging motor oil in photodegradable loop carriers. To determine whether a six-pack ring is degradable, look for a diamond embossed on the ring in the area adjacent to the finger hole.

SOURCE

The Center for Marine Conservation has prepared a series of informative pamphlets and educational materials about the impact of plastics on the oceans and the animals that live in them. For more information, contact them at 1725 DeSales Street, NW, Washington, DC 20036.

A LITTLE SOMETHING OUT OF THE ORDINARY . . .

If you're looking for a way to get away from it all and do the earth some good at the same time, select your next vacation from the following list of exotic ecological adventures.

◐ **Saving the Leatherback Turtle.** From the beginning of their lives, leatherback sea turtles are under siege—from egg poachers, animal predators, the unruly sea, beach development, and a deadly sun. Human encroachment has whittled down the number of beaches suitable for egg-laying, thereby reducing the number of leatherbacks. On St. Croix in the U.S. Virgin Islands, biologists are working with volunteer vacationers to protect nests from poachers, relocate threatened nests, help hatchlings get to the sea, and radio-track departing females. So far, well over 20,000 hatchlings have received their help. For more information about this project and hundreds of other fascinating "rescue missions," contact Earthwatch, a nonprofit organization that sponsors ecological research expeditions and publishes *Earthwatch* magazine seven times a year: Earthwatch, 680 Mt. Auburn Street, Box 403N, Watertown, MA 02272; telephone: 617-926-8200.

❍ **Reforest Nepal.** Though treks to the Himalayas have become pretty commonplace, what makes this one stand out is its emphasis on repairing the mountainsides that have in part been deforested to meet the fuel and food needs of thousands of trekkers. A portion of the trip fee goes to the Earth Preservation Fund, which makes contributions to local conservation organizations and sponsors cleanup treks, tree-planting, and cultural restoration projects. Trip participants help get the job done by spending a short portion of their total trip planting seedlings or seeds. In addition to the Himalayas, trips are offered in East Africa and South America. For more information, contact Journeys, 4011 Jackson, Ann Arbor, MI 48103; telephone: 313-665-4407.

❍ **Southern Utah Archeological Service Trip.** The southeast corner of Utah is rich in remains of the ancient Anasazi indians. This service trip focuses on surveying and mapping a number of archeological sites. Under the expert guidance of Navajo stone masons, participants stabilize and restore the ruins of the ancient Anasazi and other tribes in southern Utah. For more information, contact Sierra Club Outing Department, Dept. #05618, San Francisco, CA 94139.

❍ **The Vermont Youth Conservation Corps.** Corps participants build trails and bridges, restore historic buildings, improve timber stands, and help manage wildlife habitat. It restricts participation to those sixteen to twenty-one years old and pays them for the time they put in on the job. Their motto: "Low pay, hard work, no picnic." And they have more applicants than they have work slots. The VYCC is just one of a growing number of Youth Conservation Corps around the United States. For more information, write or call Human Environment Center, 810 18th Street, NW, Suite 507, Washington, DC 20006; telephone: 202-393-5550.

❍ **Rails-to-Trails.** Book a bicycling vacation in the United States, Ireland, or the Caribbean through Travent, Ltd., and 10 percent of the cost of the trip will be donated to the Rails-to-Trails Conservancy. RTC is a nonprofit organization that is converting abandoned railroad rights of way into a transcontinental trailway network that will preserve for the future the nation's spectacular railroad corridor system. For more information, contact Travent/RTC Bicycle Tours, Rails-to-Trails Conservancy, Suite 300, 1400 16th Street, NW, Washington, DC 20036.

❍ **Saving a Cloud Forest.** There are places in the tropics where clouds rest right up against high mountain ridges, and the animals and plants there are unique and exotic. The El Triunfo preserve is one such place. El Triunfo is the most important cloud forest in Central America. It is home to thousands of animals and plant species, including the resplendent quetzal and the rare horned guan. Like so many forests in the tropics, El Triunfo is under constant threat from development. To preserve and protect El Triunfo, Victor Emmanuel Nature Tours organizes one tour a year there. For twelve days, tourists bird-watch, learn about the natural history of the area, and meet with local environmental activists to learn what is being done to save the cloud forest. A portion of the cost of the trip is donated to the local organization, Fundamat, to manage El Triunfo. For more information, contact Victor Emmanuel Nature Tours, P.O. Box 33008, Austin, TX 78764; telephone: 512-328-5221.

O Conservation Summits. The National Wildlife Federation Conservation Summits provide great summer adventures for adults, families, and educators—and some of America's most spectacular sights, including the Colorado Rockies and the Green Mountains of Vermont. During these week-long learning vacations, adults can discover the natural history of an area through field trips and classes led by highly qualified naturalists. Separate programs are offered for teens, youths, and preschoolers. In addition, one summit each year is specifically tailored towards educators. For more information, contact Conservation Summits, National Wildlife Federation, 1400 16th Street, NW, Washington, DC 20036; telephone: 703-790-4363.

Check the appendix for listings of many other organizations that sponsor ecological getaways.

BRIGHT IDEA

The National Audubon Society's Travel Ethic

In order to protect animals, plants, and their environments while allowing people to enjoy and learn from them, the National Audubon Society recommends that companies offering natural history tours adopt the following code of ethics.

1. Wildlife and their habitats must not be disturbed.
2. Tourism to natural areas will be sustainable.
3. Waste disposal during travel must have neither environmental nor aesthetic impacts.
4. The experience a tourist gains in traveling must enrich his or her appreciation of nature, conservation, and the environment.
5. Tours must strengthen the conservation effort and enhance the natural integrity of places visited.
6. Traffic in products that threaten wildlife and plant populations must not occur.
7. The sensibilities of other cultures must be respected.

Operators of natural history tours who wish to inquire about subscribing to the Aubudon Travel Ethic should write to the Director of Audubon Travel Programs, National Audubon Society, 950 Third Avenue, New York, NY 10022.

◐ **Encourage any airline you fly to serve hot drinks in heavy paper cups, rather than cups made of foam plastic.**

CHOOSE YOUR "SOUVENIRS" CAREFULLY

Many tourists traveling abroad unwittingly buy items made from the hides, shells, feathers, or teeth of endangered species. But just because the wildlife items are on sale in abundance does not necessarily mean that they are legal. Travelers don't realize that most U.S. laws and an international treaty called CITES make it a crime to bring many of these wildlife souvenirs into our country, because the species from which they are derived are being exploited to the point of extinction. When you travel, avoid buying these products:

◐ *Reptile skins and leathers.* These are most commonly used in watchbands, handbags, belts, and shoes. Avoid products made from most crocodile skins, including black caiman, spectacled caiman, American crocodile, and Chinese alligator; lizard skin products originating in Brazil, Paraguay, Nepal, India, and Pakistan; snakeskin items originating in Latin America and some Asian countries; and *all* sea turtle products, including tortoiseshell jewelry and combs, leather, eggs, food products, and creams and cosmetics made with turtle oil.

◐ *Birds and feathers.* The survival of many wild bird species is threatened by habitat destruction and trade; as many as 70 percent of birds may die during capture, transit, and the required thirty-day quarantine period. And frequently, birds are taken from countries that ban their export to neighboring countries where falsified documents can be obtained. Prohibited from import are virtually all birds originating in Australia, Brazil, Ecuador, Mexico, Paraguay, Venezuela, and several Caribbean countries; most wild bird feathers, mounted birds, and skins; and many large parrots, including certain macaws and cockatoos.

◐ *Ivory.* Ivory from elephant tusks is traditionally carved into products such as jewelry, scrimshaw, figurines, and piano keys. Because poaching to get the ivory to make these souvenirs is killing thousands of elephants a year, elephant ivory is strictly prohibited from import into the U.S. Under no circumstances should you buy ivory souvenirs.

◐ *Furs.* Furs from the jaguar, leopard, snow leopard, tiger, ocelot, margay, and tiger cat, among other cats, as well as the furs of marine mammals like seals and polar bears, cannot enter the United States legally.

◐ *Coral.* Because coral reefs are the building blocks of important marine communities and serve as natural barriers against beach erosion, many countries in the Caribbean and Southeast Asia prohibit the collection, sale, and export of corals.

THE *SAVE OUR PLANET* GUIDE TO THE FOURTH OF JULY

On the Fourth of July, Labor Day, Memorial Day, or any other time when picnicking and outdoor fun are the order for the day, follow these suggestions for a low-impact, high-reward celebration:

○ **Choose a place for your picnic that requires minimum transportation.** Bike, walk, or car pool with friends.

○ **Alternatively, participate in an outdoor "benefit" for an environmental organization or a cause.** Many groups organize day-long rafting trips, bird-watching excursions, beach cleanups, sails, or mountain hikes and devote a portion of the trip's fee to a worthwhile project.

○ **When shopping for picnic fare, choose products with minimal packaging that come in reusable or recyclable containers.** Avoid plastic, aluminum, and individually wrapped products. If you're taking food out from a deli, ask that it be wrapped in paper instead of plastic wrap. Favor a large bottle of juice and small paper cups over individual-portion juice boxes that come wrapped in cellophane and coated paper.

○ **If you can, take a tablecloth, reusable dishes, glasses, and silverware from home.** If you must buy disposables, buy paper plates and cups rather than those made from hard or foam plastic. Cloth napkins are an excellent alternative to paper towels and napkins. Bring along garbage bags or, preferably, burlap sacks to save cans and bottles for recycling.

And choose fresh fruit, which is packaging-free, over a treat that comes in a throwaway bag or box.

○ **When the barbecue is over, clean up.** Bottles and cans should go in appropriate bags for recycling, while paper and other trash should find their way to the nearest garbage can.

Check for restrictions on coral trade before you buy.

○ *Plants.* Like animals, plants can be smuggled, improperly documented, or otherwise tainted to get them out of one country and into another. As a result, many plant species face extinction and receive protection under U.S. law. Species prohibited from import into the United States include many cycads, orchids, and cacti.

SOURCE

For more information and a helpful brochure you can take on your trips abroad, contact TRAFFIC (U.S.A.), World Wildlife Fund, 1255 23rd Street, NW, Washington, DC 20037.

DON'T FORGET TO VOTE!

We have an enormous opportunity to improve the health of our communities and the state of our world just by exercising our basic right to vote. Environmental voters have elected candidates who will fight to protect the planet and defeated those who put pollution before people. And "citizen legislators" across the country have gone to the polls to successfully stop nuclear power plants, pass bottle bills, control overdevelopment, and restrict toxics. Here are some ways you can use the voting booth to help save our planet.

○ **Vote for candidates who pledge to protect the environment.** Attend community election forums and ask candidates how they stand on local, regional, national, and global environmental issues.

○ **Compile voting charts on officials running for re-election to help inform other voters.** All official votes are a matter of public record. Tally up environmental votes of candidates running for re-election and release them at a news conference to your local media. You can also put the results into a flyer for door-to-door distribution or to hand out at a town meeting. Ask candidates without a voting record to complete an environmental survey.

○ **Hold an environmental town meeting.** Prior to the elections, invite all candidates to a town meeting to discuss their environmental views.

○ **Once a candidate is elected, monitor his or her voting record.** If an elected official supports a measure to undermine the environment, send letters to the official and request an explanation in writing as well as an in-person meeting.

○ **Educate yourself about "green" ballot measures and initiatives.** It's especially important to get out and vote on such measures if they're being put to the electorate during a "special" election (rather than the normal general election), when voter turnout may be low.

○ **Volunteer for candidates or campaigns.** Many "green" candidates and environmental ballot measures struggle against well-funded opponents supported by polluting companies. You can help offset the dollar differences by helping to staff phone banks and get-out-the-vote efforts, posting signs and banners, or organizing a letters-to-the-editor campaign, among many campaign tasks.

○ **Join organizations that help elect environmental candidates,** such as the Sierra Club and the League of Conservation Voters.

You can find out how your member of Congress voted on key environmental legislation by reading *The National Environmental Scorecard,* a voting chart published every two years that rates Congress on environmental and energy issues. The Scorecard can be obtained for $15.00 from the League of Conservation Voters, 2000 L St., NW, Suite 804, Washington, DC 20036.

APPENDIX: RESOURCES

For more information or to contact organizations and agencies involved in environmental issues important to you, consult the lists below.

PUBLICATIONS

General Information

Blueprint for a Green Planet: Your Practical Guide to Restoring the World's Environment, by John Seymour and Herbert Girardet. 192 pp. Prentice Hall, 1987.

Blueprint for the Environment: Advice to the President-Elect from America's Environmental Community. 300 pp., $13.95. Howe Brothers (P.O. Box 6394, Salt Lake City, UT 84106, or phone toll-free: 800-426-5387).

Diet for a New America, by John Robbins. 423 pp. Stillpoint Publishing (Box 640, Walpole, NH 03608), 1987.

Environmental Pollution: A Long-Term Perspective, by James Gustave Speth. 20 pp. World Resources Institute (1709 New York Avenue, NW, Washington, DC 20006), 1988.

Environmental Progress and Challenges: EPA's Update. 140 pp. United States Environmental Protection Agency (Public Information Center, PM211B, 401 M Street, SW, Washington, DC 20460), August 1988.

Our Common Future. 400 pp. The World Commission on Environment and Development, Oxford University Press, 1987.

Personal Action Guide for the Earth, by Kathleen Gildred. 12 pp., $1.00/bulk prices available. Friends of the United Nations—Transmissions Project, May 1989 (730 Arizona Avenue, Suite 329, Santa Monica, CA 90401).

"The Planet Strikes Back! 21st Environmental Quality Index" by the National Wildlife Federation. 8 pp., one copy free; bulk prices available. Reprinted from the February–March 1989 issue of *National Wildlife* magazine. (Educational Publications, National Wildlife Federation, 8925 Leesburg Pike, Vienna, VA 22184.)

Restoring the Earth: How Americans Are Working to Renew Our Damaged Environment, by John J. Berger. 214 pp. Anchor Press, 1987.

Shopping for a Better World: A Quick & Easy Guide to Socially Responsible Supermarket Shopping. 126 pp., $4.95. Council on Economic Priorities (30 Irving Place, New York, NY 10003).

State of the World 1989, by Lester R. Brown *et al.* 256 pp. W. W. Norton, 1989.

A Vegetarian Sourcebook: The Nutrition, Ecology, and Ethics of a Natural Foods Diet, by Keith Akers. G. P. Putnam's Sons, 1983.

Acid Rain and Air Pollution

Air Pollution, Acid Rain, and the Future of Forests, by Sandra Postel. 54 pp., $4.00. Worldwatch Institute (1776 Massachusetts Avenue, NW, Washington, DC 20036), March 1984.

Breathing Easier: Taking Action on Climate Change, Air Pollution and Energy Insecurity, by James J. MacKenzie. 23 pp., $5.00. World Resources Institute (1709 New York Avenue, NW, Washington, DC 20006), 1988.

Exhausting Our Future: An Eighty-Two-City Study of Smog in the 80s. The Public Interest Research Groups (215 Pennsylvania Avenue, SE, Washington, DC 20003), $10.00.

Ill Winds: Airborne Pollution's Toll on Trees and Crops, by James J. MacKenzie and Mohamed T. El-Ashry. $10.00. World Resources Institute (1709 New York Avenue, NW, Washington, DC 20006).

Trends in the Quality of the Nation's Air. 19 pp. United States Environmental Protection Agency (Office of Public Affairs—87–019, Washington, DC 20460), May 1988.

Deforestation

In the Rainforest, by Catherine Caufield. University of Chicago Press, 1986.

Keep Tropical Forests Alive, by Lani Sinclair. 12 pp., free. World Resources Institute (1709 New York Avenue, NW, Washington, DC 20006).

Reforesting the Earth, by Sandra Postel and Lori Heise. 66 pp., $4.00. Worldwatch Institute (1776 Massachusetts Avenue, NW, Washington, DC 20036), April 1988.

Saving the Tropical Forests, by Judith Gradwohl and Russell Greenberg. 206 pp. Island Press, 1988.

"Tropical Deforestation: The Causes, Consequences and First-Step Solutions to a Global Disaster That Is Impoverishing People, Soil, the Gene Pool, Even Our Climate." $2.50. Reprint of *American Forests* special magazine issue. American Forestry Association (P.O. Box 2000, Washington, DC 20013).

Tropical Nature: Life and Death in the Rain Forests of Central and South America, by Adrian Forsyth and Ken Miyata. 248 pp. Charles Scribner's Sons, 1984.

Energy

Breathing Easier: Taking Action on Climate Change, Air Pollution and Energy Insecurity, by James J. MacKenzie. 23 pp., $5.00. World Resources Institute (1709 New York Avenue, NW, Washington, DC 20006), 1988.

Building on Success: The Age of Energy Efficiency, by Christopher Flavin and Alan B. Durning. 74 pp., $4.00. The Worldwatch Institute (1776 Massachusetts Avenue, NW, Washington, DC 20036), March 1988. Also from The Worldwatch Institute: *Renewable Energy: Today's Contribution, Tomorrow's Promise,* by Cynthia Pollock Shea. 68 pp. January 1988. *Rethinking the Role of the Automobile,* by Michael Renner. 70 pp. June 1988.

Cut Your Electric Bills in Half, by Ralph J. Herbert. 152 pp., $9.95 paperback edition. Rodale Press.

Energy Efficiency: A New Agenda, by William U. Chandler, Howard S. Geller, and Marc R. Ledbetter. 76 pp. The American Council for an Energy-Efficient Economy (1001 Connecticut Avenue, NW, Washington, DC 20036), July 1988.

"Energy Saver's" series. Includes *How to Weatherize Your Home or Apartment; All About Insulation; Oil and Gas Heating Systems; Saving Energy and Money with Home Appliances; Solar Ideas for Your Home or Apartment; Financing Home Energy Improvements; Superinsulation: An Introduction to the Latest in Energy Efficient Construction; Home Heating with Wood and Coal.* Massachusetts Audubon Society (Environmental Science Department, South Great Road, Lincoln, MA 01773). Individual copies, $3.50; set of eight, $20.50.

"Energy Security in the 1990s," by Daniel Yergin. *Foreign Affairs,* Volume 67, No. 1, Autumn 1988.

Tips for Energy Savers. Department of Energy Conservation and Renewable Energy Inquiry and Referral Service (P.O. Box 8900, Silver Spring, MD 20907; or call toll-free 800-523-2929—800-233-3071 in Alaska and Hawaii). Free.

Global Warming

Changing Climate: A Guide to the Greenhouse Effect, by Lani Sinclair. 9 pp., free. World Resources Institute (1709 New York Avenue, NW, Washington, DC 20006). January 1989.

Cooling the Greenhouse: Vital First Steps to Combat Global Warming. 72 pp., $5.00. Natural Resources Defense Council (1350 New York Avenue, NW, Suite 300, Washington, DC 20005).

"The Greenhouse Debate: New Problems, New Solutions," by Curtis A. Moore. 16 pp., one copy free; additional copies available in bulk prices. Reprint from *International Wildlife* magazine (Department GWR, National Wildlife Federation, 8925 Leesburg Pike, Vienna, VA 22184), 1989.

"The Greenhouse Effect: How It Can Change Our Lives." *EPA Journal* January/February 1989. 52 pp. United States Environmental Protection Agency (Office of Public Affairs, A-107, Washington, DC 20460).

Policy Options for Stabilizing Global Climate: Draft Report to Congress. U.S. Environmental Protection Agency (PM 221, 401 M Street, SW, Washington, DC 20460), February 1989.

The Potential Effects of Global Climate Change on the United States: Draft Report to Congress (Executive Summary). 51 pp., free. U.S. Environmental Protection Agency (PM 221, 401 M Street, SW, Washington, DC 20460), October 1988.

Reducing the Rate of Global Warming: The States' Role, by Sheila Machado and Rick Piltz. 33 pp., $7.00. Renew America (1001 Connecticut Avenue, NW, Suite 719, Washington, DC 20036), November 1988.

Indoor Air Pollution

The Healthy House Catalog. 111 pp., $15.00, plus $2.50 postage and handling. The Healthy House (4115 Bridge Avenue, Room 104, Cleveland, OH 44113; or call toll-free 800-222-9348).

The Inside Story: A Guide to Indoor Air Quality. 32 pp. U.S. Environmental Protection Agency (Office of Air and Radiation, Washington, DC 20460).

Radon: The Citizens' Guide. 24 pp., $2.00. Environmental Defense Fund (257 Park Avenue South, New York, NY 10010).

Ozone Layer

Atmosphere (quarterly publication). $15.00/year. Friends of the Earth (218 D Street, SE, Washington, DC 20003).

"Can We Repair the Sky?" 5 pp. Reprint from *Consumer Reports* (P.O. Box CS 2010-A, Mount Vernon, NY 10553), May 1989.

Protecting Life on Earth: Steps to Save the Ozone Layer, by Cynthia Pollock Shea. 26 pp., $4.00. Worldwatch Institute (1776 Massachusetts Avenue, NW, Washington, DC 20036), December 1988.

Protecting the Ozone Layer: What You Can Do. 33 pp., $2.00. Environmental Defense Fund (257 Park Avenue South, New York, NY 10010), 1988.

Saving Our Skins: Technical Potential and Policies for the Elimination of Ozone-Depleting Chlorine Compounds, by Arjun Makhijani, Annie Makhijani, and Amanda Bickel. 167 pp. Environmental Policy Institute and the Institute for Energy and Environmental Research (218 D Street, SE, Washington, DC 20003), 1988.

Saving the Ozone Layer: A Citizen Action Guide. 8 pp. Natural Resources Defense Council (122 East 42nd Street, New York, NY 10168).

Stones in a Glass House—CFCs and Ozone Depletion, by Douglas G. Cogan. 147 pp., $35.00. Investor Responsibility Research Center (1755 Massachusetts Avenue, NW, Suite 600, Washington, DC 20036), 1988.

Pesticides

The Chemical-Free Lawn, by Warren Schultz. 194 pp., $26.95. Rodale Press, 1989.

Defusing the Toxics Threat: Controlling Pesticides and Industrial Waste, by Sandra Postel. 69 pp., $4.00. Worldwatch Institute (1776 Massachusetts Avenue, NW, Washington, DC 20036), September 1987.

The Encyclopedia of Natural Insect and Disease Control, Robert B. Yepsen, Jr., ed. 490 pp. Rodale Press, 1984.

How to Grow Vegetables Organically, by Jeff Cox. 320 pp. Rodale Press.

Sensible Pest Control: A Handbook of Integrated Pest Management. 46 pp., $7.65. Massachusetts Audubon Society (Educational Resources Office, South Great Road, Lincoln, MA 01773).

Silent Spring, by Rachel Carson. Houghton Mifflin Company, 1962.

Spunky Squirrel Gypsy Moth Fact Sheet. Free. American Forestry Association (P.O. Box 2000, Washington, DC 20013).

Those Damned Mosquitoes! 20 pp., $2.00. Massachusetts Audubon Society (for address, see *Sensible Pest Control,* above).

Recycling

Become an Environmental Shopper: Vote for the Environment (plus list of 400 items in recyclable or recycled packaging). 20 pp., $5.00. Pennsylvania Resources Council, Inc. (25 West Third Street, P.O. Box 88, Media, PA 19063), December 1988.

Beyond 25 Percent: Materials Recovery Comes of Age, by Theresa Allan. 134 pp., $40 prepaid, $25 for community groups. Institute for Local Self-Reliance (2425 18th Street, NW, Washington, DC, 20009), 1989.

Coming Full Circle: Successful Recycling Today. 162 pp., $20.00. Environmental Defense Fund, Inc. (257 Park Avenue South, New York, NY 10010), 1988.

Mining Urban Wastes: The Potential for Recycling, by Cynthia Pollack. $4.00. Worldwatch Institute (1776 Massachusetts Avenue, NW, Washington, DC 20036), April 1987.

Proven Profits from Pollution Prevention: Case Studies in Resource Conservation and Waste Reduction, by Donald Huisingh *et al.* 315 pp., $25.00. Institute for Local Self-Reliance (2425 18th Street, NW, Washington, DC 20009), 1986.

Recycling: Treasure in our Trash. 6 pp., free. National Solid Wastes Management Association (1730 Rhode Island Avenue, NW, Washington, DC 20036).

Waste: Choices for Communities. 32 pp., $3.00. Concern, Inc. (1794 Columbia Road, NW, Washington, DC 20009).

Waste Not, Want Not: State and Federal Roles in Source Reduction and Recycling of Solid Waste, by Carol Andress. 63 pp. Northeast-Midwest Institute (218 D Street, SE, Washington, DC 20003), February 1989.

Wrapped in Plastics: The Environmental Case for Reducing Plastics Packaging, by Jeanne Wirka. 159 pp.; $10.00 individuals and nonprofit environmental organizations; $20.00 government and educational institutions; $30.00 industry. Environmental Action Foundation (1525 New Hampshire Avenue, NW, Washington, DC 20036), August 1988.

Toxics

America the Poisoned: How Deadly Chemicals Are Destroying Our Environment, Our Wildlife, Ourselves—and How We Can Survive! by Lewis Regenstein. Acropolis Books, 1982.

Chemicals in Your Community: A Guide to the Emergency Planning and Community Right-to-Know Act. United States Environmental Protection Agency (Washington, DC 20460), September 1988.

Danger Downwind: A Report on the Release of Billions of Pounds of Toxic Air Pollutants, by Jerry Poje, Norman L. Dean, and Randall J. Burke. 47 pp. National Wildlife Federation (1400 16th Street, NW, Washington, DC 20036), March 22, 1989.

Hazardous Chemicals. United Nations Environment Programme Environment Brief No. 4.

Hazardous Waste Fact Pack. 16 pp., $4.95. Citizens Clearinghouse for Hazardous Wastes, Inc. (P.O. Box 926, Arlington, VA 22216), Summer 1986.

Hazardous Waste in America, by Samuel S. Epstein, Lester O. Brown, and Carl Pope. 593 pp. Sierra Club Paperback Library, 1982.

Nontoxic & Natural: How to Avoid Dangerous Everyday Products and Buy or Make Safe Ones, by Debra Lynn Dadd. 289 pp. Jeremy P. Tarcher, Inc., 1984.

Secondary Containment: A Second Line of Defense (A Citizens' Series on Leaking Underground Storage Tanks). 22 pp. Environmental Defense Fund (257 Park Avenue South, New York, NY 10010).

Shadow on the Land: A Special Report on America's Hazardous Harvest. 41 pp. National Toxics Campaign (29 Temple Place, Boston, MA 02111; telephone: 617-482-1477).

"Superfund: Looking Back, Looking Ahead." *EPA Journal,* January/February 1987, pp. 13–35.

Water

The Chesapeake Bay Foundation Homeowner Series: Water Conservation, Household Hazardous Waste, Detergents, Your Boat, Oil Recycling, Soil Conservation, Septic Systems. The Chesapeake Bay Foundation (162 Prince George Street, Annapolis, MD 21401).

A Citizen's Guide to Plastics in the Ocean: More Than a Litter Problem, by Kathryn J. O'Hara, Suzanne Iudicello, and Rose Bierce. 131 pp. Center for Environmental Education (1725 DeSales Street, NW, Suite 500, Washington, DC 20036), 1988.

A Citizen's Guide to Protecting Wetlands, by Jan Goldman-Carter. 64 pp. National Wildlife Federation (1400 16th Street, NW, Washington, DC 20036), single copy free.

A Citizen's Guide to River Conservation, by Rolf Diamant, J. Glenn Eugster, and Christopher J. Duerksen. 113 pp. The Conservation Foundation (1250 24th Street, NW, Washington, DC 20037), 1984.

Controlling Nonpoint-Source Water Pollution: A Citizen's Handbook, by Nancy Richardson Hansen, Hope M. Babcock, and Edwin H. Clark II. 170 pp. National Audubon Society and The Conservation Foundation (950 Third Avenue, New York, NY 10022), 1988.

Danger on Tap: The Government's Failure to Enforce the Federal Safe Drinking Water Act, by Norman L. Dean. 70 pp. National Wildlife Federation (1400 16th Street, NW, Washington, DC 20036), October 1988.

Drinking Water—A Community Action Guide. 31 pp., $3.00. Concern, Inc. (1794 Columbia Road, NW, Washington, DC 20009), 1988.

Is Your Water Safe to Drink? by Raymond Gabler. 390 pp., $16.00. Consumers Reports Books, 1988.

Medical Waste: EPA Environmental Backgrounder. Environmental Protection Agency (Office of Public Affairs, A-107, Washington, DC 20460), November 1988.

Safety on Tap—A Citizen's Drinking Water Handbook, by David G. Loveland and Beth Reichheld. 68 pp; $5.95/members, $7.95/non-members. Washington, D.C., League of Women Voters Education Fund (1730 M Street, NW, Washington, DC 20036), 1987.

Surface Water: The Student's Resource Guide. 30 pp. Water Pollution Control Federation (601 Wythe Street, Alexandria, VA 22314-1994), 1988.

Water: Rethinking Management in an Age of Scarcity, by Sandra Postel. 65 pp., $4.00. Worldwatch Institute (1776 Massachusetts Avenue, NW, Washington, DC 20036), 1984.

Your Water, Your Life. Video: VHS, $29.95—buy; 16mm, $29.95—rent. Public Interest Video Network (1642 R Street, NW, Washington, DC 20009).

Organic Gardening

Banquets for Birds. 24 pp. National Audubon Society (950 Third Avenue, New York, NY 10022), 1983.

The Chemical-Free Lawn: The Newest Varieties and Techniques to Grow Lush, Hardy Grass, by Warren Schultz. 208 pp. Rodale Press.

Common Sense Pest Control Quarterly. Bio Integral Resource Center (P.O. Box 7414, Berkeley, CA 94704). Membership, including quarterly, $30/yr; publication catalog $1.00 plus legal-size self-addressed, stamped envelope.

The Encyclopedia of Natural Insect and Disease Control: The Most Comprehensive Guide to Protecting Plants—Vegetables, Fruit, Flowers, Trees, and Lawns—Without Toxic Chemicals, by Roger B. Yepsen, Jr. 496 pp. Rodale Press.

The Encyclopedia of Organic Gardening. 1,248 pp. Rodale Press.

The Organic Garden Book: The Complete Guide to Growing Flowers, Fruit and Vegetables Naturally, by Geoff Hamilton. 288 pp. Crown Publishers, Inc., 1987.

The Rodale Guide to Composting, by Jerry Minnich, Marjorie Hunt, and the editors of *Organic Gardening* magazine. Rodale Press, 1979.

Rodale's Landscape Problem Solver: A Plant-by-Plant Guide, by Jeff and Liz Ball. 448 pp. Rodale Press, 1989.

COMPANIES THAT SUPPLY ORGANIC GARDENING PRODUCTS

Biologic, 418 Briar Lane, Chambersburg, PA 17201; telephone: 717-263-2789. Free brochure. Offers biological insecticides that kill soil and boring insect pests without harming plants roots.

W. Atlee Burpee, 300 Park Avenue, Warminster, PA 18974; telephone: 215-674-4900. Catalog free. Products include animal traps, netting, Tanglefoot, insecticidal soap, and beneficial insects.

Gardener's Supply Company, 128 Intervale Road, Burlington, VT 05401; telephone: 802-863-5693. Catalog free. Products include organic insecticides like Bt, sabadilla, and Safer's Insecticidal Soap.

Harmony Farm Supply, P.O. Box 451, Graton, CA 95444; telephone: 707-823-9125. Catalog $2.00. IPM monitoring tools, yellow sticky traps, fly traps, pheromone traps, insecticidal and fungicidal soaps, and beneficial organisms are among the products offered by this company.

Nature's Way Product, Earlee, Inc., 2002 Highway 62, Jeffersonville, IN 47130; telephone: 812-282-9134. Catalog free. Nature's Way offers Bt, milky spore powder, rotenone, insecticidal soap, and a variety of other organic pesticides.

The Necessary Trading Company, 602 Main Street, New Castle, VA 24127. Catalog $2.00, refundable with first order. The Trading Company's items include rotenone, Bt, beneficial insects, herbs and herbal oils, Tanglefoot, insecticidal soaps, and preventive pest management systems.

ENVIRONMENTAL PROTECTION AGENCY
Regional Offices

EPA Region 1
JFK Federal Building
Boston, MA 02203
617-565-3234

**EPA Region 2
(2AIR:RAD)**
26 Federal Plaza
New York, NY 10278
212-264-4418

Region 3 (3AH14)
841 Chestnut Street
Philadelphia, PA 19107
215-597-4084

EPA Region 4
345 Courtland Street, N.E.
Atlanta, GA 30365
404-347-2904

EPA Region 5 (5AR26)
230 South Dearborn Street
Chicago, IL 60604
312-886-6165

EPA Region 6 (6T-AS)
1445 Ross Avenue
Dallas, TX 75202-2733
214-655-7208

EPA Region 7
726 Minnesota Avenue
Kansas City, KS 66101
913-236-2893

EPA Region 8 (8HWM-RP)
999 18th Street
One Denver Place, Suite 1300
Denver, CO 80202-2413
303-293-1648

EPA Region 9 (A-3)
215 Fremont Street
San Francisco, CA 94105
415-974-8378

EPA Region 10
1200 Sixth Avenue
Seattle, WA 98101
206-442-7660

ORGANIZATIONS WORKING TO SAVE OUR PLANET

Organization	Problems Addressed						Materials Available										Membership
	Acid rain	Deforestation	Garbage overload	Global warming	Water pollution	Toxics	Classroom materials	Issue/legislative updates	Posters	Publications	Slides	Speakers	Technical reprints	Tourism/trips	Videos	Newsletter/magazine	
American Council for an Energy Efficient Economy 1001 Connecticut Ave., NW Washington, DC 20036 202-429-8873	✓	✓	✓	✓	✓	✓		✓		✓							professional organiz.
American Forestry Assoc. 1516 P St., NW Washington, DC 20005 202-667-3300		✓		✓			✓	✓	✓	✓		✓	✓	✓	✓	✓	$24 yr. individ.
American Oceans Campaign 2219 Main St. Santa Monica, CA 90405 213-452-2206			✓	✓	✓	✓		✓					✓	✓		✓	non-member- ship mailing list
Better World Society 1100 17th St., NW Suite 502 Washington, DC 20036 202-331-3770		✓	✓	✓	✓	✓	✓		✓	✓					✓	✓	$25 individ.
Center for Marine Conservation 1725 DeSales St., NW Washington, DC 20036 202-429-5609			✓	✓	✓	✓	✓		✓	✓	✓	✓			✓		$20 basic
Center for Science in the Public Interest 1501 16th St., NW Washington, DC 20036 202-332-9110			✓		✓	✓			✓	✓						✓	

Organization	Acid rain	Deforestation	Garbage overload	Global warming	Water pollution	Toxics	Classroom materials	Issue/legislative updates	Posters	Publications	Slides	Speakers	Technical reprints	Tourism/trips	Videos	Newsletter/magazine	Membership
Citizens Clearinghouse for Hazardous Wastes, Inc. P.O. Box 926 Arlington, VA 22216 703-276-7070	✓		✓		✓	✓				✓		✓	✓			✓	
Clean Water Project 317 Pennsylvania Ave., SE Washington, DC 20003 202-547-1196		✓	✓	✓	✓	✓	✓	✓		✓		✓	✓		✓		$24 individ.
Concern, Inc. 1794 Columbia Rd., NW Washington, DC 20009 202-328-8160			✓		✓	✓	✓		✓	✓							$20/yr. individ.
Conservation Foundation—World Wildlife Fund 1250 24th St., NW Washington, DC 20037 202-293-4800	✓	✓	✓	✓	✓	✓	✓	✓	✓	✓✓	✓	✓	✓	✓	✓	✓	$15 individ.
Conservation International 1015 18th St., NW Suite 1000 Washington, DC 20036		✓		✓	✓	✓	✓	✓	✓	✓	✓	✓	✓	✓	✓	✓	$15 individ.
Cousteau Society 425 E. 52nd St. New York, NY 10022 212-826-2940	✓	✓	✓	✓	✓	✓	✓	✓	✓	✓	✓	✓	✓	✓	✓	✓	$20/yr. individ. $28/yr. family
Earthday 1990 P.O. Box AA Stanford University Palo Alto, CA 94605 415-321-1990	✓	✓			✓	✓				✓		✓	✓			✓	$25

Organization		Membership
Environmental Action, Inc. 1525 New Hampshire Ave., NW Washington, DC 20036 202-745-4870 (lobbying)	✓	$20/yr. basic
Environmental Action Foundation 1525 New Hampshire Ave., NW Washington, DC 20036 202-745-4871 (research and education)		$20/yr. basic
Environmental Defense Fund 257 Park Ave. South New York, NY 10010	✓	$20/yr. basic
1616 P St., NW Washington, DC 20036 202-387-3500		
Friends of the Earth 218 D St., SE Washington, DC 20003 202-547-5330	✓ ✓	
Global Tomorrow Coalition 1325 G St., NW, Suite 915 Washington, DC 20005-3104 202-628-4016	✓	
Greenhouse Crisis Foundation 1130 17th St., NW, Suite 630 Washington, DC 20036		
Greenpeace USA 1436 U St., NW Washington, DC 20009 202-462-1177	✓	$15 basic
Institute for Local Self-Reliance 2425 18th St., NW Washington, DC 20009 202-232-4108		

Organization	Problems Addressed: Acid rain	Deforestation	Garbage overload	Global warming	Water pollution	Toxics	Materials Available: Classroom materials	Issue/legislative updates	Posters	Publications	Slides	Speakers	Technical reprints	Tourism/trips	Videos	Newsletter/magazine	Membership
Izaak Walton League of America 1401 Wilson Blvd. Level B Arlington, VA 22209 703-528-1818	✓	✓	✓	✓	✓	✓	✓	✓	✓	✓	✓		✓	✓	✓		$20/yr. individ. basic
Island Press 1718 Connecticut Ave., NW Suite 300 Washington, DC 20009	✓	✓	✓		✓	✓				✓							
League of Women Voters 1730 M St., NW Washington, DC 20036 202-429-1965					✓			✓		✓							
National Audubon Society 950 3rd Ave. New York, NY 10022 212-832-3200	✓	✓	✓	✓	✓	✓	✓		✓	✓	✓	✓	✓	✓	✓	✓	$35 individ.
National Center for Appropriate Technology 3040 Continental Dr. P.O. Box 3838 Butte, MT 59702 406-494-4572			✓							✓			✓				
National Coalition Against the Misuse of Pesticides 530 7th St., SE Washington, DC 20003 202-543-5450							✓			✓		✓	✓			✓	$20 individ.; $12 low-income

National Geographic Society
1145 17th St., NW
Washington, DC 20036
202-857-7000 — $18/yr. individ.

National Parks and Conservation Association
1015 31st St., NW
Washington, DC 20007
202-944-8530 — $25/yr. individ. basic

National Toxics Campaign
37 Temple Place, 4th Floor
Boston, MA 02111
617-482-1477 — $25/yr. basic individ.

P.O. Box 28171
Washington, DC 20005
202-291-0863

National Wildlife Federation
1400 16th St., NW
Washington, DC 20036
202-797-6800 — $15/yr. basic/mag, $20/yr. 2 mags

Natural Resources Defense Council
40 West 20th St.
New York, NY 10011
212-727-2700 — $10/yr. basic individ.

1350 New York Ave., NW
Washington, DC 20005
202-783-7800

Nature Conservancy
1815 N. Lynn St.
Arlington, VA 22209
703-841-5300 — $15/yr. individ., $25/yr. family

Rainforest Action Network
301 Broadway, Suite A
San Francisco, CA 94133
415-398-4404 — $15/yr. student; $25/yr. individ.

Organization	Acid rain	Deforestation	Garbage overload	Global warming	Water pollution	Toxics	Classroom materials	Issue/legislative updates	Posters	Publications	Slides	Speakers	Technical reprints	Tourism/trips	Videos	Newsletter/magazine	Membership
Rainforest Alliance 270 Lafayette Street, Room 512 New York, NY 10012 212-941-1900		✓		✓			✓	✓	✓	✓	✓	✓	✓			✓	$20/yr. individ.; $35/yr. family
Renew America 1001 Connecticut Ave., NW Suite 719 Washington, DC 20036 202-466-6880			✓	✓	✓	✓		✓		✓		✓	✓		✓	✓	$25/yr. individ.
Rocky Mountain Institute 1739 Snowmass Creek Rd. Old Snowmass, CO 81654 303-927-3851		✓		✓	✓					✓			✓			✓	
Safe Energy Communication Council 1717 Massachusetts Ave., NW Washington, DC 20036 202-483-8491	✓	✓	✓	✓		✓	✓	✓	✓	✓		✓			✓		non-membership
Sierra Club 730 Polk St. San Francisco, CA 94109 415-776-2211	✓	✓		✓	✓	✓			✓	✓		✓		✓		✓	$33/yr. individ.
Smithsonian 1000 Jefferson Dr., SW Washington, DC 20560 202-357-1300						✓	✓		✓	✓		✓	✓	✓	✓	✓	$20/yr. individ.
Trout Unlimited 501 Church St., NE, Suite 103 Vienna, VA 22180 703-281-1100	✓	✓		✓				✓	✓			✓		✓			$20/yr. individ.

Problems Addressed · Materials Available

Organization															Notes
Trust for Public Land 116 New Montgomery Ave., 3rd and 4th floors San Francisco, CA 94105 415-495-4014	✓	✓			✓	✓	✓			✓	✓	✓	✓		non-membership; nonprofit
Union of Concerned Scientists 26 Church St. Cambridge, MA 02238	✓	✓					✓	✓	✓	✓	✓	✓		✓ ✓	donation, no particular amount
1616 P St., NW, Suite 310 Washington, DC 20036 202-332-0900				✓									✓		
U.S. PIRG 215 Pennsylvania Ave., SE Washington, DC 20003	✓	✓	✓	✓	✓			✓	✓	✓	✓	✓		✓	
Wilderness Society 1400 I St., NW, Suite 550 Washington, DC 20005 202-842-3400	✓			✓	✓	✓	✓	✓	✓	✓	✓	✓	✓	✓ ✓ ✓	$15/yr. individ.
World Resources Institute 1709 New York Ave., NW Washington, DC 20006 202-638-6300		✓		✓		✓	✓	✓	✓				✓		
Worldwatch Institute 1776 Massachusetts Ave., NW Washington, DC 20036 202-452-1999	✓	✓	✓	✓				✓					✓		
Zero Population Growth 1400 16th St., NW, Suite 320 Washington, DC 20036 202-332-2200	✓	✓	✓	✓	✓	✓	✓	✓	✓	✓	✓	✓	✓	✓	$20/yr. with discounts

INDEX

NOTE: Resources listed on pages 189–194 of the Appendix are not included here.

"Abby" virus, 93
Academy for Educational Development,
    136
Acid aerosols, 17
Acid rain, 17–19, 32, 112, 135
Aerosol propellants, 15
    acid, 17
    banning of, 16, 51
Agriculture
    crop rotation in, 79
    intercropping in, 78
    pesticide use in, 8
    runoff in, 2–3
    shifting planting dates, 80
    wise use of land for, 125–26
    See also Gardening
Agriculture, U.S. Department of
    Insect Pathology Lab, 94
Air, community efforts to clean up, 166–67
Airborne toxic chemicals, 18
Air cleaning devices, 175
Air conditioner
    automobile, 107–8, 109, 110, 168
    cleaning condensers, 136
    efficiency, 50
    proper use of, 29
    replacement of filters, 29
    room units versus central, 28
    selecting energy efficient model, 28
    setting thermostat for, 29
    shading of unit, 28, 29
    use of fan with, 29
    room, 49
    market analysis of, 30
Airplanes, conservation programs for, 182
Air quality
    in apartments, 175
    in homes, 37–41
    in offices, 145, 147–48
Air-to-air heat exchangers, 37
Alachlor, 8
Algae, 16
Aluminum, recycling, 66–67, 112–13, 114
American Academy of Pediatrics, 19

American Council for an Energy Efficient Econ-
    omy, 46, 49, 50, 151
American Forestry Association, 22, 28, 89, 90,
    170
American Lung Association, 19, 100
Americans for Safe Food, 122
Animals, endangered species among, 36
Ants, controlling, 63, 94–95
Apartment
    air quality in, 175
    building ecology center in basement, 174
    energy conservation in, 175–77
    pest control, 174
    and planting of trees, 177
    setting up recycling project in, 174–75
    sharing of appliances in, 175
    use of roof for garden, 174
    using exhaust fan in, 173–74
    water conservation in, 174
    weatherizing, 173
Aphids, controlling, 94–95
Appliances
    energy guide labels for, 50–51
    sharing, 175
    See also specific entries
Aqua Glass, 113
Aquifers, 2
Asbestos, at schools, 132–33
Asbestos School Hazard Abatement Act, 132–33
Atrazine, 8
AT&T, office paper recycling program of, 144
Attic
    insulation of floor of, 24
    ventilation of, 39
Aurora, Colorado, energy conservation in
        schools in, 135
Automobile
    air conditioning for, 107–8, 109, 110, 168
    buying, 106–8
    and fuel efficiency, 99–100, 107
    maintenance for, 108–10
    new fuels for, 102–3
    parking, 103–4
    washing, 109

203

Baby Bunz & Co., 60
Bathroom, 52
  and medicine storage, 56–57
  and personal hygiene, 56–57
  water consumption in, 52–54
Batteries
  disposal of, 67–68
  rechargeable, 68, 118
Beach, organizing cleanup of, 182
Ben & Jerry's Homemade Ice Cream, 117
Benedict College, 138
Benomyl, 85
Bhopal, 18
Bicycling, 104–6
  on vacation, 184
Bike-to-work days, 105–6, 107
Biobottoms, 60
Biodegradable products, 56, 114, 115, 121, 127
Bio Integral Resources Center, 87, 171
Biological contaminants, 39–40
"Bird bath" for insects, 81
Birds
  feeding, 82–83
  protecting, 164–66, 186
Body heat, 25
Body Shop, 115
Bottles, mandatory bills for, 153–54
Boulder, Colorado
  bike-to-work days in, 106
  roadster bikes in, 105
Bromine, 16
Bugs
  beneficial, 9
  purchase of, 81
BugVac, 82

California, University of, at San Francisco, 138
California Action Network, 124
California Energy Commission, 150
Cameras, throwaway, 116
Camping, 179–80
Canadian Standards Association, 127
Cancer
  and formaldehyde exposure, 40
  lung, 39
  and pesticide residues, 7–8
  and radon exposure, 37–38
  skin, 16
Captan, 85
Carbon, role of rain forests in global recycling
  of, 13
Carbon dioxide (CO_2), 14–15
  buildup of, 13
  and tree planting, 89–90, 163
Carbon monoxide, 18, 40
Carpets, drying and cleaning of water-damaged,
  39
Car pooling, 101, 151
Catalytic converters, 18

Center for Marine Conservation, 139–40, 183
Center for Science in the Public Interest, 41
Chemical resistance, 9
Chemical spills, 6
Chesapeake Bay, pollution of, 4, 164
Chicago Faucet Company, 55
Chlorine, 117
Chlorofluorocarbons (CFCs), 15–16, 51
  community restrictions on, 168, 169
  identifying and avoiding, 118
Chlorpyrifos, 85
Christmas tree
  artificial, 71–72
  live, 71
  recycling, 72
CITES, 186
Citizens Clearinghouse for Hazardous Wastes,
  Inc., 156, 159, 160
Clean Air Act, 19
Cleaning products
  alternative, 61–63
  toxic, 60–61
"Clean Sweep" program, 45, 68, 162
Climate
  and clothing choice, 25
  effect of, on lifestyle, 13–14
Clothes dryer
  efficient use of, 57
  gas versus electric, 57
  "solar," 57
  venting, 39
Clothes washer
  and choice of detergent, 58
  energy-efficient, 48, 50
  front-loading, 57
Cloud forest, saving, 184–85
Cloud seeding, 3
Coal, and release of carbon dioxide, 15
Coalition for Recyclable Waste, 116
Cockroaches, controlling, 63
Cogeneration, 139
Cohen, Ben, 117
College campuses, environment movement on,
  137–38
Colorado River, 2
Community
  building energy-efficient buildings in, 172
  "Clean Sweep" project in, 45, 68, 162
  and de-icing of streets in, 162
  dumping of toxic chemicals, 162
  garbage dump in, 159–61
  litter control in, 163
  pollution prevention programs in, 161
  promotion of least-cost utility services in,
  171–72
  protecting local water supply, 161–64
  protecting wetlands in, 162–63
  reducing pesticide use in, 170
  tree planting by, 163–64

waste disposal in, 152–55
water conservation program in, 170–71
Community Products, Inc., 117
Compassionate Consumer, 63
Composting, 65, 75, 76–78
Compressed natural gas, 102
Computers, 143
   laptop, 151
Concerned Neighbors in Action, 156
Congressional Office of Technology Assessment,
   9
Congressional Research Service, 154
Conservation program, adoption of model, 22
Con-Serv Inc., 54
Contact lenses, throwaway, 55–56
Convection oven, 47
Cooling, hints for, 30. *See also* Air conditioner
Copper fungicide, 81
Coral, protecting, 187
Council on Economic Priorities, 119
Crawl spaces
   insulation of area over, 24
   ventilation of, 39
Curare, 12

Daylight, use of, 30, 33
Deforestation, 10, 12–13, 35–36, 73
   effect of, on water availability, 3–4
Desalinization, 3
Desertification, 13
Diapers
   alternatives to plastic pants and pins, 60
   cloth, 59
   disposable, 58–59
   washing at home, 60
Diaper services, 59
Diatomaceous earth, 80
Diazinon, 85
Dicofol, 85
Diesel oil spill, 6
Dimmers, 34
Diosgenin, 12
Dioxin, 6, 117
Dishwashers
   detergent choice for, 58
   energy-efficient, 46, 48, 50
   water-saving, 45
Disposable cameras, 116
Disposable diapers, 58–59
Disposal products, objecting to, 116–17
Doors
   storm, 23, 176
   testing for leaks, 23
Drapes, 176
Drip irrigation, 84
Drought, plants for, 83
Duck, R., Company, 60
Dutch elm disease, 170

Earth Care Paper Company, 68, 145
Earth Day, 129, 137–38, 139
Earth Preservation Fund, 184
Earthwatch, 183–84
Earthwatch magazine, 184
Earthwatch Teacher Fellowships, 140
Ecology center, setting up, in apartment,
   174
Ecology Club, 128–29
Economy of Energy Conservation in Educational
   Facilities, 136
Education, environmental, 139–41
Educational Facilities Laboratory, 134
Electricity, saving energy on, 35
Electric resistance heat, 49
El Triunfo preserve, 184
Emergency Planning and Community Right-to-
   Know Act, 160
Emetine, 12
Endangered species, 36
Energy, leaks, 22, 23
Energy, U.S. Department of, 29, 151
Energy audit
   for apartment buildings, 172
   for house, 23
   for school, 135
   for supermarket, 127
Energy conservation
   in apartments, 175–77
   and kitchen appliances, 46–49
   in offices, 148, 150–51
Energy consumption
   and automobile usage, 99–100
   need to reduce, 15
Energy guide labels, 50–51
Energy leaks, 176
Energy management and control system
   (EMCS), installation of, in office, 150–
   51
Energy Miser bulbs, 34
Energy sources
   coal, 15
   need for new, 15
   nuclear energy, 15
   solar, 31, 32
Environmental Action Coalition, 174
Environmental Action Foundation, 66
Environmental Defense Fund, 13, 155
Environmental education, 139–41
Environmental Hazards Management Institute,
   42
Environmental Products Corporation, 114
Environmental Protection Agency (EPA), 5, 7,
   8, 16, 18, 37, 38, 39, 40, 43, 68, 119,
   121, 131, 132, 133, 140, 148, 159, 160,
   167
Estuaries, 4
Exhaust fans, 39, 173–74
Exxon Valdez, oil spill by, 6

Fan
exhaust, 173–74
use of, with air conditioner, 29
whole-house ventilating, 28–29
Farmer's markets, 118–19
Faucets, and water conservation, 54
Fertilizer
all-natural, 88
organic, 74–75, 87–89
overuse of, 88
synthetic, 76, 88
Fire, building, while camping, 180
Fire extinguishers, halon, 51
Fireplace
in apartment, 176
in house, 25
Fire safety, and placement of insulation, 24
Fishing, 181–82
impact of pollution on, 4, 6
Fleas, controlling, 63
Flies, controlling, 63
Flow-control aerator, 54, 55
Fluorescent fixtures/bulbs, 33, 34, 135–36
Food and Drug Administration, 8, 9
Food products
disposal of, 64–65
packaging for, 111–12
and use of pesticides, 119, 121–22, 124
Formaldehyde, 40–41
Fossil flowers, 80
Fourth of July, *Save Our Planet* guide to, 187
Freezers, energy efficient, 47, 48
Freon, 15
Fresh Kills landfill (Staten Island, N.Y.), 10
Friends of the Earth, 12
Frosted bulbs, 34
FSC Paper of Chicago, 157
Fundamat, 185
Furniture, and deforestation, 35–36
Furs, and endangered species, 187

Gainesville, Florida, biking in, 105
Garages, insulation of area over, 24
Garbage barge, 10
Garbage dump, 159–61
Gardening, 73–74
on apartment building roof, 174
and birds, 82–83
composting, 65, 75, 76–78
mulch for, 75, 83, 92
organic, 74–76
perennial beds in, 81
and pest control, 76, 78–81
planting of flowering plants, 81
shifting planting dates, 80
tools for, 97–98
use of physical barriers in, 80–81
watering, 75–76, 83–84
See also Agriculture

Garden State Paper Company, 145
Gas furnace
buying proper size of, 25
energy-efficient, 49
Gels, 56
Gibbs, Lois, 160
Gifts, creative selection of, 72
Gift wrap
alternatives to, 68
recycling, 68
Girardet, Herbert, 44
Glass, recycling, 66–67
Glendale, Arizona, water efficiency program in, 171
Global Releaf, 89–90
Global warming, 13–16, 16, 22, 112, 135, 169–70
Grass clippings, 78, 87–88
Great Lakes, toxic pollution of, 7, 18–19
Greenhouse Crisis Foundation, 109, 126, 140
Greenhouse effect, 13, 14–15, 16, 32–33, 102, 103
Greenpeace, 61
Guppy, Nicholas, 10
Gypsy moth, controlling, 92–94, 170

Halon, 15–16
Halon fire extinguishers, 51
Harnik, Peter, 173, 175
Hazardous wastes. *See* Toxics
Heating system
changing filter on, 28
fireplaces, 25, 176
gas furnaces, 25, 49
maintenance of, 24, 40
oil furnaces, 25–26, 49
solar, 31, 32
Heating, zone map, 26
Heat islands, 169–70
Heat pollution, 3
Heat pump, 24, 49
Hewlett-Packard, recycling by, 144
Hiking, 179–80
Hill Air Force Base, and energy conservation, 161
Hirschhorn, Joel, 9
Holidays, and waste disposal, 68, 71–72
Home
air conditioning for, 28–30
building/buying, 31–32, 39–40
furniture for, 35–36
heating system for, 22–28, 31–32, 40, 49
indoor air pollution in, 37–41
insulation for, 23–24
lights in, 32–35
radon in, 37–38
vacationing at, 179
Horticultural polymers, 84

Hunter Energy Monitor, 29
Hydrofluoric acid spill, 6

Iceberg, potential of melting, 3
Incineration, of wastes, 10, 153
Indoor pollution, 37, 175
  in apartments, 175
  biological contaminants, 39–40
  formaldehyde, 40–41
  from heat sources, 40
  lead, 41
  radon, 37–38
  smoking, 39
Industrial water use, 3
Infrared radiation, 14
Insecticidal soap, 81
Insects, "bird bath" for, 81
Institute for Local Self-Reliance, 153
Insulation, 23–24
  for new house, 31
  R-values for, 23–24
  with CFCs, 51
Intercropping, 78
International Decade of the Environment, 22
Ipecacuanha roots, 12
Irrigation, 3
  drip, 84
Irvine, California, restrictions on use of chloro-
    fluorocarbons in, 169
Ivory, and endangered species, 186–87

Jacobson, Judith, 19

Kielbaso, James, 169–70
Kitchen
  energy-saving appliances for, 46–49
  and water safety, 41–46

Ladybugs, 81
Landfills, 9
Landscaping
  design tips for, 90, 92
  and tree planting, 89–90, 91
  See also Lawn care
Laptop computers, 151
Laundering
  of cloth diapers, 60
  detergent choice for, 58
  dryer selection, 57
  washing machine selection, 48, 50, 57
Lawn care, 85–87
  bug control, 87, 90, 92–94
  fertilizing, 87–89
  mowing, 86
  watering, 86
  weed control, 85, 86–87
  See also Landscaping
Lawn Institute, 87–89
Lawrence Berkeley Laboratories, 32

Lead
  consumption of, 41
  in drinking water, 2, 43, 44, 133
  in packaging, 124
Lead emissions, sources of, 18
League of American Wheelmen, 107
Leaks
  faucet, 54
  toilet, 53
Leatherback turtle, saving, 183–84
Light bulbs, 32–34
  alternatives to, 34
  and use of dimmers, 34
Lighting, solar solution to night-time, 97
Lights
  fluorescent, 135–36
  turning off, 177
Los Angeles
  cleaning up of air in, 167
  use of trip reduction ordinances in, 105
Love Canal, 6
Lovins, Amory B., 101
Lovo Products Division, 54
Lygus bugs, 82

Margosan, 87
Martha's Vineyard, waste disposal in, 163
Maryland, recycling paper in, 157
Massachusetts Audubon Society, 97, 176, 177
McDonald's, and recycling, 156
Meat, consumption of, 125–26
Medical wastes, disposal of, 4, 56–57
Medicine cabinet, 56–57
Medicines, rain forest as source of many, 10, 12,
    165
Mercury poisoning, 6
Methanol, 102–3
Methoxychlor, 85
Methyl isocyanate, 18
Minnesota, recycling in, 154, 155
Montreal protocol, 16
Morro Bay, California, water efficiency program
    in, 171
Mosquitoes
  controlling, 95–97
  sources of, 96
Mothers and Others Against Pesticides, 123
Moths
  controlling, 63
  protecting natural fibers from, 64
Motor oil, recycling, 108
Mountain bikes, 180
Mousses, 56
Mulch, 75, 83, 92

National Academy of Sciences, 8, 12, 181
National Audubon Society, 82, 140
  travel ethic of, 185
National Cancer Institute, 12

National Coalition Against the Misuse of Pesticides, 9, 122
National Council of Churches, 140
National Geographic Society, 140
National Institute for Occupational Health and Safety, 148
National Science Teachers Association, 140
National Toxics Campaign, 52
National Wildlife Federation, 7, 54, 139, 140
  Conservation Summits, 185
Natural Resources Defense Council (NRDC), 8, 123, 124
Neenah Paper, 145
Nepal, reforesting, 184
Newspapers, recycling of, 65, 127, 144, 158
New York City's Office Paper Recycling Service, 145
Nitrogen dioxide, 40
Nitrogen oxides, emission of, as cause of acid rain, 17
Non-aerosol sprays, 118
Northern States Power Company, 172
Northwest Coalition for Alternatives to Pesticides (NCAP), 134
Nuclear power, 15
Nursery
  and energy consumption, 58–59
  use of cloth diapers, 59
  use of diaper services, 59
  use of disposable diapers, 58–59

Ocean outfalls, 4
Offices
  air quality in, 145, 147–48
  energy conservation in, 148, 150–51
  installation of energy management and control system at, 150–51
  recycling at, 143–45
  smoking in, 148, 149
Ogallala Aquifer, 2
Oil furnace
  energy-efficient, 49
  proper servicing of, 25–26
Oil spills, 6
Omaha, "underground" schools in, 135
Omni Products, 55
Organic, definition of, 123
Organic Foods Production Association (OFPANA), 123
Organic gardening, 73–74, 76
  hints for, 74–76
Organic Wholesalers Directory and Yearbook, 124
Osage, Iowa, energy efficiency and conservation in, 22, 168
Outboard Marine Corporation, 183
Overfertilizing, 88
Overfishing, 19
Overgrazing, 19
Ozone, 16, 17–18

Ozone hole, 16
Ozone layer, 15–16
  protecting, 51, 168

Pacific Northwest Power Planning Council, 171
Packaging
  best choices for, 120
  lead in, 124
Packaging materials
  disposal of, 65–67, 111–12, 114–19
  plastic as, 66, 67, 112, 114, 156
Palmer, Arnold, 88
Paper, recycling of, 130, 143–45, 157
Paradichlorobenzene (PDCB), 63
Parking, problems with, 103–4
Passive smoke, 39
Pennsylvania Resources Council, 117
Perennial beds, 81
Periwinkle, 165
Periwinkle Project (Rainforest Alliance), 165
Personal hygiene, and water conservation, 54–56
Pest control
  ants, 94–95
  in apartment, 174
  aphids, 94–95
  in garden, 76
  gypsy moths, 92–93, 94
  and home repairs, 64
  intercropping in, 78
  in lawns, 87
  low-toxicity, 92
  mosquitoes, 95–97
  nontoxic, 63–64
  in schools, 134
  toxics in, 79–81
  weeds, 85, 86–87
Pesticides, 7–9
  agricultural use of, 8
  integrated program for, 78, 125
  reducing use of, 170
  safe, 81
  in supermarket, 119, 121–22, 124
Phosgene, 18
Photovoltaic cells, 97
Pilot light, 174
Planting dates, shifting, 80
Plants, protecting, 187
Plastic can, 116
Plastics, 144
  banning foam, 67, 155
  disposal of, 4–5, 9, 65–67, 111–12, 114–19
  legislation requiring degradable, 183
  recycling, 113, 156
Plastics Recycling, Inc., 113
Pollution
  air, 166–67
  business of exporting, 7
  growth of, 21

heat, 3
packaging, 114–19
plastics as form of, 4–5
water, 2–7
See also Indoor pollution
Polyvinylchloride (PVC) plastic, 112
Population growth, and need for water, 3
Praying mantids, 81
Precipitation, 3
Prince William Sound, oil spill in, 6
Project ROSE (Recycled Oil Saves Energy),
    108, 109
PTA
  setting up Environment Committee, 129
  and waste reduction, 130
Puget Sound, pollution of, 4
Pyrethrum, 81

Quassia, 81

Radial tires, 109
Radiator, cleaning of, 28, 176
Radon, 8
  at home, 37–38
  in schools, 131–32
Rails-to-Trails Conservancy, 107, 184
Rainforest Alliance, 36, 165
Rainforest Crunch, 117
Rain forests, 10, 11
  destruction of, 12–13, 35
  role of, in global recycling of carbon, 13
  as source of medicines, 10, 12, 165
Razors/blades, disposable, 56
Recycled packaging, identification of, 117
Recycling
  of aluminum, 66–67, 112–113, 114
  of bottles, 114, 153–54
  community programs for, 22, 145, 153
  of glass, 154–55
  and McDonald's, 156
  of motor oil, 108
  of newspapers, 114, 127, 144, 158
  of paper, 130, 143–45, 157
  of plastics, 113, 144
  at school, 129–30
  setting up apartment-building program for,
    174–75
Reflector bulbs, 34
Refrigerators
  cleaning condensers in, 136
  energy-efficient, 46–47, 48
Reptile skins and leathers, 186
Reserpine, 12
Resources, consumption of, 19–20
Reverse vending machines, 114
Rhode Island, recycling in, 154
Ringer Corporation, 74
Ringer Natural Lawn and Garden Products, 89
Rockford, Illinois, recycling in, 154

Rocky Mountain Institute, 172
Rodale Press, 82
Roofs
  garden, 174
  for new house, 31–32
  ventilators for, 31
Rosenfeld, Art, 90
Rubber Research Elastomerics, Inc., 154
Rubber soaker hoses, 83–84

Safe Drinking Water Act, 43
Sampson, Neil, 170
Sand, for de-icing of streets, 162
Schneider, Claudine, 150
Schools
  asbestos in, 132–33
  conservation programs for, 128–31
  construction of "underground," 135
  energy audit for, 135
  and energy conservation, 134–37
  environmental education in, 139–41
  heating, ventilating, and air-conditioning sys-
    tem, 136–37
  radon in, 131–32
  recycling programs at, 129–30
  and water conservation, 133–34
Scopolamine, 12
Sea turtles, 181
Seattle, Washington, recycling in, 22, 154
Seldman, Neil, 153
Seventh Generation, 121
Sewage, as cause of pollution, 4
Seymour, John, 44
Shea, Cynthia Pollock, 157
Showers, water conservation in, 52, 53–54, 134
Sierra Club, 140–41, 153, 181, 184
Skin cancer, 16
Smoking
  in homes, 39–40
  corporate programs for stopping, 149
  in offices, 148, 149
Smurfit, 145
Soft soap, 81
Solar energy, 31, 32
Solar Energy Industries Association, 32
Southern Utah Archeological Service Trip, 184
Sprinklers, 83
State University of New York at Stony Brook,
    138
Storm windows/doors, 23, 176
Stoves, energy-efficient, 47–48
Strawberry plants, vacuuming, 82
Streep, Meryl, 123
Styrofoam, 15
Sulfur dioxide, emission of, as cause of acid rain,
    17
Sunergy, 98
Superfund Law, 7

Supermarket
  and biodegradeable products, 127
  and buying in bulk, 115
  energy audit for, 127
  and environmental awareness, 126–27
  and meat consumption, 125–26
  and packaging pollution, 114–19
  paper versus plastic bags, 115
  pesticides in, 119, 121–22, 124
Super saver bulbs, 34
Synted Company, recycling by, 143

Telecommuting, 151
Thermal draperies, 23
Thermogram, 23
Thermostat
  for air conditioner, 29
  automatic clock, 25
  proper setting for, 24–25, 176
3M program, for pollution prevention, 161
Ticks, controlling, 63
Times Beach, Missouri, 6
Tips for Energy Savers, 30
Tirecycle, 154
Toilet dams, 53, 133
Toilets, water conservation in, 53, 133
Top floor ceiling, insulation of, 24
Tourist attractions, minimizing impact on, 179
Toxics, 5–9
  contamination, 112
  household hazardous wastes, 69–71
  in pest controls, 79–81
Toxic Substances Control Act, 132
Traffic, methods of curbing, 102
Transportation
  and air pollution, 166–67
  biking, 104–6
  and parking problems, 103–4
  and traffic control, 102
  See also Automobiles
Trees, planting, 89–90, 91, 137, 163–64, 177
2, 4-D, 85

Ultraviolet radiation, 16
Unbleached paper, 117
United National Environment Programme, 15
Utility services, promoting least-cost, 171–72

Vacation
  choosing place for, 179
  choosing unusual, 183–84
  fishing, 181–82
  flying on, 182
  hiking/camping, 179–80
  at home, 179
  souvenirs for, 186–87
Vegetarian cookbooks, 126
Ventilation
  of attic, 147
  of crawl space, 39
  of dryer, 39

  fan for, 28–29
  of office space, 147
  roof, 31
Vermont Youth Conservation Corps, 184
Victor Emmanuel Nature Tours, 184–85
Vulcan Chemical, 18

Wall outlet, and energy leaks, 176
Washington, D.C., tree planting in, 170
Washington State Department of Ecology, 139
Waste disposal
  batteries, 67–68
  in community, 152–55
  compost, 65
  and exportation, 9–10
  food/organic wastes, 64–65
  incineration, 10
  medical wastes, 4
  packaging, 65–67
  problem of solid, 9–10
  suggested ways for, 69–71
Water, 2–3
  bottled, 42, 44
  community programs for conserving, 170–71
  conservation of, 44–45, 174
    in schools, 133–34
  contamination of, 43
  drinking, in schools, 133
  for garden, 75–76, 83–84
  keeping clean, 45
  for lawns, 86
  lead contamination of, 2, 43, 44, 133
  new sources of, 3–4
  pollution of, 2–7
  protecting local supply of, 43, 161–64
  quality of, 2–3
  recycled, 84
  safety of drinking, 41–42
Water consumption, in bathroom, 52–57
Water faucet, filter for, 44
Water heaters, energy-efficient, 49
Water Sense Wheel, 42
Waxman, Henry, 18
Weeds
  chemical resistance of, 9
  control of, 85, 86–87
Well contamination, problem of, 2
Wellman, Inc., 113
Wetlands, 4
  protecting, 162–63
Windows
  for new house, 31
  in schools, 137
  storm, 23, 176
  testing for leaks, 23
Working Assets, 166
Worldwatch Institute, 99, 157
World Wildlife Fund, 36, 141, 188

Zero Population Growth, 20